Books to be written

CW00501895

A non-fictions author's how-to guide to writing, publishing & marketing you own books

Allan Kelly

Books to be written

A non-fictions author's how-to guide to writing, publishing & marketing you own books

Allan Kelly

ISBN 978-1-912832-22-4

Contents

II   Writing

III   Production

What people are saying about *Books to be Written*

"When I first started self-publishing my own books in 2014, Allan was a great source of knowledge to me. I've badgered him for years to write this book and I'm glad it's happened!" Steve Smith, author of *Measuring Continuous Delivery*

"I can honestly say that without Allan's advice I would never have published my book – I am so glad he has now put that wisdom into an easy-to-read and highly practical book. Rather than offering up a get-rich-quick fantasy, *Books to be Written* clearly explains what outcomes you can expect as well as why and how to do it, all based on first-hand, real-world experience. And, as always, Allan covers this in an entertaining and highly readable way. Writing, publishing and promoting a book will never be easy, but with this guide in your hands you will be able to get started right away and make the process as simple as possible." David Daly, author of *Better Agile*

"It's amazing, I'm writing a book myself (my first) and this is timed perfectly for me. So much great advice in there and your honesty is refreshing." Sean Luke

"Awesome page turner. Read it in two days. Admire how open you are mentioning your dyslexia – kudos for that." Björn Schotte

"It is great to read about your experiences on book writing and I wished I had all that advice before writing my own book" Christopher Preschern, author of *Fluent C*

"*Books to be Written* is a straight-forward, and easy to digest roadmap and one I am sure I will revisit as my story progresses, both to refresh my memory, but to also test my hypotheses to ensure I am on track. The genius of this book is that you will likely continue to re-read it as you move through your story process." Gilbert B. Hammer

Preface

Follow the path of the unsafe, independent thinker. Expose your ideas to the danger of controversy. Speak your mind and fear less the label of 'crackpot' than the stigma of conformity.

Thomas J Watson Jr, CEO of IBM 1914-1956

What do you think about when you think of writing a book? You probably think of long hours at a keyboard, you probably think of a mighty manuscript with tens of thousands of words. Maybe you see the creation of that manuscript as a marathon.

When books are 70,000 words long and publishers handle everything once the draft is delivered, then a marathon is a reasonable analogy. Of course there is the small matter of marketing the book – but surely that is akin to a lap of honour to soak up the glory?

By contrast when you write your own book, arrange production to a high standard, publish it yourself and then market the hell out it, the metaphor is not a marathon. When you are writer, publisher and marketeer, writing a book is more akin to a triathlon. First you write, then you produce and publish, then you market.

This book describes my experience of writing, both self-publishing and working with a publisher, and marketing the finished works. Here is one secret that I can share right now: publishers might help with marketing, but most marketing comes down to you one way or another.

Before you start your triathlon, it helps to do some training, so I'll describe a training regime. As there are times when you will feel like giving up, I'll also discuss some of the benefits you might get from writing.

One recurring theme is the way in which the publishing landscape has changed since the start of the millennium. Digital tools have changed writing, changed publishing, changed buying and even changed book consumption.

Not all publishers have grasped the opportunities offered by these changes, while others are struggling to adapt their business model. Whether you aim to self-publish or to work with a publisher, I hope this book will prepare you to be a successful author in the digital age.

Why write a book?

A few of you will answer that question with 'To make money'. In case you haven't heard, for every J K Rowling there are not just ten or 100 budding authors – there are 1,000 or even 10,000. So, first of all: you probably won't make much money.

If you do want to make money then you are reading the wrong book. I won't ignore the subject of writing for profit, but I am sure there are better authors out there to read for that. I've read a few myself.

The basic formula for writing a best-seller will be recognizable to many readers from other fields: identify a market, identify a subject, identify a compelling need to buy. Perhaps even test your market *Lean Start-up* style, then write for that market.

You don't even need to be knowledgable in the subject you write about. Identify the best-selling books in the field, read a few of them and write your own version based on what you have learned.

Therein lies my first piece of advice: you don't need to have an original idea for a book, you don't need to have something unique to say. After all, despite the thousands of love stories out there, people keep writing love stories.

From a classic business perspective, the fact that many books might exist about a specific topic suggests a crowded market that one should avoid. On the other hand it can also be viewed as a validated market: if people are buying such books it suggests a subject people do want to read about.

If you are from an academic background what I have just said may sound horrifying: the aim of most academics – and certainly PhD students – is to find and describe new knowledge. If you are an academic, or original knowledge is your goal, then you too are probably reading the wrong book. Still, you might nevertheless find useful advice here. I'll discuss academic writing later.

So who is this book for?

My key audience, the people for whom I am writing this book, are my friends. While I haven't met some of you yet, others have already heard this advice. Indeed, I'm writing this book to save myself time. A few times a year people come to me and say "Allan, I'm thinking of writing a book, you've written a few books, can I get your advice…". (Steve, I'm thinking of you.)

A variation on this is David, who said "I've written this book…", to which I replied "Publish!". Then last month there was Trevor, who I haven't seen for years and who has written what looks like a really interesting book, so I just couldn't help sending him a note saying "Have you thought of…?".

These friends write because, like me, they have something they want to say. The other things they have in common is that we all come from a technical background. While few of our books are deeply technical, they may still appear technical to a non-technical reader.

So, while I'd like to think this book is interesting to a wider audience, those coming from a technical background may find it especially interesting. It also means I should apologise to the non-technical reader if my technical bias comes through.

My first book, *Changing Software Development*, was written because I wanted to say "Hey world! Have you ever looked at it like this…". True, I was looking for something to write as a book – like many others, 'writing a book' is on the bucket list in my head of things to do. For someone moving into the consultancy field a book adds credibility. A author friend of mine was told by a very successful author "A book is an extended business card".

My second book, *Business Patterns*, was written for similar reasons: "Hey world, you can use patterns for business strategy". (In fact the *EuroPLoP 2009 proceedings* might have counted as my second book, but it was more of a compilation exercise.)

I wrote book three, *Xanpan*, because I wanted to play with the LeanPub platform. It started life as some repurposed essays and grew. When people starting paying for my unfinished book it motivated me to continue. I'm saying *Xanpan* was book number three, but it might have been four or five if you include the *Agile Reader* series, which I never marketed, assigned an ISBN to or had copy-edited.

Book four, *A Little Book of Requirements and User Stories*, was written because, like this one, I kept giving the same advice to people again and again. I eventually found time to write that advice down on a flight from London to Dallas, but instead of a 4,000 word essay it came to 27,000 words, of which about 20,000 on the flight.

Books five and six were one book that I split in two. *Project Myopia* says "World: this project management thing is wrong", while *Continuous Digital* attempts to describe what to do instead.

I wrote *The Art of Agile Product Ownership* because *A Little Book of Requirements and User Stories* needed a companion. Then a publisher got involved and it became something different.

My last and eighth book started as notes to myself, but then Covid happened and it became my lockdown project. It is with this title, *Succeeding with OKRs in Agile*, that I finally feel

I've cracked it: I know not only how to write, produce and publish a book, I now also know what needs to be done to make it sell.

There is a story behind each of my books, but the common uniting theme is that *I had something to say, something I wanted the world to know.*

Having written one's masterpiece, it's great to make a little money from it. So please read this book if you have something to say and would like to make a return from it.

Actually, while I and my bank manager appreciate the money, I would still be better off putting my time into other work – such as taxi driving. But money is information as well as spending power. When I receive money from book sales it carries an important message: people are buying my books. In other words, my messages are getting out there and people are listening.

With three book produced through publishers and another four self-published and on sale via Amazon and elsewhere, I'm now making a few hundred pounds a month (that's a few hundred dollars a month or few hundred euros a month.)

I'm still not making enough money to cover my mortgage, but I'm making more than enough to buy a few drinks in the pub. I'm making enough to have to remember to mention it on my tax return.

But there is a final motivator for writing: *to learn.*

Notice I say learn, not teach. As much as any of us want to educate the world, the person who learns most from writing is the author, not the reader. Writing – putting your ideas down in words, words which kind-of fit together and make sense – forces you to straighten out your thinking. Writing highlights where you are making jumps in logic and where your thinking is weak. Writing will challenge you to find out more.

If any of this sounds like you, please read on.

Subscribe to hear more

For Allan's latest updates, blog posts, speaking appearances and more please subscribe[1].

Subscribers are the first to know of Allan's latest workshops and receive discounts to books, workshops and other events, plus occasional give aways such as audio books.

As a thank you new subscribers receive an e-book – currently *Continuous Digital*.

[1]https://allankelly.net/newsletter/

Foreword

I don't remember when I met Allan Kelly. I'm sure it was at a conference, and I was impressed with his straightforward and practical approach to agility.

Fast forward a few years and Allan suggested he write a series of articles for AgileConnection.com. At the time, I was the technical editor for the site. I said something like "Of course!" and gave him the site's parameters.

We were off and running. Allan wrote a number of articles for AgileConnection.com and I enjoyed reading them. They were straightforward and practical.

Allan's written several books over the years, and each of them share that straightforward and practical approach to the topic. Now you too can learn from Allan's approach to writing, publishing and marketing a book.

Many people think they have a book in them, but somehow that book never exits in their brain. That's because many would-be authors get stuck. They have many questions about writing, publishing and marketing. How can they start? What's the process? And how do they decide how to publish the book?

Allan wrote this guide for the people who don't know how to start and finish writing a book. Starting with why to write a book, Allan suggests that we learn from our writing. I certainly do, as do my writing students.

Allan offers many gems on how to start, maintain and finish writing a book. One of the big problems with this process is that writers learn as they write. Allan offers options for you to use indirect feedback about your topic to refine your book as you write. If you take Allan's suggestion to use leanpub.com as your writing platform, you can also integrate that feedback as you write.

Allan acknowledges that 'Once you have finished writing the work really begins'. (The first sentence of Chapter 20.) Allan's guidance continues with the ins and outs of how you can produce and market an excellent book, one that represents your thoughts and brand.

In Allan's deft hands you can read everything he knows about writing, creating books in various formats, publication and marketing, especially if you are willing to use leanpub.com. I use LeanPub for my nonfiction books and recommend it highly for all nonfiction book writers.

Allan then does a deeper dive into various possible delivery formats, including audio, perfect bound versus hardcover and so on. I have realized that my audio 'readership' is not the same as my e-book readership, and that both of those groups seem to be different from those who prefer paper copy.

Don't stay stuck. Help your ideas find their place in the world, so that your readers can use those ideas. Use *Books to be Written* as a terrific guide to write your book and help your readers.

— Johanna Rothman, Author of *Free Your Inner Nonfiction Writer: Educate, Influence, and Entertain Your Readers*

I A brave new world

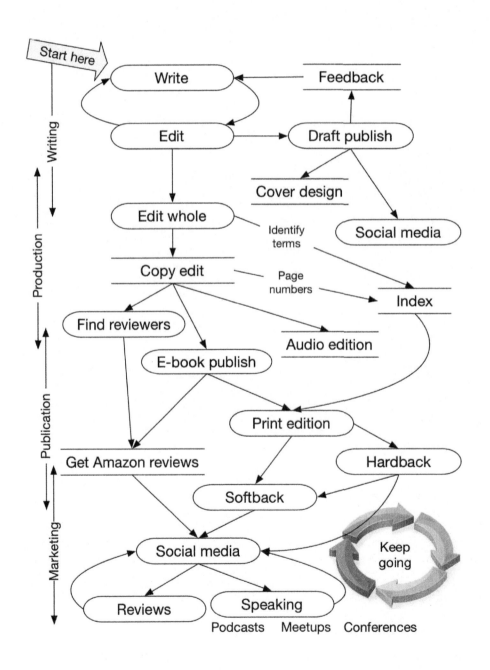

1. What is a book?

More books are being published now than ever before in history. The rise of digital publishing has not killed traditional books, but rather has grown the market. The growth of audio books is doing something similar. It is not just that authors are writing more books: there are more authors than ever before.

There are more publishers too. Most of the publishing imprints you might have heard of are ultimately owned by a few mega-publishers such as Bertelsmann, Axel Springer and News Corp, but there are many more small publishers, and probably millions of solo author-publishers such as me.

But this profusion of books, authors and publishers raises the question: *what is a book?*

Twenty years ago this was easy to answer: a book was words printed on paper, bound together and normally stored on a bookshelf. On the spine it bore a distinguished name such as Wiley, Bloomsbury, HBS, Oxford, Addison-Wesley, Pearson, Orbit.

Today a book can be electronic: is an e-book version of Harry Potter any less of a book than the 500-page print version?

If I write 50,000 words and give away PDF versions, is it a book?

If I have it copy-edited and typeset but only ever give away electronic versions, is it a book?

If I add an ISBN number, does that make it a book?

If I print and sell copies, is it a book?

If I pay a publishing house to do the hard work of editing, typesetting, adding an ISBN, printing and putting it in bookshops, is it a book?

In short, at what point does a *book* become a *book*? What are the defining features of a book?

Once you step into the world of modern digital publishing, the very notion of a book changes.

I have lots of books on my shelves. Some old favourites like *Lord of the Rings* and *Catch-22*, and more serious books like *How Buildings Learn* and *The C++ Programming Language*. Without a doubt these are books. They are published by publishing houses (Harper Collins, Vintage Classics, Penguin, Addison-Wesley), they have an ISBN, they are printed on paper and were mostly bought in bookshops and carried home.

Most of these books are also available in electronic form for my Kindle or iPad, but that doesn't mean they aren't books. If the same content was only available electronically, would it still be a book? Is being printed the defining feature? If I only ever own *Lord of the Rings* in an electronic format, does that mean I don't own the book?

Or perhaps it is the involvement of a publishing house. Although self-publishing has existed for many years, it has traditionally been seen as the domain of the vain. There is a certain snobbery in having a publisher involved: a publisher adds credibility – although some publishers are more credible than others. Having worked with publishers I find it hard to see what else they add.

My first book, *Changing Software Development: Learning to be Agile*, is undoubtedly a book. It contains about 90,000 words, was published by John Wiley and Sons, has an ISBN number and print versions appeared before electronic ones.

A year or so later I self-published the EuroPLoP 2009 conference proceedings. Michael Weiss and I are listed as editors, but in truth we did very little editing of any of the 600+ pages.

The proceedings have an ISBN number (978-1-4466-9363-6) and are available in print or electronic versions. There may be a few dozen electronic versions around, but I don't think there are more than a dozen print versions in the world. The wonders of print-on-demand technology mean you can go to Lulu.com and order a copy today.

I also used Lulu.com to self-publish a book titled *Agile Reader*. It contains a collection of essays on software development that I used to give away when I delivered training courses. People could also buy copies, but I never publicized the book. Still, it made me a little money.

Unlike my other books, *Agile Reader* has been through three editions, at one point it was in Lulu's top-ten sellers list, and probably more copies have been printed and distributed than any of my other books, but I'm not especially proud of it. *Agile Reader* was not polished, never copy-edited and the typesetting was crude – only Microsoft Word. It filled a need.

Agile Reader was never given an ISBN and no copies were sent to deposit libraries, but they are printed and most people would consider them books. Perhaps a better term would be a pamphlet:

> *pamphlet*: noun, a small booklet or leaflet containing information or arguments about a single subject. Apple MacOS dictionary

Which raises a question: *how many pages or words do you need before a written work can be considered a book?*

John Wiley paid me an advance for *Business Software Patterns*, my second book – or third if you count *Agile Reader*. It runs to over 110,000 words. I find it hard to imagine ever writing a book that long again. In contrast my shortest book, *Project Myopia*, contains only 22,000 words.

After *Business Software Patterns* I vowed 'never again', but my attitude changed when Laurent Bossavit told me about LeanPub. With LeanPub you can write and sell a manuscript before it is finished. This raises more questions: if a manuscript is only available as an e-book, is it a book? If it is never finished, is it a book?

Since then I have produced seven books with LeanPub and started a couple of other book projects that I subsequently abandoned.

Two of those books became a book called *Art of Product Ownership*. Then Apress publishing came along and said "We like your book on LeanPub, would you like to publish it with us?".

Art of Product Ownership was less of a book than *The Art of Agile Product Ownership* because the former was never finished. Copies sold, but it was removed from publication and became *The Art of Agile Product Ownership*. Was the original version less of a book because it was electronic only? Because it was self-published? Because it didn't have an ISBN?

An odd thing happened with *The Art of Agile Product Ownership* after I delivered the final manuscript: I lost interest in it. There was still work to do: index, copy-editing, typesetting, printing and so on, but I was largely a bystander. This feeling was reinforced when the copy-editing turned out to be awful but I felt I couldn't veto publication.

So I lacked motivation to publicize *The Art of Agile Product Ownership* because I'd lost ownership – ironic, really. When the pandemic hit a couple of months later the book was largely forgotten, but 18 months later royalty cheques arrived. Apress had given me a small advance, and unlike my Wiley books this time the royalties more than covered the advance. Publishers still have power when it comes to sales.

While I was busy forgetting about *The Art of Agile Product Ownership* I was writing *Succeeding with OKRs in Agile*. With that book I felt that I'd finally got it right.

The topic is more popular than I ever though it would be.

I've learned to write. I've kept it short and to the point.

I paid for a professional copy-edit – the same editor Wiley commissioned to edit and typeset *Business Software Patterns*, who I keep returning to. I paid for professional artwork – again I have a regular artist.

I quickly got electronic and print versions onto Amazon, and Amazon is where most sales are made.

I received reviews on Amazon at the book's launch, I publicized it on social media and I did a virtual book tour – perhaps something that was easier and faster because the book was published in the middle of the pandemic.

And the book sells.

The publishing industry defines a book as almost anything with an ISBN number, which means that *Succeeding with OKRs in Agile* is actually three books: printed paperback, an e-book and an audio book. In fact, though, *Succeeding* is actually just one title with three editions.

My formula

- Publish early, even before you think you are ready to publish.
- Publish often. Write iteratively, publish often and make social media noise when a new version is available.
- Keep your book short, less than 200 A5 pages and/or less than 30,000 words. Split it into two or more books if you have more material than will fit into this length. Or maybe release extra material as another book, or as an appendix or extra, and forego the usual production polish and publicity.
- Keep the price low for e-books, 'under 10' – that's under $10, £10, €10. Charge more for the print version, an extra 5 but maybe just 10, so an £7.50 e-book would be a £17.50 printed book, a $9.99 e-book a $19.99 printed book. (My printed books outsell my e-books.)
- Have an audio version of the book recorded. You might choose to do this yourself, or you might get someone else to voice the book. Audio versions sell themselves and lead to more overall sales.

2. Why write a book?

I think my motivation for my first book was the desire many have 'to write a book', to see my name on a book cover, to say "I've written a book", just to show that I could do it.

If I'm being honest, there was also a part of me that felt that the 25,000 words I'd written in my Masters dissertation deserved a wider audience. Something I have to relearn with every successive book, however, is that one shouldn't be scared to throw work away, even if it is well-developed.

Not for the money

One reason nobody should write a book is *to make money*. Most authors would earn more flipping burgers or stacking shelves. True, a few, such as J K Rowling, do make money, but they are the exception.

Commercially speaking, writing a book is seldom a profitable use of time. Having said that, though, there are exceptions. Clearly Jo Rowling makes a lot of money, but we're talking about novels. If you *are* writing a novel, please still read this book about books, as I'm sure you will learn something, but please be aware that I'm not thinking principally of you.

If you already have a platform – perhaps you are on TV – then I imagine there are people who will buy your book and benefit you financially. If you have been privy to public events – perhaps you worked for a politician who was at the centre of some scandal – then I'm sure there are people who would love to hear your story. In both cases you might want to find a commercial agent.

So, discounting vanity and money, *why write a book?*

Learning

Top of the list is to learn. The truth is that the person who learns most from a book is not a reader – it is the author. Putting your thoughts in order, putting them into words, forcing yourself to make sense and be understood brings order to your own thoughts. It uncovers flaws in your reasoning, it makes connections you have overlooked, it drives you to read more, to follow up leads on interesting information and more.

Fulfilment

Reason number two flows from learning: writing a book is very fulfilling. Looking at a tome you have created and knowing you created it is a fantastic feeling, and if you ever get the opportunity to see your book on the shelves of a distinguished bookstore it is ten times better!

Credibility

Next is professional credibility: a book marks you out as someone who knows their stuff, a book with your name on it is a sign of credibility and builds towards a reputation. Books also provide a marketing platform: in marketing your book you are also marketing yourself. When you are invited onto a podcast to talk about your book you are saying "Please buy my book", but you are also saying "Here I am! If you like what I am saying maybe you want to hire me?".

That said, I suspect 80% of that benefit comes from having one book, another 18% comes from your second book, 1% the third, and by the time you get to the fifth or sixth you're probably losing credibility!

Credibility can help in landing a job. Although a warning: this doesn't automatically happen. People do not say "Wow, I must hire them because they wrote a book", or "I must hire the person who wrote this book". I've even heard of one company that views authors negatively: they reason that authors are more interested in acquiring material for another book than in doing their job.

A calling card

A book might not land you a job, but it can help to secure an assignment. As a consultant, particularly an independent consultant, the credibility of books goes a long way. It could be argued that a book makes money, not by selling copies, but by marking you out as someone who is worth working with.

Books are useful as calling cards – why give someone a business card when you can give them a book? Books impress clients; they are more substantial. So maybe selling copies of your book won't provide you with much of an income stream, but it might mean that you get hired more often and earn more as an expert in your field.

Books can also serve as a platform to sell from. I'm sure that my books have opened doors that have allowed me to sell training workshop places. My books have also secured me speaking opportunities at conference and meet-ups that have later led to consultancy engagements.

I haven't yet succeeded with it, but you can also build products around a book, such as online or in-person training programmes, or tools that can be used to follow recipes in your book – software, playing cards, worksheets and more.

I'm sure there are other reasons why you might want to write a book that I haven't thought of, but these are perhaps the most common. If it helps, write down your own reasons – but equally don't be worried if you don't know why, you just know that you want to write. Just do it: these days writing a book is cheap even if it is not easy. What is the worst that can happen? You give up? Or you publish and nobody buys?

Something to say

One final reason, perhaps the real reason I write, or at least keep writing, is that I have something to say. When you have something to say it makes writing much easier. Blame it on being a big-mouthed Liverpudlian – well Birkenhead, actually. Blame it on being dyslexic and seeing the world differently. Or blame it on a feeling that I can change the world.

However you look at it there are things I want to share, things I want to tell people, things I want to point out. If you are writing for one of the reasons above but don't have much to say, you are going to find it a longer and harder process.

So write about what you want to share with people – it is so much easier.

Giving my knowledge away?

A friend once told me that "I worry that if I write a book people can do it themselves and they won't hire me as a consultant".

Perhaps he is right. I once did some consulting in Leeds where one of the managers said "You're *that* Allan Kelly!" and proceeded to show me his copy of my 'little red book', *An Agile Reader*. "At my last place we based our version of agile on your book".

The manager had never been on one of my training courses, but someone on his team had. That someone had a copy of my red book and they used that as a guide when implementing their own version of agile. So, if I had not written the book, would they have hired me?

I suspect not: the company concerned has a reputation for penny-pinching, so I don't think they would have hired anyone. If they had hired someone they would have haggled for a low price, so the work would have only been marginally profitable. More importantly, there was no guarantee I would have secured the work: if the book didn't exist they might never have heard of me.

As an expert and consultant you can never write down everything you know, readers can never absorb everything you say, and many real-life cases defy explanation anyway. A book can only contain *explicit knowledge*, it can never hold *tacit knowledge*. Yet that tacit knowledge is essential.

If someone reads one of my books and can 'follow the instructions' then I'm delighted. If my book helps people to solve their problems without me then I am happy. I am succeeding, I am helping people and I am making work better.

But no matter how much I write, and how clearly I write it, people will find it hard to implement what they read. That is where consultancy and training comes in, and that is where there is money to be made.

A book shares knowledge and it builds credibility. It is also a marketing tool that opens more doors than it closes.

Some of the people who buy your book won't read it. They will however be impressed. They might not pick up the phone immediately and call but your name will register in their mind. Years later they may call. Or, when faced with a choice of several potential consultants, they may remember your book and note that the others haven't published anything.

Of course this book is an exception. I write it to share what I have learned: I don't have any plans to offer services for budding authors.

Not yet, anyway.

3. It's digital now

Thirty years ago I would shop for books on Charing Cross Road in London. A shopping trip could result in multiple purchases, both novels and technical books. Now those shops are gone and my books overwhelmingly come from a Seattle-based company I both love and hate.

The world of publishing has changed, and you probably won't be surprised that the change is called *digital*. However, fears that digital books and e-readers would do away with books were misplaced: more new books are published today than ever before.

In most countries book sales boomed during the pandemic – the UK and Australia experienced in excess of 10% growth. Nor was this just the result of people staying home and reading. In many other countries book sales are also growing.

Once again new technology has not rendered an industry obsolete, but rather has increased consumption. One of the ways in which it has done this is by lowering costs. Another is by making writing and publishing tools accessible to more people. Technology allows you to carry your library in your pocket and to listen to books rather than read them.

This is a book about writing your own book, so will be bought by people who want to write and publish their own books. Until recently this was such a niche market that it didn't make sense to create such a book. Until recently people like me wouldn't have the experience to write about it, and until recently the cost of writing and publishing such a niche book would not justify the effort.

But these changes have played out in ways you might not have realised.

The bookshop

In technical publishing it used to make sense to write big books and sell them for a high price. Publishers like Wrox and Apress would produce thousand-page tomes that sold for upwards of £40 or $60 when £40/$60 was a lot of money. Amazon still lists Wrox's 1056-page *Professional Microsoft SQL Server Analysis Services 2008*, with a recommended price of £39.99 and five authors.

Back then most books were sold through actual bookshops. People like me would wander in, browse the shelves, choose a book, pay for it and take it home. The bookshop might never see me again. Even if I returned the staff wouldn't know I was a regular until I'd been in many times. Even if I had a relationship with the shop I probably wouldn't have one with the publisher. I might meet authors at conferences or book signings, but it is unlikely that they would let me know if they had a new book out.

In those days it made sense for the author, the publisher and the shop to take as much of my money as possible for each transaction. To justify a higher price a book needed more pages, and more pages meant more authors or a longer gestation period.

In some fields taking longer to write a book doesn't matter much, but in technology it does. If Wrox's *SQL Server Analysis Services 2008* had been written by a single author it might only have been completed in time for *SQL Server 2010* to be released.

Oddly, bigger books don't necessarily cost more to print. I'm sure Wrox 1,000-page tomes do cost more in paper than Pinal Dave's 110-page *SQL Server Interview Questions and Answers: Updated 2021*, but the cost doesn't increase proportionately. Paper is only part of the cost of printing a book: the publishing process – selection, editorial choices, marketing and so on – is the same whether a book has 100 or 1,000 pages.

So when books were bought in shops it was a big event and largely a one-off. Today the strategy is reversed: you need to aim for multiple sales, price low to remove the barrier to a sale, and reduce the size of the book because a) several smaller books can earn more than one big book, and b) small books are quicker to produce and get onto the market.

Why write 20 chapters of 50 pages each when you could write two chapters, put a 100-page book on sale and bank some cash while working on the remaining chapters?

When books are bought online it need not be a one-off event: the seller knows who you are and what you bought, authors and publishers will encourage you to share your name and email – 'register your book' or 'download additional material'. Every purchase is on at least one database.

Because they have your contact details they can sell to you again. Buying a book ceases to be an isolated transaction and, if managed correctly, becomes the start of a relationship. Seller, author and publisher can now tell you that 'Your favourite author has a new book' – 'People who bought SQL Server 2008 also bought...' and so on.

Now the seller collects not just your money but also valuable information: your contact details and your preferences. This helps them to sell to you again and again. The sale is just the start of a relationship, and that information is valuable in itself. So rather than sell 1,000 pages of one book for £40, it makes sense to sell ten books, each of 100 pages at £5 each.

Simultaneously, selling these books has become cheaper: digital technology means that shops can check their own stock online without searching the store, ordering a book no longer requires paper or a telephone request, and because books are instantly available, bookshops no longer need to carry large stocks.

But that is not all. Print-on-demand means publishers no longer need warehouses and vast stocks of books to support future sales. Money is saved on warehouses, storage costs, printing costs and other capital costs because there is no longer a need to invest in infrastructure before books are sold.

We haven't even got to the effect of e-books, Kindles and iPads. Nor have I mentioned Amazon yet.

Amazon

Amazon changed everything.

Most books are now sold through a single retailer, a retailer that is ruthless at driving down costs and exploiting economies of scale. A retailer that knows every purchase you have ever made from them and has honed its skills in using that data to offer up the next thing you will buy before you know yourself.

Many bookshops no longer need to keep stocks because many bookshops no longer exist. Much of the traditional book logistics 'tail' is now optional. Novels may still be printed cheaply and shipped to many small bookshops in the hope of sales, but professional books only need to be shipped from printing plant to one warehouse.

When my first book was published I was proud to see it in Foyles on Charing Cross Road. Even in 2008 you wanted your book to be on the shelves in shops so that customers could see it, and a good publisher was one who could get your book on the shelves of as many shops as possible. Bookshops have limited space, so this is a battle, and publishers may be asked to pay for prime locations in shops.

Now, particularly in technical publishing, there is just one shop that matters. Publishers no longer need to spend money on sending salespeople to visit many bookshops. For the author that also means that one reason for using a publisher has gone: as long as your book is on Amazon you will get your sales. You will certainly sell more copies if you can get it listed with Waterstones, Borders, Powell's, Daunt books and all the other chains and single local bookshops, but those extra sales are unlikely be worth the effort.

Amazon has changed the world of book reviews too: previously your book would be lucky to get one review in a specialist publication. People would flip through the book and decide for themselves in the shop. Now reviews on Amazon are a big deal: the more reviews the better: don't even tell people your book is on sale until you have reviews.

You still want to seek out reviews elsewhere. Technology has changed this: there are myriad of online journals for every niche, there are bloggers and multiple social media sites where people might review or name-drop your book. There are also dedicated review sites like GoodReads, although these might not be as independent as they appear: Amazon owns GoodRead.

It is worth repeating that Amazon knows what you have bought and what you have reviewed. Amazon can tell if new edition of a book is released or an author has published a new book, and Amazon can tell you about other books you might want to read.

Electronic

I know bookshops still exist, but there are a lot fewer than there were 20 years ago. As a reader, book buyer and high-street shopper, I don't think that is necessarily a good thing.

I don't consider Amazon a paean of virtue – some of its sales and employment practices are questionable. But it is nevertheless dominant, and as authors this is the world you and I find ourselves in.

As a consumer you can choose not to buy from Amazon, but as an author you don't have much choice. Fortunately Amazon is very good at what it does – few of their competitors do a better job.

All the changes mentioned so far are the result of digital technology. Without modern computers and the internet there would be no Amazon, no easy self-publishing, no CRM systems and mailing lists, no online reviews and no GoodReads. Instead, publishers would employ more people to publish fewer books, on paper, for sale in bookshops.

We still haven't mentioned e-books.

4. Publishers

Digitization has not only changed what it means to be a book, but also who publishes books. Previously self-publishing was mostly considered the preserve of the rich and vain: real writers had publishers. Today digital tools make both writing and publishing easier.

You may now ask *why use a publisher?*. If you are not asking that question, then at least think about it.

I admit that I might come over as a little biased against publishers. There are good reasons to use a publisher, but there is more to say about self-publishing – if only because there is more work to do when self-publishing. So please forgive me if I write more about self-publishing and don't argue the case for using a publisher too strongly. Once you understand what is involved you will be better placed to make your own decision as to whether to self-publish or to work with a publisher.

When writing my first book I was glad to have a publisher, I was glad to have their advice, guidance and for them to take on a lot of the administration involved in publishing. That continued into my second book – I was more capable by then, but it was a complex book.

Change

Two things have changed. First, as already noted, digital tools make self-publishing and marketing much more accessible and less work.

Second, publishers have changed. In recent years publishers have shed a lot of staff and offer a lot less traditional hand-holding. Publishers expect authors to do more, especially where marketing is concerned.

Publishing was always a game of finding a few big sellers to offset the mass of books that just broke even. By reducing their costs publishers can reduce the break-even point, so they can take more chances in the search for the elusive best-seller. Those cost reductions mean less support for authors.

My first book came about because I met and talked to a publisher. Back in the early 2000s publishers used to send editors to conferences. The EuroPLoP conference usually had editors from two publishers in attendance, one English and one German. EuroPLoP is really a writers conference and has generated several dozen books, including several best-sellers. (I have more to say about EuroPLoP when I discuss writers conferences).

I got to know Gaynor at EuroPLoP and talked through some ideas. I saw her again at the ACCU conference and after a while the idea for my first book came together. She guided me through the proposal and provided advice when it was accepted.

When I came to write my second book Birgit had replaced Gaynor, but a similar pattern played out. Except that, to our surprise, the proposal was turned down. Birgit didn't give up, however: she found out why the proposal was turned down and we reworked it. On the second try it was accepted.

During the production process my editors read early drafts and gave feedback. Thanks to the publishers I learned about image copyright and navigated the necessary permissions. They arranged the book covers, copy-editing, typesetting and marketing aids. Most importantly of all, they got it into bookshops.

The sad thing is that new authors need this help most of all. So it is new authors who have suffered most as publishers reduced the staff that provide a lot of the editorial support.

Repeat authors are more likely to be offered help and be in a stronger position to ask for it. Because repeat authors are less of an unknown risk, publishers are prepared to allocate more of their scarce resources to them.

Services

Almost all the services traditionally provided by a publisher can either be replaced by technology (for example typesetting) or bought yourself (such as editing and copy-editing). Even when buying technology services, you can still contract a copy-editor anywhere in the world, communicate over email and pay via PayPal – they no longer need to sit in a publisher's office.

Access to retailers has been replaced by access to Amazon – you don't need to get your books onto shelves anymore. If you do want to sell beyond Amazon, then Amazon will help you to do so, or you can buy that service too (check out IngramSpark).

I'd like to say that publishers help with marketing. They do – a little, but not enough. Even with a publisher authors should expect to market and advertise their own books. Although again there is support if you can justify paying for it.

Credibility

Perhaps the biggest single reason for using a publisher is the credibility they bring. Saying "My business patterns book is published by John Wiley" carries a lot more weight than if I say "I self-published my OKRs book".

Self-publishing is still seen as inferior to a brand-name publisher. Being associated with a well-known brand, a brand that dates back over 200 years, a brand with a reputation for quality, rubs off. You may never have heard of me or my books but you have probably read a book published by John Wiley and Sons.

Of course not all brands have the same credibility, but if credibility is important to you then make sure you work with a credible brand. For some authors credibility is important. New authors especially benefit from being associated with a known brand, while academics also benefit from the credibility of their publishers.

Does that credibility reflect in sales? Maybe, it also reflects on you, which is important if your motivation for writing a book is to boost your own credibility.

A book on financial markets published by Financial Times Publishing, or Harvard Business Press, may not sell any more copies than a self-published book. But if the author is aiming to increase their credibility as a financial services consultant, then being published by the FT or HBP is going add a lot more weight.

Royalties and advances

Ten percent seems to be the standard royalty from a publisher. Some may pay more: you might get lucky, but then again you might be unlucky.

Advances rarely seem to happen for first-time authors, but once you have a book under your belt you stand a good chance of getting one. That said, don't expect a lot of money. The advance might be paid when the book proposal is accepted and contract signed, or it might be on delivery of the draft manuscript.

The most I have ever received for an advance was £2,000. Since I can occasionally earn that in a day – although usually it takes me longer – it is obviously not enough to justify writing the book.

Advances are loans that need to be paid back, normally by deduction from sales royalties. Only when your royalties exceed the advance will you see more returns. If you already have an existing book with the publisher you might also find royalties from that diverted to pay off your advance.

That said, I'm not sure how long publishers give you to pay back the advance. It's entirely possible that it is never paid back and they never ask for the money back. I'm not sure, but from my own experiences and conversations I think publishers only start to get concerned when the advance is big and the book is seriously not selling.

Some authors can secure large advances and higher royalty payments. For this you need a story to tell, a hot topic or a track record of writing books which sell, or all three. I have yet to meet anyone in the technology community who has achieved this.

So don't expect an advance, but be thankful for anything you do get. Similarly, don't expect more than 10% royalties. (Later in this book I go through some pricing calculations which suggest that 10% isn't such a bad number really.)

To use a publisher or not?

Why use a publisher	Why self-publish
Credibility	Retain copyright
Advance	Higher royalties
Editorial support	Option to buy your own quality support
Administration support	Keep control yourself
Access to markets	Optional DRM
Quality control	Quality control

To use a publisher or not may sound like a big decision, but you don't have to make it now – you can decide later. In fact I advise you to do so, and focus first on writing your book.

If you start self-publishing – via LeanPub or some other mechanism – you retain the right to sign up with a publisher later because you still hold the copyright. You can write, publish, earn money, even iterate with several improved versions, and only then think about a publisher. Indeed, if you are self-publishing early versions as you go your efforts might attract the interest of a publisher. This happened for me with both *Xanpan* and *The Art of Agile Product Ownership*.

Even if your book doesn't attract a publisher by itself, you are in a stronger position to approach one. Having a partially complete manuscript, some sales and perhaps reviews puts you in a much stronger position when you talk to publishers. In fact, I'd recommend you start your book this way and decide on a publisher once you better understand your work.

However, once you have signed with a publisher, going the other way – to self-publishing or another publisher – is hard, because you have signed away your copyright. So focus on your book and your writing, and decide about a publisher later.

The self-publishing challenge

The challenge in self-publishing is simple: *you are responsible for everything*. Consciously or not you are constantly making effort-benefit calculations.

Yes, my e-books would sell more if *I* listed them on the Apple bookstore but *I* need to do that. Yes, *I* should investigate hardback versions, but will it sell enough to justify *my* time? Yes, my books would sell more if *I* ran adverts, but that too takes time and money. While *I* could hire a marketing person to help *I* still need to find them, *I* still need to work with them and *I* still need to follow through on their suggestions.

That is a lot of my time. I only have 24 hours in a day – I guess you do too – and I have other things to do. Consequently many of the things I could do to boost my sales are undone, because it's just me.

Working with a publisher shares a lot of this workload. Make no mistake, though – the publisher will still need you to do a lot.

5. Reasons to work with publishers

I may come across as anti-publisher, but I'm not – I'm just disappointed in the publishers I've worked with. That might be my fault, I might have had unrealistic expectations, or it might be theirs for not setting expectations correctly. Ah well, you live and learn.

There are good reasons for working with publishers. They do pick up a lot of the post-writing work: graphics, copy-edit, layout, indexing, distribution, price-setting, sales accounting and so on. You can always buy these services yourself, often from the same people, but until you have those connections and contacts that can seem daunting.

Undoubtedly I benefitted and learned a lot from having a publisher for my first two books. I'm glad I did and would do the same again. Especially with my first book, the publisher ensured that I produced a far better book than if I had done it all myself. I'm also sure that, thanks to the reputation of the publisher and their distribution network, it sold more copies than I could have done on my own.

My second book, *Business Patterns*, benefitted too: this was a complex book in terms of content, layout and market positioning. I was probably over-ambitious, but this book wouldn't be what it is without the publisher: I needed their help. Given that, and that the book had an eight-year gestation period, had I used LeanPub and incremental publishing it would have been a different book.

There is more value in having a publisher for your first book, when you are new to writing and publishing, but this is when you are least attractive to a publisher. *Are they sure you can write? Will your book sell? Can you publicize it?*

My first book was published 15 years ago, an aeon in digital terms. Not only has technology moved on and made production easier, but digital technology has also changed marketing: much more of it occurs online via social networks. At the same time publishers have been on a drive to cut costs, which can translate into less support to authors.

Publishers are not homogenous

Of the two publishers I've worked with I would consider working with one of them again. That said, I'm not sure that that publisher offers the best marketing channel for my work or, today, have the staff in place to provide the same level of support. The other publisher has surprised me with the revenue they have delivered, but the publishing experience was something I would not like to repeat.

I don't have experience of other publishers, so I don't know what support they offer. I know people who have sung the praises of Dorset House and O'Reilly. Part of me would love to publish a book with Addison-Wesley, but I don't know what they are like to work with.

There are also half-way-house publishers. Before the digital revolution there were 'vanity' publishers – who I assume still exist – who undertook to produce, print and distribute a book for a fee paid by the author. If necessary they could even arrange for a ghost writer. One could consider self-published books as a successor to vanity publishing. If so, then it is very much low-budget vanity!

Then there is 'contract publishing', which is similar but commands more respect. An individual or organization commission a book (that is, pays a fee). The publisher may even create the content or have the manuscript ghost-written.

There are also publishers in between who do some of the work but leave some to you. Such publishers make their money from fees rather than royalties. Thus the author takes more risk, but has a bigger potential upside if the book sells.

Publishers only

Although most of the traditional activities undertaken by a publisher can be done by a self-publishing author or subcontracted, there are some things publishers do that I have failed to reproduce. Some of these might be possible if I invested more time, but then the question arises: *would that time be more profitably spent doing something else?*

So here are some things publishers can do which I haven't found a way of doing.

Publishers such as Amazon have access to more tools and options, that is clear, but what those tools are I don't know. They do appear to be able to get reviews on unpublished books.

The Amazon Vine programme in particular is something I wish I could access. Vine allows publishers to offer books free to a panel of regular Amazon reviewers. My publisher put *Business Patterns* in the Vine programme and it generated some great reviews.

While Amazon, Lulu, IngramSparc and others allow print-on-demand books to be made available in the book distributions systems that bookshops buy from, this does not guarantee that books are sold. Just because a book is in a distribution system does not mean someone will buy it. They can order it from any bookshop, but will they know to order it?

Traditionally publishers invested a lot of effort in salespeople who encouraged shops to stock books. This is particularly important for big bookshop chains like Waterstones and Barnes & Noble, for which one sale might consist of several thousand copies.

Like any good retailer, booksellers have a variety of tricks for selling books. The books at the front of the shop aren't there by accident: price reductions and those 'recommended' stickers on some books might be better titled 'sponsored by'. Many of these tactics are paid for by the publisher.

Sometimes booksellers take this too far. Under James Daunt shops in the Waterstone's chain (which now almost includes Barnes & Noble) have moved away from 'head office know best' to a more distributed approach in which individual shops make more decisions.

Either way, as a self-publisher you might struggle to get your book in pole position. That is not to say you shouldn't try – maybe your local bookshop would like to host an author signing?

Similarly, how books get into libraries is a mystery to me. I would not be surprised if a similar salesforce approach was at work here too. Professional books are unlikely to find their way into a public library by accident and probably struggle to get into a university library without a sponsor.

Indeed, one academic did request my books be stocked in his university's library. However, even though the book was available in global distribution systems, the library struggled to buy it. If I recall correctly they were eventually persuaded to buy from Amazon.

Then there are electronic libraries like Safari Tech Books Online. Safari started at O'Reilly but now includes books from other publishers such as Que, Sams and Prentice-Hall. Other publishers offer their own online libraries or are part of other such as Kindle Unlimited. Rather than making money from selling books, their publishers and authors make money from renting books.

Again I know of no way of getting my book into a digital library without a publisher – the exception being Kindle Unlimited, which I discuss in another chapter. So this line of revenue remains closed.

Although it may sometimes feel as if bookshops are dead, that everyone buys online and e-books reign supreme, that is not the case. When combined brick-and-mortar bookshops outsell Amazon. Physical books regularly make up 50% or more of my sales, and other authors tell me that is on the low side.

For the self-publisher it doesn't make sense to chase anything but the very biggest booksellers – and probably not even them. Put all your energy into Amazon. Step out of that world and there is a bigger market to sell to, but doing so requires resources and effort beyond the self-publisher, so if you really want a best-seller you may well be better off with a publisher.

Which makes most money?

I don't know.

– Self-publish and take 70-80% of the revenue, but pay the production costs with your own money and time.

– Sign up with a publisher and accept 10% royalties, but have them pay the production costs and organize distribution.

– Pay a contract publisher to do the boring bits, but keep most or all of the revenue yourself.

Option one gives you a big cut of every sale, but option two potentially gives you a smaller cut of a bigger pie. Option three is the best or worse of both worlds, depending on how you look at it.

I don't know which is best because while I've worked with two publishers, written six self-published books and spoken to many more authors and publishers, this isn't a laboratory and no two experiments are the same.

So while I'm very happy with my book sales, and very happy with the money I receive from Amazon every month, I cannot know *whether I would have had even more success with a publisher* and, like everyone else, I wish they would generate a little more money.

6. Publisher checklist

Have worked with two publishers and also self-published, there are a lot of things I'd want to understand before working with another publisher before I work with them. So here is my checklist. I'm not sure what the 'right' answers are; I also know that in any relationship there is always compromise. A publisher might fall down on one of these points but be strong enough on others to compensate.

Editorial

Will I be working with an editor?

If so, who?. Try and talk to them in advance and find out what they expect to be doing and what they expect from you.

Will there be a review panel?

Some or maybe all chapters may be passed through a review panel. They will provide you with feedback and the publisher with evidence that the book is worth publishing. If there is to be a review panel, ask who will choose the members – it's probably you.

Who will do the copy-editing?

How much time will I have to check the copy-edit?

What tools or systems will be used?

You should also enquire into what happens if you are not happy with the copy-edit. The quality of copy-editing can vary massively; I've been really disappointed by offshore copy-editing.

Once it is complete the publisher may expect you to approve it within a few days. On one book I was temped to refuse it, but didn't know what would then happen. Once the copy-edit has been completed you are close to the end of the publication process, and the publisher may be keen to get the book printed and onto bookshop shelves, so time might be tight.

That particular publisher also used an awful online tool, some inferior version of Adobe Acrobat that meant I had to sit at a machine connected to the internet to approve any copy-edit. It was painful.

Can I use my own copy-editor? If you have worked with a copy-editor before and had a positive experience, it might be worth finding out whether you can work with them again.

How will I pay for image and excerpt fees? If you need to pay for an image it will probably come out of your royalties, but ask.

Marketing

What marketing help will the publisher provide?

The answer may well be 'none', but you should determine this when you sign up. They may arrange to have flyers printed for your book, they may be able to introduce you to book publicity agents (although you may need to pay the fees), or maybe assist with interviews.

How will review copies be handled?

How many printed copies will you provide for review? Will you post them or will I?

Can you put the book into the Amazon Vine programme or similar?

As I have said, Amazon reviews are really important, yet publishers are loath to share copies with reviewers, especially printed copies. As only about one in three reviewers will post a review, you need to 'spray and pray', so you need a publisher who will play along and not see every review copy as a lost sale.

Publication

Will the book be published in all countries simultaneously?

Will the e-book and printed book be published simultaneously?

Will you be using DRM technology?

Assuming you are going to publicize your book on social media, you want both book and e-book appearing simultaneously in all markets at once. Social media and your follower base are boundless. It is very frustrating when you tweet that your book is available with a link to your local Amazon site and someone replies 'I wanted to buy your book but Amazon US lists it as available next month'.

Although books are produced electronically, the e-book version may follow a different process to the printed book. I remember the print version of *Business Patterns* appearing months before the e-book. I had people on social media telling me they wanted to buy the e-book but couldn't.

Will they put the book in any online library systems? For example Safari. How will you be remunerated?

For the author

How many copies will I get and what about an electronic version?

Normally a publisher will give you ten printed copies. Getting a digital copy out of them can be more difficult, especially one which is DRM-free or can be loaded onto a Kindle.

What is my discount?

As an author you will get a discount on copies of your own book from the publisher. If you want to use the book as part of your marketing efforts or course literature you might need many more than ten.

A 10% discount on the recommended retail price probably means you are better off buying your own book from Amazon, which would also give it a boost in their ranking.

Can I distribute e-books myself? and **Can I offer discounts on my books?**

If your book is going to form part of your personal or corporate marketing, you want to be able to share copies – or at least make them available at a discount to selected clients.

How often will I be paid royalties?

Will I have access to sales figures, and how?

I have a pretty good idea how many copies my first two books have sold, but no idea of how many copies my third has sold. That particular publisher is impenetrable.

Royalty rate

You don't need to ask about the royalty rate: they will be sure to tell you. It is probably 10%. You can ask for more, but unless you are a bit of a name you are unlikely to get it.

Author rights

You don't need to ask about copyright, as this will be in the contact and almost certainly transfers it from you to the publisher once you deliver the manuscript.

Will I be able to offer excerpts for publication elsewhere?

You might want to do this either as part of the marketing publicity or for professional publications. If you can offer excerpts to publications, find out **how many words can you use**.

Audio

What about an audio version?

Will the publisher arrange for an audio version of your book? Will they pay for production? Do they expect you to create it?

If not, will they let you arrange an audio version? What permissions need to be given? By whom? What is their procedure?

As I discuss in another chapter, not only do audio books earn money, they also create sales of print and e-books, so you do want an audio version of your book. Not all publishers have woken up to this yet.

Pricing

How how much will it sell for? What about discounts?

Are you happy to leave this to the publisher or do you want a say? Make sure you are happy with the market segment they are targeting.

Find out too if there is a mechanism for you to offer discounts to selected groups such as your course attendees. Publishers may see discounts as lost revenue, but I don't – to me discounts encourage people to buy right now, and help you look good.

End of life

How long will the book remain on the publisher's list?

Will copyright revert to you at any time in the future?

(If the book is batch printed) **How long will the print run be retained for? Will you get a chance to buy any unsold (remaindered) books before they are pulped?**

(If print-on-demand) **Will the e-book and print-on-demand mean the book never goes out of print?**

Can I exit the contract and reacquire the copyright?

If the production process is not satisfactory you might want to pull out. At the other end of the cycle you might want to reacquire the rights and recycle the material later.

7. Digital publishing: selling before you have finished

Printed books need to be printed before you can sell them. This means the book needs to be finished before you can sell it. While that might seem obvious, it is not the same with electronic books: you can start selling an electronic book before you have finished writing it.

The economics of printing books, and the fact that, once printed, you can't change them, has led to a particular publishing process that digital books don't need to obey. Creating a digital book is a lot more like creating software.

Traditional publishing

Because physical books are printed, they can't be changed later. This means that everything needs to be 'right' before they are printed: the author needs to say everything they want to say, the book need copy-editing, the images need to clear copyright checks, the text needs to be typeset and the index needs to be produced with correct page numbers.

Because there are economies of scale in printing, it makes sense to print all the predicted sales in one go. Most books never sell enough to justify a second print run, let alone a second edition. Actually, many books don't even justify a first print run, but publishers only learn that later. Therefore, while it makes sense economically to have a big print run, it also makes sense to print as few as possible to save printing, shipping, storing and pulping books that don't sell.

Ideally you don't want to print any copies that won't sell, so you need to be pretty sure the books will, at least, not lose money. So publishers want to see evidence that an author and their book will sell.

Digital publishing

There are no printing costs to digital books, although I discuss download costs later. Plus I can change them after they are published. No digital book need ever be 'finished' – indeed actually knowing when you are finished can be difficult.

When I start selling a book using LeanPub it isn't finished. I continue adding chapters, editing existing content, changing graphics and so on. Those who buy my book are entitled to free updates – just like an app you buy from the Apple AppStore for your phone. Every time I push out a book update buyers get an email saying 'Allan just updated his book, download the latest version for free'.

Every time I release an update is a marketing opportunity, and social media makes it easy. All it requires is a battery of tweets announcing a new chapter, or a status update telling my LinkedIn connections that a chapter has been extended or edited. Were I on Instgram I could also make noise about the diagrams, graphs and illustration I'm adding and changing.

My recent books have earned around $1,000 even before they were finished. People know they are buying an unfinished product, but that has its own value: they get to be the first to read the book and they get an opportunity to give feedback.

To be honest, while in theory early versions of my books should generate feedback, I don't get much. The best feedback I get is the sales, the payments. Not that $3.50 changes my life, but I know that someone, somewhere, thinks that what I am writing is worth money. That is a special form of feedback.

When to stop?

Traditional publishers ask authors to complete book proposal forms when considering a book. These forms detail the book's title, synopsis, table of contents, target audience, competitor books, estimated word count and proposed delivery date.

A lot of that information is designed to allow the publisher to assess the size of the book's market. The list of competitors is there, not so that publishers can check that your work is better, but so that they can see how the competition sells. If you are proposing a book on 'Safety critical systems in PHP' and there are no competitors, or competitors that have only sold a dozen copies, it might be that there is no market. (Nielsen and other book distribution systems allow publishers to see sales figures on rival books. How much information they can see I don't know.)

The word count and deadline are there to define the book and determine when it is 'done'. The delivered tome is expected to have a structure not too far from the table of contents, which means that a) the author has thought this through in advance, and b) there is limited opportunity to change the contents.

When writing and publishing yourself you probably don't create your own book proposal, although it might be useful. An author may decide for themselves to stop writing when, after six months, nobody has bought a draft copy of 'Safety critical systems in PHP' or whatever. But since there is no editor or project manager, no word count or table of contents, an author could just keep writing.

I faced this problem with my first self-published book, *Xanpan*. I had plenty of ideas but I didn't know when to stop. Eventually I stopped because I wanted to pursue other projects. However, because people are still buying the book, the temptation to continue remains.

Batch processing

Traditionally when writing is finished it is time to move a book to production. Copy-editing is the first process here, followed by typesetting and indexing, then printing. It doesn't make sense to start these processes before writing is finished because the text will inevitably change.

In the digital world indexes are rather a thing of the past, as readers can search the text electronically.

Modern digital tools reduce the need for typesetting, but they don't produce the quality a skilled typesetter would. My copy-editor, Steve, also typesets, and I can hear him groan every time I politely decline his offer to typeset my book. Yes, a professional typeset would make my book look better, but to my eyes modern tools deliver 80% of the quality for 10% of the cost.

However, cost-benefit is not the only problem typesetting faces. Traditional typesetting laid out books on paper, but in the digital world printed books are but one of many formats. There is PDF, Mobi, ePub and others I have never heard of. A book that is brilliantly typeset on paper may look awful on ePub or vice-versa. If quality is important to you then you may need to do several typesets.

However, modern digital publishing tools can easily produce multiple formats. It may only be 80% of the quality of print, but it's 80% on all platforms. This is very much like software: I spent a large part of my programming career porting software between Windows and Unix – and not just one Unix version, but Solaris, SCO, Interactive, AIX, TruUnix and so on.

Copy-editing remains. I'm sure some authors are pretty good at grammar, spelling and all that stuff. If I were more confident that my chapters would remain stable I could have chapters copy-edited one at a time, but I frequently find myself delving back into a chapter and changing it – even moving vast chunks to other chapters.

Cover design needn't be a batch process; it can be done at pretty much any time. Having a good-looking cover can only help sales even if the book isn't finished. If you are using social media to generate interest and sales in your unfinished book, having a professionally designed cover gives your message more impact.

One new process has inserted itself into the digital age: the creation of audio books. Only when the text is stable do I have have a narrator record the book, although in theory I could have Stacy record the chapters one by one as I finish them.

Publisher cost-cutting

In recent decades publishers have striven to drive down publishing costs. Books are printed in far-away countries where it is cheap. This increases shipping costs, and more trouble introduces a time delay. It is unlikely that your heavy books are going to be airfreighted overnight – six weeks in a shipping contain is much more likely.

Copy-editing and typesetting have also been moved to offshore locations. While publishers clearly feel that the quality of both is as good in their chosen low-cost location as it is in their more expensive home country, not all authors agree with them. While I'm prepared to compromise on typesetting and layout, I am unwilling to compromise on copy-editing.

I may have been unlucky, but of the three books I published with traditional publishers two were copy-edited in a low-cost location. Being dyslexic I need more copy-editing than most, and I'm sorry to say I wasn't happy with the quality of either.

During the copy-edit of the second of those two book I toyed with rejecting the copy-edit. I had no idea what would happen if I did, so I didn't. I wish I had.

Conversely, one of my books was edited here in the UK. The copy-editor was not an employee of the publisher – like many copy-editors he was and still is freelance. Any publisher can hire him, and I do too. Steve has copy-edited almost all my books and I'm very happy with him. Judge for yourself. I know authors who use cheaper copy-editors, but I value his standards and he has got to know my quirks.

Print-on-demand

Digital technology has also changed the economics of printing. Economies of scale still mean that printing 1,000 books in one run is cheaper than printing one book individually a thousand times. If only 100 out of those 1,000 books sell and the other 900 get pulped, however, the economics change.

Not only do those 900 wasted copies cost a lot to print, they also cost to store while the publisher hopes someone will buy them. All that incurs charges, but perhaps more importantly it requires organization and administration. Someone needs to rent warehouse space and employ the warehouse staff.

Individual print-on-demand copies may cost more to print than a bulk-printed book, but they don't require capital to be locked up in stock or the administration of storage or staff. There must be a point below which it makes sense to print each book on demand and above which it makes sense to bulk-print, but I have no figures or experience. Certainly as a self-publisher print-on-demand is much simper.

Power to small publishers

Publishers once had access to unique resources and skills that made them the guardians of what was published. Today digital technology means many of these specialist capabilities are now available to anyone.

Unlike their own employees, the freelancers who publishers use – for copy-editing, type-setting, indexing and artwork – are available for hire. Your money and mine is as good as Addison-Wesley's or Penguin's.

Put all this together and the self-publishing author can match traditional publishers, and even better them in places.

8. Copyright

Self-publishing means that you to keep the copyright to your work. That might not seem a big deal if your aim is to make money by selling books, but if your aim is to use the book as a calling card or as the basis for other products, it might be. In fact, because publishers don't yet seem to understand the way the digital world has changed, their restrictions – designed to protect copyright – may actually hinder sales.

As a consultant I find it incredibly useful to own the copyright to my work. Whether it is giving e-books to potential clients or using parts of books in marketing, the content I self-publish gets reused while the books I sold to a publisher get ignored.

Everything you write is copyright. You only lose copyright if you explicitly disown it, by declaring the work to be in the public domain or by applying a Creative Commons licence[1]. When you self-publish you keep the copyright, while when you work with a publisher you transfer your copyright to them. That is how they make their money.

Publishers regard the content and copyright as their source of revenue, thus it is to be guarded.

Want to publish a 'teaser' excerpt from your book in a magazine? Or recycle some of the book into journal articles? You will have to check with the publisher first. When I did this with one book I was limited to 1,000 words – any more than that and the publisher wanted payment.

Want an audio version? Unless the publisher wants to do this – and take most of the revenue for themselves – then you may need to pay the costs yourself and yet still pay the publisher.

Translations? Publishers might find a foreign language publishing house which will buy the translation rights, just don't expect much in the way of payments yourself. They won't give translation rights for free.

Conversely, when you own the copyright you can allow anyone you choose to translate the book. You could pay your own translator, or you could come to a revenue-sharing deal or any other arrangement. The same goes for second editions and repackaging – say using excerpts from one book as part of another.

---

[1] https://creativecommons.org/

Give it away

Want to give away copies to potential clients? You can probably buy your own printed books at a discount, normally 20%, 40% if you are lucky. Once you have bought them they are yours to do as you see fit.

Giving away electronic copies? There must be a way of doing this, but you will probably need to buy a book to give it away. Publishers apply DRM to e-books, so you might have to ask the recipient to install the software mandated by your publisher.

Giving away copies may well be in your own interests, perhaps to generate online reviews or to impress potential clients. If you own the copyright then giving away e-books is cost-free. Even printed book costs are low when you are the publisher, although you need to add in postage.

Post-Brexit, UK residents face the additional burden of import taxes throughout Europe, which are applied somewhat erratically. E-books can sail unnoticed across the internet, but printed books sometimes incur import duties higher than the full sale price of the book.

I frequently give books to potential clients when replying to an enquiry. Being able to say "Thanks for your enquiry... we should talk some more, in the meantime please check out my book, this is a link to a free download". If I sold the book I might make a few pounds, but if they buy my consultancy or training services I might make several thousand.

Electronic books also make a great give-away for mailing list subscribers: 'Join my mail list and receive a free e-book'. Or raffle them off when you do a public talk, which is a great way to remind people that if they enjoyed your talk, they may enjoy the book.

But perhaps the overwhelming reason for giving books away is to generate reviews, particularly reviews on Amazon. I discuss this elsewhere so I won't repeat myself, save to say publishers don't always 'get' this.

A good Amazon review is worth more than the book itself, but publishers restrict how many copies you can give away. One of my publishers was reasonably happy for me to distribute pre-copy-edited PDF versions of the book, but only wanted to circulate ten final copies for review. They even raised difficulties when one reviewer asked for a printed copy instead of an e-book.

Sell it

Perhaps best of all, if you own the copyright you can sell it to a publisher.

Twice I have had publishers approach me about 'adopting' my self-published work. The first time was with *Xanpan*: this was mostly finished – being my first e-book it had a long gestation after I decided not to write any more – when a publisher came along and asked "Would you be interested in publishing with us?".

I went through the formal application process, but at the end of the day the publications committee decided against adopting the book. At least that motivated me to 'finish' the book properly.

It would have been nice to see Xanpan formally published by a reputable publisher, but I wouldn't then have been able to do half the things I've done with it. It has been recorded, it has been my mailing list give-away and it has become my standard additional reading text when I deliver a training course.

From time to time I toy with the idea of doing a second edition, or a 'Xanpan XL' version. Both of them would require reusing the text from the existing book, so I would have needed a publisher's permission. I would probably only get it if the publisher wanted to publish the new book themselves.

This happened again when the work-in-progress *Art of Product Ownership* was found on LeanPub by Apress. I did a formal book proposal, but this time they did decide to publish.

You can start writing your book today before you have a publisher agreement. You can approach a publisher at any time, or if you are lucky they might approach you. Owning the copyright retains your option to work with a publisher at a later late. The reverse sometimes also happens.

Keep it in print

Books go out of print because publishers no longer consider it meaningful to keep stocks of printed copies. If your print run was 3,000 there is every chance that three years later 2,000 are sitting in a warehouse somewhere. A few copies a year may sell, but those 2,000 cost to store, and at some time the publisher is going to want that space for another book.

When a publisher wants to get rid of surplus books they get 'remaindered'. They may simply be pulped and the paper made into new books, or they may be defaced in some way and sold on cheaply – say the cover torn off or pages cut. The expectation is that the books are now worthless, but such books have a habit of turning up. If you think this is going to happen to your book you might be want to buy the printed copies from the publisher before they get pulped.

Electronic books don't have a 'cost of carry', so will probably never go out of print, but electronic publishing is too new to know for sure. Print-on-demand books needn't go out of print either.

If a book is only printed when someone buys a copy, then there is no cost of carry. The only cost comes from the disk space the print image file occupies, and as the cost of storage continues to fall that gets closer to zero every year.

Bringing back copyright

You will want to check your contract to see whether you have any right to the copyright after a book is remaindered, or whether you can buy it back. Those contracts I have seen are time-limited; say, after ten years copyright is released. In the IT field the vast majority of books are going to be irrelevant by that stage.

If you have produced a book with a publisher and think people are still interested in it, you might be able to reacquire the copyright and set it up on a print-on-demand system yourself. If you are really lucky you might even be able to get hold of the typeset files for printed copy.

As publishers themselves adopt print-on-demand and small-batch size printing technology, remaindering and reacquiring copyright are likely to disappear. The good news is that also means your book may never go out of print.

9. Money from writing

Most of this book discusses how to make money from your own writing and publishing, whether with or without a publisher. Basically you write, your book gets published and you earn money from sales.

Of over 45,000 'unique titles' published in the US during the year 2021–2022 less than 1% sold over 100,000 copies, while 86% of books sold less than 5,000 copies. Perhaps more worryingly for a new author, 15% of books sold less than 12 copies[1].

The 5,000 figure is significant because, certainly in the US, this is the point at which publishers consider a book to be profitable. Publishers accept that most books will lose money, so they aim to make enough from big sellers to cover their losses. They therefore aim to publish many books in the hope of finding a best-seller and reducing the costs of producing those that don't sell. This is why publishers always seem to be reducing costs.

None of my books have sold 5,000 copies, but I still make money from writing. Authors can make money even while a publisher is losing it. Three of my books have sold only in the hundreds, four have sold over a thousand copies, one will break a thousand soon and another has – or will – cross the thousand barrier, but I lack data on it so I can't be sure.

So while a publisher may see my book sales as a failure, I don't. Nor are book sales and royalties the only way to make money out of writing.

As I've already mentioned, writing a book can support other revenue streams such as consulting and training. A book gives you credibility and boosts your non-book income. While *Xanpan* has only sold a few hundred copies, it has become a key element of my consulting practice. If you have a successful book you can create additional revenue-earning material around the book, for example an online course that helps people acquire the ideas and practices in the book.

You can also earn money directly from writing. Such opportunities are not very common, but they do exist. In the past I have been asked to contribute chapters to other people's books. Such chapters, or sometimes forewords, seldom pay, but they are about boosting your credibility and possibly publicizing your own books on the back of someone else's.

---

[1]The figures quoted here are taken from the BBC radio programme More or Less: 'Do half of new books really sell fewer than twelve copies?', broadcast October 22 2022 and available as a podcast.

Very occasionally I have been asked to contribute a chapter to a book and have been paid for it. It doesn't happen very often, but it can happen. I have also been paid to contribute to magazines and journals. This also isn't very common, as most magazines and journals today expect free contributions. While there may be no money on offer, contributions are again about credibility and publicity. Sometimes I get paid, and even if it is only $200 it is nice, particularly if I retain the copyright and can use the material again elsewhere.

More recently I was approached by a consultancy company that wanted fresh content for their website. While they were prepared to pay for posts, I decided the amount on offer wasn't enough to justify the time required.

I have also met someone who earns money from posts on Medium. Personally I've never understood Medium: it seems to be half blog site and half newspaper. However, I have failed to find another Medium blogger who makes it pay, so it is still a mystery to me.

A word of warning about reusing material online. Google doesn't like repetition on the web and penalizes it in their search algorithms. So if your website only contains blog posts of things you have published elsewhere on the web, Google will not rank it highly.

Should people come to see you as an authority on a subject you might also find publishers approaching you, not to write for them, but to review book submissions and early chapters of books. This occasionally pays, although not large sums. Alternatively publishers may reward you with a selection of books from their catalogue.

I used to regularly review books for publishers but I've mostly stopped now. Finding the time to review a book, or even a few chapters, can be hard. The last time I reviewed a book the publisher gave me four or five books of my choosing, which I then failed to read for lack of time.

Books sales are my main source of writing income. While there are other paid writing opportunities, they are rare – but then I haven't gone looking for them. After all, there are plenty of professional journalists and copywriters who make a living from writing, so the opportunities are there if you do go looking.

10. The *Little Book* story

I once wrote a book on a flight from London to Dallas. To be honest, it was only a first draft, and those ten hours didn't include any editing or production. I didn't set out to write a book, and I when I saw how much I had written I didn't know what to do with the manuscript. Eventually that manuscript ended up as my best-selling *A Little Book about Requirements and User Stories*.

For years I had been looking in envy at Mike Cohn's *User Stories Applied* and thinking 'How does he get 200 pages and a best-seller out of something so simple?'. If I'm being completely honest I didn't think much of *User Stories*. In fact I had spoken to Rachel Davies, who was on the team that invented user stories, and she told me that they didn't expect them to last either!

Still, I found clients kept asking about user stories and I found that I was giving the same answers again and again. 'I must write this down', I kept telling myself, 'then I can just give people a printout and have done with it'.

Eventually the time came when a client asked me to Louisiana. Ten hours in the air – I could write down my user story notes. I expected to spend a couple of hours writing, eat a meal, watch a film and sleep a bit on the flight. As it was, my laptop came out shortly after takeoff and I didn't stop until "Prepare cabin for landing" was announced.

The words just flowed. I was writing down what I had already told people, so I knew what I was going say – it was almost a transcription exercise. Looking at the text a few days later in a Houston hotel room I didn't know what to do with it.

I had over 20,000 words. Too many for a journal article, far more than I expected to give clients, not enough for a book (and I didn't want to write a book about user stories!) but too much to waste. *What was I going to do?*

At the time I was contributing occasional pieces to the online journal *Agile Connection*. I asked the then editor, Johanna Rothman, if she would like a series of articles on user stories. I can't remember her exact reply, but it was very quick and meant something like 'Is the sky blue?'.

Johanna set two rules: pieces were to be no more than 1,200 words and to be written in the active voice. She already knew that I tended towards the passive voice. Whether it is because active/passive is a hard thing to grasp, or whether it is my dyslexia, I find it all mumbo-jumbo.

Like the noun-verb thing, I can understand the concept of active voice and passive voice while I work with the definition and think about it, but ask me two minutes later what the difference is and I don't know. Fortunately Johanna also knew of a text editor with a plug-in that could help me.

Basically, passive voice means you use 'be' a lot. The text editor would highlight everywhere I used 'be' (and a couple of other guilty words) and I would rewrite the sentence. Rewriting those sentences was pretty much random; I would just keep trying different formulations of words that said the same thing but didn't use 'be'. Like an infinite monkey I eventually got my Shakespeare: I came to see patterns of how I needed to change sentences, but please don't ask me to recall any now.

Johanna was a great editor. Not only did she give me these two rules, but she also read my material and gave me non-judgemental feedback. When she was done my articles were handed off to Beth, who did a copy-edit on them. Fantastic!

Agile Connection wasn't paying for pieces but their production standards were – and still are as far as I know – high. Their standards were higher than just about any other online and several print journals I've contributed to.

I broke the 20,000-word manuscript down into a series of 1,200-word pieces, each focused on a different aspect or problem with user stories and requirements more generally. In the end the series ran to about 12 or 14 articles and ran from July 2015 to March 2016. Not all the original ideas made it into articles and one or two more were added along the way, but basically it was the same material.

By this time I'd already published *Xanpan* with LeanPub and I started to wonder if I could recycle my user stories articles. After writing *Xanpan* I'd adopted Markdown as my standard medium and was using basic text editors rather than Microsoft Word. The loss of formatting distractions was liberating and allowed me to focus on what I wanted to say.

I'd not signed a copyright agreement with Agile Connection, so I still owned the copyright, but I was shy about telling Johanna or Beth, so it started as an experiment. I also wondered whether, when the articles were free to download from Agile Connection, anyone would buy a book.

Having carved my airplane manuscript into 1,200-word blocks the book was easy to put together. I added a couple of other chapters that weren't in the series, and an old essay as an appendix to go deeper into one specific question.

The book sales immediately surprised me! The content was free online already, but people nevertheless bought the book on LeanPub. To be honest I was a little embarrassed because, as I said, I didn't think much of user stories.

Unlike my three earlier books, *Little Book* is not trying to change the world: it does not contain a single unified idea that everything else supports. *Little Book* is much more of a 'Sixteen things to improve your user stories' book. I now know that '*n* things' books usually sell better than big ideas.

After a while I decided to take the book to Amazon Kindle Direct, KDP. This is where I really started to see sales and I realized that, as good as LeanPub is, most people don't know it exists. I realize now that the book sells on Amazon because it's a popular topic, it's a '*n* things' book, it's cheap and, because it sells well, it sells well – sometimes it was just below Mike Cohn's book in the category tables!

Amazon has a lot of visitors, and Amazon algorithms are very good at spotting that someone who has bought one of my earlier books might like another. Its algorithms also spot that people who buy *User Stories Applied* might buy *Little Book*, so those who buy Cohn's work might well find Amazon saying 'People who bought *User Stories Applied* also bought *Little Book*'.

As I had done with *Xanpan*, I created a Lulu print version, and that sold well. Even fewer people go to Lulu than go to LeanPub, but because Lulu will push a book into global distribution systems, including Amazon, it becomes widely available.

Unfortunately the fees Lulu and booksellers take means that if your book is priced low you see very little money from a sale. Eventually I moved the print version of *Little Book* onto Amazon's own print-on-demand service and I now see more returns from its sales.

My first foray into audio books was *Project Myopia*. The results were a little disappointing but I found the processes relatively easy. I'd been reading a lot about the power of audio books, so I decided to have Stacy record *Little Book* for me.

A few weeks after the audio book went live I saw book sales jump markedly. The sales boost eventually worked its way through the system, but a couple of years later I got to do another experiment.

The *Agile on the Beach* conference, of which I am a cofounder and still an organizer, decided to give its mailing list subscribers a Christmas present. I offered the audio version of *Little Book*. In mid-February sales went up and stayed up for several weeks.

Both these events lead me to conclude that audio book sales increase sales of actual books, both electronic and print. When someone listens to *Little Book* on Audible I make a little money, but a few of them will go on to buy the e-book and I make a little more money.

All books see sales decline over time, but I've just checked and today, seven years after publication, *A Little Book about Requirements and User Stories* is still selling. Last month alone it sold 19 copies on Amazon, the majority print editions, bringing in over $50 of royalties. In addition there will be revenue from ACX/Audible and maybe a few LeanPub sales.

In truth *Little Book* took more than the LHR-DFW flight time to write but, as usual, most of the time was not writing the manuscript, but editing it. Perhaps because I didn't have high expectations of *Little Book* I've taken chances and undertaken experiments with it. These have paid off and the book has consistently – and somewhat embarrassingly – sold. The next experiment should be a second edition.

II Writing

11. When you know what you want to say

It is easier to write if you know what you want to say. If you *feel* the message you are trying to convey, if you can imagine the argument you are trying to make and if you can see the people you want to speak to in your mind's eye.

Sometimes I know what I want to say, but while I might not know the words I'm going to use I have a clear idea of the message I want to convey with those words. It is hard to say how I have that clear idea: it is just there, in my head, I can conceive the thing – the whole is a 'thing'. Sometimes I can draw it, and sometimes trying to draw it gives me the words. At other times I have to ask myself "What is it you are trying to say?", then write and iterate.

I used to think that this was the way everyone's mind worked – after all, I only have experience of my own mind, so I extrapolated to everyone else. However, having spoken to a few people, I now think my dyslexic mind may go further in seeing the whole. All I can say is, just try and write down your ideas. If you can't write them, draw them, even if all you end up with is a collection of bubbles with words in them.

The original draft of *Project Myopia* was very much an idea. I just knew that projects were wrong and I wanted to explain my thinking. As I wrote down the problems inherent in projects I was able to see different problems laid out before me and I was able to name them. As as I wrote it became clear that what I was actually talking about was the *project model*.

If you feel it helps to write something down that states your core message, do so. Equally, if you have an audience in mind, write that down. In fact, make them part of your book: put a statement of target audience at the beginning, or write an introductory chapter.

You might drop these sections later as the book takes shape, but to start with they serve to remind you what you want to say. That said, I usually find that I can't write such a statement until near the end of a book, when I understand it well enough to write a short summary.

My way

As with the rest of this book, this section describes what I have found to work for me. While I hope you will find techniques and inspiration to help you write here, I suspect we each need to find our own way to express our voices. I know that many people find the actual writing far harder than I do.

So don't just read what I say about writing. Chapter 14 briefly describes Gerry Weinberg's *Fieldstone technique*; if you like what you read, then move on to reading his book *Weinberg on Writing* (2006).

The foreword to this book is written by Johanna Rothman, who also has a book about writing, *Free your inner nonfiction writer* (2022). Since Johanna's book is entirely about the actual writing, she has more advice, more techniques and goes into more depth than I do in this section.

Talk, then write

At other times I know what I want to say because I've already told someone. Some of my best pieces have been the result of talking a problem through with a client or colleague. Shortly afterwards, while it is still fresh in my mind, I sit down and write it up.

One variation on this technique is to talk to yourself – like the *Cardboard Programmer* pattern. I find this works best if I am walking or speaking into a voice recorder, or both. Sometimes I will record the same speech multiple times to get my thoughts in order, then sit down and type. The voice recorder is actually superfluous – I almost never listen to the recording!

I wrote a lot of *Succeeding with OKRs in Agile* during the 2020 Covid lockdown, on my morning walks around Acton Park that serve as my daily exercise. My fellow early morning walkers must have wondered about this strange man wandering around the park talking into a recorder.

I use this approach too when creating new presentations, so it might not be a surprise when I say another variation on the technique is to create a PowerPoint of the things you want to say. Normally it works the other way round – my presentations draw on something I have already written.

Much of this book is simply my writing down what I have said to people: Steve Smith, David Daly, Peter Wendorff and others. I don't remember the exact words, but I remember the topics and how it felt. I just have to project myself back to those conversations.

Introductory chapter

Introductory chapters can be interesting. An introduction often summarizes the whole book and acts as a rallying cry. I find them one of the hardest chapters to write, simply because there is so much I want to say in them – the whole book in fact! But, perhaps because they set the tone and preview what is to come, introductory chapters are often the best chapters in a book.

Sometimes I end up with more than one introductory chapter simply because I find some great opening paragraphs. That's why some of my books have an Introduction *and* a Preface, and maybe a Prologue too. Or why some are divided into parts with each part having its own introduction.

As a general rule more people are going to read the early chapters of a book than the later ones – there will always be some readers who abandon a book. Of those early chapters, it is the Introduction that is most likely to be read. So it is the Introduction which a) expresses your message to the greatest number of people, and b) is your opportunity to grab the reader's attention and make them want to know more, to read the rest of the book.

Editing

Writing is not the hard part – editing is. And it is boring: very very boring.

Reading over one's own work, asking oneself if it is clear enough, changing words, moving commas, aligning tenses, changing all the 'we' to 'you', 'me' or 'one', or perhaps removing all the 'you' and 'me' and changing them to 'we', and so on. Not just once but twice, three times, four times. Discovering that you wrote the same idea in two different chapters, sometimes even in the same words, or even the same idea twice in one chapter.

Perhaps because I'm dyslexic, most of my writing is read and edited many times. Two or three immediate edits are not uncommon. Put to one side, read and edit a week later. Then, maybe, let it mature for a few more weeks and repeat. Although with this book I'm doing far fewer read-edit cycles than usual: it's a little experiment.

In recent years I've started using the voice synthesizer on my Apple Mac to read my text to me, as I can hear mistakes that I can't see. This might be a dyslexic thing, but I'm forever assembling the right letters into the wrong word, and that's before it gets anywhere near a professional copy-editor.

Hit delete: less is more

Perhaps the hardest part of editing, both individual pieces and the whole book, is removing work. Sometimes I can write a really great paragraph and then, during editing, I realise I've made the same point in another great paragraph. If I'm lucky I can merge them, or I can say 'To put it another way...' or some other formulation, but sometimes – often – the right answer is to strip out the duplication.

This problem appears too at the whole book level. While you are less likely to write two whole chapters that say the same thing, you may well find that removing a chapter, or simply not developing an idea, makes the book more wholesome. That is to say, what you leave out can be as important as what you leave in.

However, it *can* sometimes help to explain something a second time. If you want a message to sink in then you might want to repeat it. You might make the same point in different ways several times in a book.

If you want a book to be really focused then you can't afford too many repeats or diversions – you have to keep to the core material. If on the other hand you are trying to write an *everything you might need to know* reference guide, then sure, add more in – but then why not write in instalments? Each book in the series could form part of the 'ultimate' reference guide.

Even if you are prepared to let your book lose focus and make some digressions, remember that readers might find more pages off-putting, and more pages means higher costs. More words are more words to have copy-edited. More pages mean more pieces of paper to be printed and shipped. Even electronic books cost more to ship when you have to pay download charges for bigger files.

I find deciding what to leave out harder than what to leave in. At some stage during book development the book will sprout a 'surplus' or 'extra' subdirectory where discarded chapters and ideas get stored. I can always get them back if I need them, but with them out of the way I can see the whole more clearly.

Sometimes I tell myself they will be used in a sequel or a Volume II. I've yet to actually follow through on the idea, but both Xanpan Appendix[1] and Succeeding with OKRs in Agile Extra[2] come close.

One of the options offered by LeanPub is to store documents in GitHub. The big advantage of using such a source control system is that nothing is ever completely deleted or lost – you

---

[1]https://leanpub.com/xanpan2
[2]https://leanpub.com/agileokrsextra/

can always go back in time. Of course if you are not from a programming background and are not familiar with such systems, you may well find the administration overhead off-putting. (You can use Git or another source-code control system whether you are using LeanPub or not.)

Authors learn most

Perhaps the best-kept secret about any book is that it is the author who learns more than anyone else. Your book may be designed, like this one, to share what you know with a wider audience, and you may strive to make the book readable and accessible, but it is the author, during the act of writing, who learns the most.

The act of putting words down, stating what you think you know, making it fit together, making it coherent, working through the anomalies in your own thinking, plus any research, all means that the person who learns most from any book is the person who writes it: you.

I'm learning from writing this book. Learning is one of the reasons I keep writing.

Development editing

When you know what you want to say – like this book – the writing comes easily. As you write you see what is needed, know what needs to be included and what to leave out. It isn't always like that. Sometimes you have ideas but it is less clear what needs to be said, what should be included and what merely clutters the message. This is where *development editing* comes in.

For my first book, *Changing Software Development*, I had help from the publisher's computer science editor. While she didn't write any of the words she was the first reader, she commented on the drafts, made suggestions, asked me to expand some parts and questioned if some sections were needed. One might say that she guided my work. While the message and content were most definitely my own, she 'shaped' the work.

This guiding and shaping mainly related to the earlier chapters – as the work progressed I had less assistance. Undoubtedly the book was better for this help – although like all my books I would do it differently today!

My second book, *Business Patterns*, benefitted from similar help – by now a new editor, Birgit, was in place, although the long gestation of the book meant that most of this help occurred before it was officially approved. Most of *Business Patterns* was peer-reviewed at EuroPLoP and VikingPLoP conferences over eight years.

Birgit had been one of those reviewers, and she and I had many conversations about the book before it reached the proposal stage. As I recount in another chapter, the book proposal needed two attempts to be accepted, which also led to long conversations about content.

Only recently did I learn that this kind editorial help is called *development editing*, and is quite normal when working with publishers. That said, my last publisher provided little support here, which might be either a sign that my ideas were well-formed or a sign that not all publishers take it so seriously.

While self-publishing authors can hire a development editor to help them with their ideas, I have never done so, nor am I aware of anyone who does. The role requires an understanding of publishing and the target market, what makes good (readable) writing, some familiarity with the subject matter and the ability to give feedback without crushing its recipient.

Given the skills and knowledge required it is perhaps understandable why such editors are more likely to be found in publishing houses. Over time editors get to build up market knowledge and understand their specialism, which increases their value to writers.

As a writer it is up to you to decide whether you feel the need for a development editor. If you do, then the obvious thing to do is to work with a suitable publisher. Just remember to check in advance what help you will get before you sign the contract. As I said, I had very little help from my second publisher.

Alternatively you might find a development editor for yourself[3]. Before you start an open search it would be worth talking to other authors, asking for recommendations and getting an idea of what you expect an editor to do for you before you hire someone.

In retrospect I realise that I struck lucky with my fourth book, *A Little Book about Requirements and User Stories*. As the long original essay was broken into sections for serialisation, Joahnna Rothman gave feedback and guidance on each instalment. Over time a tone and style emerged and gaps in the original were plugged. Johanna filled the development editor role.

However, luck is not a strategy, so if you want to find a Johanna you need to be proactive. Rather than seeking out a professional development editor, you perhaps might ask a trusted peer to help guide your book. What they lack in editing skills might be made up for in subject knowledge. You could pay them directly, or credit them as a co-author. After all, co-authors need write an equal numbers of words or take equal cuts of any royalties.

---

[3]A quick search on Upwork.com finds several dozen.

12. Learning to write

I'm sure some authors just sit down one day and write a book. For most of us, though, it helps to work up to it. A book is a marathon, or perhaps a triathlon if you are both writing and self-publishing. If you are going to attempt an endurance event it helps to practice on a smaller scale beforehand.

I have been lucky to find forums where I have been able to practice my writing and discover my own voice. Actually, while I say 'lucky', it wasn't all down to luck: I grabbed opportunities, took risks and sought out places to write, publish and get feedback. Such places do exist, although my places might not be the right places for you.

Some of the help I get from others is because I seek it out. At other times people just offer suggested edits, ideas or questions. I am reminded of Tennessee Williams' character Blanche DuBois in *A Street Car Named Desire*: "I have always depended on the kindness of strangers".

A few people have played really important roles in making me the writer I am today. I'm sure I've thanked John Merrells and Johanna Rothman in print before now, but Alan Griffiths, Reg Charney, Kevlin Henney, Linda Rising, Lise Hvatum and Klaus Marquardt have all played more than minor parts in my growth.

Writing for journals

The world is full of journals and magazines – all the publications you see in a newsagent or bookshop. There are all the academic publications to be found in libraries, then all the online publications. I won't mentioning blogging and medium.com for now.

All these publications need content, which means they need writers. Some of them will have high quality thresholds – think of the blind reviewing that academic journals use. But there are plenty that are just scraping by, desperate for writers to contribute.

The world of online journals varies massively. A few will pay for your work – although it won't be much, maybe $200. A few others will expect you to pay *them* for the privilege of publication.

Indeed, one such appeared in my mailbox this morning, a journal I'd never heard of seeking contributions. A quick Google revealed others who had received similar requests and discovered that it cost $65 to publish with them. If you are looking to practise writing there are much cheaper options.

I got my start writing for the ACCU journal *Overload* in the late 1990s. ACCU started life as the *Association of C and C++ Users*, so the journals I published focused on programming in the C family of languages: C, C++, C#, Java and so on. I'd joined the ACCU, read the articles and thought 'I'd like to share, and I think I'm as good as some of these.'

John Merrells was the editor at the time and was very welcoming. He accepted almost everything I wrote and was very gentle in his feedback. In time John handed over to Alan Griffiths, who was equally welcoming, even when my articles started to stray a long way from C++.

Some of my articles were recycled into chapters for *Changing Software Development* and a few found their way into *An Agile Reader*. So *Overload* was a great place to collect 'field stones' (which I'll talk about later).

In the end I contributed to *Overload* for over ten years. Even as I started blogging and writing books I continued to contribute. During that time I also started to place articles occasionally in other journals. Not long after my contributions to *Overload* ceased I became a regular in *Agile Connection*.

At *Agile Connection* Johanna Rothman challenged me to write small articles: the long meandering pieces of *Overload* were no more. This was and still is a challenge. One of the nice things about writing a book is that you have space to explore and expand your ideas – although that also means you can get lost.

Both *Overload* and *Agile Connection* gave me the opportunity to learn to write. My early *Overload* pieces were written more like a school essay or work documentation. My *Agile Connection* pieces are more focused and hold fewer and better-formed ideas.

Blogging

My other great training ground became my blog. I started blogging in 2005 and I'm still going now. The challenges of a blog are different. While there is no strict word limit, shorter is better, although I regularly break that rule.

Blogging is more frequent too, although it doesn't have to be. I produce two or three blog posts a month now. There are times when I would produce twice that many and there have been months with nothing. The catch with blogging is that no matter how many times I edit my content is still full of dyslexic English. (I'm fantastically grateful to Richard Howells, who has provided free after-publication copy-edit suggestions.)

With a blog I can write anything I want: there is no editor to tell me I'm writing rubbish, or that "nobody wants to know this". That probably shows in some of my early articles while I was learning what form my blog should take.

Blogging has taught me to write more and the importance of staying focused. My blog stays on-topic now, but the range of topics I feature reflects my wide-ranging interests.

Perhaps I should move from blogging to Medium[1], but to be honest I can't work out what the point of Medium is. Functionally Medium appears to me to be a blog. Part of me knows it is more, but as yet I haven't worked out where it fits into my writing. Similarly, LinkedIn provides blog-like features which I haven't really grasped.

Presentations

Writing articles, blogs and books is a little like being a script writer creating a story to be acted out. By contrast, presentations, at conferences and elsewhere, is like being a stand-up comic. You need to work out some material, but you then need to deliver that material using your own voice.

There are synergies between presenting publicly and writing. Both require you to develop a story you can share, which means that you need to organize your thoughts, remove any surplus and ensure you have a coherent narrative.

Presenting also provides rapid feedback. More often than not you can see your audience, you can see whether they are engaged or falling asleep, you can see if they laugh at your jokes or have puzzled looks on their faces. If you are lucky you will get questions, and people will even come up to you to chat after you have finished.

I started writing and delivering presentations round about 2001 and they have formed part of my learning journey in writing. I got my start in the ACCU, this time thanks to Reg Charney, who ran the Silicon Valley group. I quickly moved onto ACCU conferences when I was back in England.

Giving presentations helps in another way too: once you have a book available, you want to promote it. Appearing at conferences and local meet-ups is an effective way of getting your message to a wider public and encouraging book sales.

---

[1]https://medium.com/

Strunk and White

If you hang around authors for long there is one book that inevitably gets mentioned: *The Elements of Style* by Strunk and White[a]. Many writers hold this book in awe.

When I was starting out in writing I bought a copy and read it – or rather I tried to read it. It was like being back in school: use verb for this and a noun for that, never put a pronoun after an adjective[b], infinitives must not be split. I spent most of my time checking the meaning of words like 'verb' and 'infinitive', and simply parsing the meaning of the writing. Gobbledygook.

I might be the only writer in the world who has failed to comprehend what Strunk and White are talking about. I blame my dyslexia. So I took the Vogon route: 'What nature refused to give to them, they did without. Until their myriad anatomical deficiencies could be rectified with surgery.'[c]

Strunk and White went to the charity bookshop a long time ago. My brain doesn't work like that.

[a]Or *Skunk and White*, as I always think of it.
[b]I'm making these rules up, they kind of sound right but I don't know!
[c]*HitchHiker's Guide to the Galaxy*, Douglas Adams.

13. Writers conferences

It was at a former monastery about an hour outside Munich that I learned to write over a period of 12 years: EuroPLoP.

While most people who have heard of EuroPLoP think of it as a *patterns conference*, it is really a *writers conference*. One of the earliest pattern aficionados in the technology world, Richard 'Dick' Gabriel, brought writers workshops to the nascent pattern conference movement.

For me it started in 2002, when I asked on the ACCU-General mailing list if anyone else had seen a program design technique I had used twice. I asked if other people knew of it, did it have a name? Is it a *pattern*?

The replies amounted to 'Yes we've seen it, No it isn't a documented pattern, perhaps you should write it.' I decided to take up the challenge.

Kevlin Henney was also a participant in the discussion. He was already an established author, pattern writer and attendee at EuroPLoP. Kevlin offered to shepherd me as I developed the idea.

'Shepherding' is a coaching-like process used in the patterns community. Authors draft a pattern paper, then a shepherd works with the author to help them improve the pattern. If you are not familiar with patterns, think of them as a form of extended poetry that deals with problems and solutions.

I will always be indebted to Kevlin; he worked with me for several months to improve the paper. In the end I said "What do I do with the paper next?" and he said "Submit to EuroPLoP 2003". So I did.

Once a paper is accepted for a patterns conference it is assigned a shepherd. In my case this was Frank Buschmann – someone else I will always be indebted to. Frank worked with me for several more months to improve the paper. By the time I got to the Swabian hideout that hosts EuroPLoP I had a brilliant paper. Well, at least I thought so.

EuroPLoP – and other pattern conferences – are unlike other conferences you may have been to. There are no speakers, no keynotes, no PowerPoint and no name badges. The conference opens with a rain dance, after which you learn the names of the other 50 or so attendees.

The core of pattern conferences are the writers workshops, where writers receive feedback on their papers. Most people in the workshops are authors and everyone has read their papers beforehand.

Each writer takes a turn to introduce their paper and then turns their back on the group. For the next hour, under the direction of a moderator, the group discuss the paper while the author takes notes.

Authors are not allowed to speak. Any urge to say "You misunderstand me" or "You didn't read the bit where I said..." must be swallowed. You learn that the reader, not the writer, interprets the words and decides on their message. It is not that people misunderstand you, but that you have not explained yourself as well as you thought you had.

In between sessions we play games – non-competitive games, games that are fun and build trust. You need this trust to take the feedback.

On the first day my workshop decided to take my paper first – that felt like an honour. I introduced my paper and turned my back. For the next 15 minutes or so I was in Heaven. People loved my paper, it addressed a real problem, it was readable, it contained good examples – wonderful.

Then the moderator said "Now can we turn our attention to suggestions for improvement". That was when the knives came out – or it felt like that.

Thirty minutes later we moved to summaries. I was invited back, everyone stood, thanked me and clapped for me. My emotions were mixed to say the least. After coffee it took real willpower to return to the room and go through the same process with another author's paper.

After lunch I went into the garden, cried and started to recover. I understood that everything that was said would improve my paper.

The conference would reconvene with a game of invisible frisbee, or maybe tick-tock or huggy bear. It is impossible to hold grudges after playing one of those games.

The next night Frank Buschmann won the shepherd of the year award for his work with me on my pattern.

When I got home and processed my notes I incorporated as many comments as I could. Although I also found that reviewers didn't agree and I had to make decisions. The workshop didn't kill me – it made my paper stronger and me stronger.

The paper was included in the conference proceedings and went on to be included in *Pattern Languages of Program Design* Volume 5. Quite an achievement for a first-time author.

I returned to EuroPLoP the next year with the first of my business patterns. Ten patterns conferences later I published *Business Patterns*: 35 of the 36 pattern in that book had been workshopped at EuroPLoP or VikingPLoP.

Business Patterns took me about eight years, and in some of those I went to two patterns conferences a year. Taking a paper through this cycle takes six to 12 months, so it is a slow way to write a book.

In 2004 I shepherded my first paper, something I still do today. I must have shepherded a couple of dozen patterns papers by now, for EuroPLoP, VikingPLoP and 'classic' PLoP. I learn from shepherding others too.

At EuroPLoP I learned a lot about writing, patterns and both giving and receiving feedback. It may have been the most significant professional event of my life – more so than the MBA I received a few months later.

As a writer, if you get a chance to attend a patterns conference or take part in a writers workshop, grab it with both hands. It might be tough, but you will learn so much: seldom will you ever get such honest, open and timely feedback. Equally, critiquing other writer's papers, looking for their strengths, weaknesses, places to improve and places to delete will also make you a better writer.

Blind review

Although most writers attending EuroPLoP today are writing academic papers, the conference differs from the usual academic publishing process in that it does not use blind review. EuroPLoP review is open.

For those of you not familiar with the process, in blind review an author's work is sent to two or more reviewers who provide anonymous feedback. Academic journals may base their decision to publish or not on that feedback.

In my experience blind review is annoying: you get comments from someone – you don't know who – which may or may not make sense. There is no opportunity to enquire into the comments or the thinking behind them. If your work is going to be blind-reviewed then it is all the more reason to have people you trust review your work and give feedback before you submit it to a journal.

14. Some writing techniques

There are plenty of books, courses and even degrees in writing. I've consulted almost none of them. The advice I am giving here and in other chapters about the actual writing process describes my own experiences. I don't mean to criticise any of those other sources: maybe if I read a book on writing I could be better!

When I know what I want to say it's not uncommon for the words to pour out of me. Once started, my main problem is stopping. I think of this as the *straight-through* technique: just start writing and keep going. However, that doesn't always happen. Usually I need to use one or more formal approach to writing.

A more formal approach might be nothing more than whacking a number of points down in a text editor and then writing something for each one. This works particularly well when, like this chapter, I want to talk about a series of issues.

Sometimes I have a general idea, I start writing something, and as I write I think 'I must say something about...' I flip down the page and make a quick note, and before I know it I have a series of bullet points or section headings to write to.

Right now this paragraph is followed by the words: *Fieldstone*, *Free writing*, *Carving out stone* and *Editing*. These might be the names of section you are about to read, they might have moved to other chapters, they might have been renamed or even deleted altogether. Such ideas don't need to be section titles, they don't even need to be words you will use in the final text, they just need to be triggers to help you remember the thought you had.

Plan and organizing

I expect that most people were taught at school how to write an essay or exam answer – assuming you sat exams that were more than multiple choice questions. These techniques can be useful, but only up to a point.

Either though advice or my own inventiveness, I developed the exam planning technique further, partially using *mind maps*, so that when I set about an exam I could plan an essay and execute it in about 45 minutes.

I occasionally use these planning techniques when I'm writing, but it tends to be when I have problems, such as organizing a lot of material. More often I'll plan out a piece when I want to work through my thinking and present a careful argument to build a case.

A question

Answering a question can be a really useful technique – but of course you need a question. Questions aren't that hard to come by: they may come from clients as part of my consulting practice, or they may arise at conferences or during training sessions. Sometimes people just email or message me a question. These are all candidates to be answered in a blog post or book.

You could invent your own questions, but to do that you need to have an idea in the first place, so inventing your own questions isn't necessarily straightforward. One nice thing about questions you've been asked is that you know there is at least one person out there who actually wants an answer. Someone has given you market research.

The beauty of answering a question is twofold. First, it helps keep you focused, and second, you've probably answered it already, so you know what to say.

Time-boxed writing

I was the first person at Leicester University to be allowed to type my exam answers rather than write them. I trained myself to sit at a computer, plan an essay and type it, all in 45 minutes. When time is short there isn't much time for editing; writing words that you then throw away is a luxury.

In many ways my use of a computer was unfair on other students. Computers support cut-and-paste: I could pick a sentence up and move it somewhere else. Plus, I suspect that even then I could type faster than most people can write.

Fieldstone

The late great Gerry Weinberg described his approach to writing as *The Fieldstone Method*[1]. He likened writing to dry-stone walling, in which wall builders collect stones, then choose

---

[1] *Weinberg on Writing*, Gerald M Weinberg, 2006

stones so that they fit together. Think of it as a giant Tetris puzzle with irregular shapes. Wallers may need to knock bits off the stone, or rotate them to fit, but that is their skill.

To get started, both wallers and writers need to collect stones; for writers the stones are *ideas*. They don't need to be fully formed ideas, although they might be. Neither do they need to be fully written essays, although again they might be.

Weinberg's advice is sound and I've used it both consciously and subconsciously myself, but it's not the only approach and it's not the only metaphor I use in writing.

I just outlined some stones I've collected for this chapter – Fieldstone, Free writing, Editing. I also maintain a collection in my blogging software (MacJournal) where I list possible future blogs. Sometimes these are little more than a title, but more often they are a title and some bullet points. Occasionally they are complete draft blog entries running to hundreds of words.

I also have a back catalogue of material that I've either published in journals or used in books already. For example, several chapters in *Continuous Digital* were originally written for 'Xanpan 2'. I abandoned that book although I released a draft as the 'Xanpan Appendix'. When writing *Continuous Digital* I realized those chapters would fit in well.

Free writing

The straight-through approach echoes a well-known writing technique called *free writing*. This technique is commonly used by writers to warm up for the day by just writing what comes into their head. The idea is not so much to write a text as to get ready to write; little of what is written during free writing will see the light of day.

I got into free writing when I was writing my Masters dissertation. I don't think any of my free writing made it into the dissertation, but a lot of the ideas did. In free writing the brain makes connections and has insights.

That also happens when one is talking through one's ideas – either into a voice recorder or to another person – so you might think of free writing as a variation on talking. Although free writing, when typed, takes longer than talking.

One might describe free writing as a *stream of consciousness*. I've read and reviewed a few books written in this style and generally I'm not impressed. Authors don't always make a coherent argument or manuscript. Streams of consciousness feel as if they lack a foundation and just say what someone wants to say.

If you are writing a reference book free writing will not work. If you are trying to make a coherent proven argument over several hundred pages it will also fail, but sometimes it works fine.

Dairy/journal

I still do a bit of free writing when I keep my diary, or perhaps I should call it 'journal'. Once a week – sometimes more often, sometimes less – I take a little time in the morning, say 20 or 30 minutes, to just write down my thoughts, to brain dump.

I have a folder called 'Dairy' that contains a file for each of the past 15 years. In addition there are some voice recordings. I very rarely read the diaries or listen to the recordings; they are really write-only.

The diary serves as a free-writing exercise to practise my writing skills, but also an organizational and reflection technique to think about my work and life. Sometimes the diaries are a place to rehearse conversations – sometimes writing comes first and sometimes conversations – sometimes they are place to unload a full mind, sometimes they are a discussion with myself.

For the past eight of those 15 years I start the dairy by listing three positives in my life. I didn't invent this idea, but I forget where I picked it up. The three points might simply be 'The sun is shining, summer is arriving, children went to school happy', although I can normally do better than that. When I'm feeling down and worried, making myself think of three positives can be really beneficial.

More often or not, even if I struggle with positives one and two, I end up with five or six. I do have to restrain myself from writing 'but' on some of them: 'The sun is shining but rain is forecast', or 'Client seemed happy but they they haven't booked any more time'.

You might find material or insights in your diary to put in your masterpiece, but that is not the aim. The aim of the diary is to get into the habit of writing – although I get a lot more benefit from the reflection and offloading I do in writing it.

Orwell

One author's notes on writing have influenced my style – George Orwell and the six rules he gave in his essay *Politics and the English Language*:

1. Never use a metaphor, simile or other figure of speech which you are used to seeing in print.
2. Never use a long word when a short one will do.
3. If it is possible to cut a word out, always cut it out.
4. Never use the passive when you can use the active.

5. Never use a foreign phrase, a scientific word or a jargon word if you can think of an everyday English equivalent.
6. Break any of these rules sooner than say anything outright barbarous.

I am far from perfect at following these rules, especially number 4, but I do try.

Carving out of stone

Sometimes I write a lot of text – I'm doing it with this book. I just go forwards, there is very little editing, ideas just come, get written or get noted. As I've said already, duplication can slip in.

This approach has advantages and disadvantages. On the plus side I am motivated, I have clear thought, I am capturing words and the words kind of look as if they make a book. However, while doing so I am building up a mass of editing: writing is the easy bit, but editing is hard and seldom fun.

There is also a danger that if I stop writing, stop moving forwards, not only will I lose momentum, but I'll also lose unity. At the moment this book exists in my mind as a complete whole, I know what I've said and I know, kind of, what I want to say. That's OK while I'm working on it.

But if I stop, if I go on holiday for a few weeks, find I'm working intensively with clients for a couple of months, then the chances are that ideas will vanish, that I'll forget what I've written and what I want to say. It will be hard to restart, and when I do I'll duplicate some of I've written already.

Whether I go through in one pass or whether I stop and restart I've yet to see, but at the end of this I'll have a mass of text that needs editing and carving into shape. It will be less of fieldstone book than a book carved from stone.

Right now I'm gambling on keeping my momentum up, keeping writing to get to some sort of 'done', before I get distracted. If I can then it will be a very quick book; if I don't it will be hard to pick up again.

Either way, I dread the granite carving that is to come. My first book, *Changing Software Development*, was absolutely carved from stone. It started life as a rewrite of my Masters dissertation; more material was written, some old journal articles and essays were incorporated, then it needed editing. My understanding of what I was trying to write changed in the process.

It might be that in the end all books are carved from stone. When you get near the end you can see the whole and you truly understand your argument, but you also see what needs to be removed and changed.

Speaking to write

Of course it is now 2022 and you don't need to physically write or type to 'write' a book that you could dictate.

You could use a speech-recognition software to change your spoken words into written words. Personally I'm not a big fan of speech recognition: I've tried it but found it lacking. Technology has advanced since I last tried it, so maybe I should try it again.

Speech-recognition software is not the only option for dictating a book – you could have someone transcribe your words. You don't need your own PA for this either, as there are online services. Companies such as Rev[a] claim to use a mix of speech recognition, AI and humans.

I originally tried using speech recognition to avoid repetitive strain injury (RSI) in my hands and arms, but I then discovered that RSI can affect the voice too. Spend too much time talking to your computer and you may end up with throat problems.

While I don't dictate my words, I do listen to them. I've found the text-to-speech facility on my Apple Mac really helps with editing. This might be a dyslexic thing, but I frequently overlook places where I've created a word very like the word I want – perhaps with all the right letters. Reading a text while the computer speaks it to me helps me spot such things and I can often fix them then and there.

[a]https://www.rev.com/

15. Incremental and iterative writing and publishing

The key advantage of incremental publishing is that it allows you to start marketing and selling you book very early. Don't be scared to *publish early, publish often*

In traditional print publishing you had to finish your masterpiece to be able to publish it. If you worked with a publisher, you would have a contract that detailed a table of contents, a word count and a delivery date. You delivered approximately that number of words following the table of contents approximately on the date specified.

In digital publishing you don't need to do that. You can publish what you have today, and republish every time you add a chapter, edit or even remove a chapter. Every republication becomes an opportunity to make marketing noise and tell people you have a book in the works.

If you are writing and publishing with LeanPub this is a trivial process – there is one button to press on the website and a few minutes later you are published. New readers can buy your new edition immediately, while your existing readers get an email telling them there is an update to download. This is LeanPub's killer feature.

Some compare this style to the weekly instalments Charles Dickens published that eventually built into a novel. Unlike Dickens' readers, however, who would need to pay for the next instalment, LeabPub buyers get the updates for free.

If you are publishing on Amazon things are a little more complicated. While Amazon allows updates of books, it is not built in a way that makes this easy. You need to produce your e-book file, upload it to Amazon and wait for the book to be approved. This might take a few hours or it might take a day or two.

Apart from the extra work Amazon requires, the delay means it is not possible to start marketing (tweeting, Facebooking and so on) your update immediately. With LeanPub you can be lining up the messages while the publication is readied, but with Amazon you need to come back when the release has occurred. Perhaps this is not a big issue, but it's worth being aware of.

Upside

There are multiple upsides to incremental writing and publishing. Firstly you get to make money sooner. Secondly there are the marketing opportunities. Every change, every chapter, every republication and every added diagram is a reason to make marketing noise. Social media channels make this easy and fast, and if you are lucky existing buyers join in.

Even if marketing noise doesn't result in an immediate sale, it still makes more people aware of your work. They may not buy the first time you tweet 'Another chapter added', but as the weeks go by your message builds, so when you eventually get to say 'Book complete, now on sale' they may part with their cash.

Nor is it only on social media that you can tell people about a book. If you are doing conference presentation or podcasts you can always say "I'm working on a book right now, if you are interested you can buy a draft or register for updates at...". This way you start sales and marketing earlier.

Getting early readers will also help with book reviews when you get to that point. I talk about book reviews in another chapter.

Finally, you get to develop your ideas as you go. Take that last paragraph. I've known since I first imagined *this* book that I would need a chapter on book reviews. As I wrote that last paragraph I was thinking 'How much do I say about reviews?... maybe it belongs in the review chapter'. I opened another file and wrote a few lines about reviews and early buyers, then saved it as 'Reviews.txt'.

That kind of thing happens all the time. Traditionally one would have to think of all the chapters and sections in advance, and if additional ideas blew the agreed word count you might have needed to think again.

Downside

Incremental publishing does have a downside. I once bought a book that was unfinished, I didn't realise it was unfinished, and so found it really brief and unsatisfying. For a couple of years whenever someone mentioned the book I felt the need to say it was underwhelming but usually bit my tongue. It was only two or three years later, after a machine upgrade, that I opened it and found the missing chapters.

My books have the additional problem that the pre-copy-edit versions are written in my dyslexic English. Undoubtedly this will put some readers off. It doesn't make me particularly proud, but it is the way I work.

I could ask my copy-editor to work incrementally too, but that would create its own problems. At the very least it is going to inject delay between my finishing a chapter and being able to publish it. (Steve, my copy-editor, confirms it has been done and it does create its own set of problems.)

I don't write linearly; chapters move around as I develop a book. So, while I might write 'As described in the previous chapter…', the chapter might well subsequently move to later in the book. Really I want my copy-editor to pick that up, but if my chapters are in flux he won't be able to do so.

Indeed, the copy-editor may end up editing chapters that are later removed altogether. Thus – and maybe you can see this coming – the copy-edit is going to cost more.

All of this could be overcome at a cost, but I don't feel it is worth it. For me copy-editing is a batch process that happens at the end, but you may disagree.

Feedback

Publishing your book incrementally should also allow for feedback. Getting feedback is better done earlier. Waiting until you have written all 20 chapters before seeking any feedback means that the feedback cycle can be very long.

When you publish early and incrementally you can get feedback on maybe just two chapters before you write all 20. One can hope, even expect, that readers will send you notes on the work so far. This does sometimes happen. I'd love to be able to that say a draft book will stimulate a lot of feedback from readers, but it won't. You will get some, but the truth is that getting feedback about a book is like getting blood out of a stone.

Few people pick up a new book, read it and think 'I really must tell the author they have made a mistake here'; fewer still will think 'I must share my story with the author'. Of those who do think something like that, very few will contact you. I have had very few people ever contact me to point out logical errors or take issue with my arguments, even when my books are controversial, such as *Project Myopia*.

Two types of feedback do arise. The first is financial, when people buy your draft book. Your book goes to them and their money comes to you. Seeing people pay for your book, seeing funds in your account, is great confirmation that you are doing something that some people value.

The other type of feedback – and I do love everyone who sends this – is on grammar, punctuation and perhaps spelling[1] that slips through the checker. While I respect everyone

---

[1] What my school-age children call 'SPAG': spelling, punctuation and grammar.

who tells me that "You have used the wrong 'were'", and I dutifully apply every grammar and spelling fix I am given, I'm much more interested in feedback on content.

I know I make grammar and spelling mistakes. I know my books would be more readable if I didn't have them. I know I would have fewer poor Amazon reviews, but what I really want feedback on is the content. *Is this book useful? What else would you like to see in the book? Which chapters are dull? What could be removed?*

At the end of the process the book will be professionally copy-edited and (hopefully) all the dyslexic English will be removed.

Perhaps the biggest downside of incremental publishing is *knowing when you are done.* There is a temptation to keep writing – especially if financial feedback is coming in and your ideas are still developing.

Publishers and feedback

If you are working with a publisher you are not going to get feedback from early buyers. If a publisher has a good reputation it is in their interests to help authors improve their work. They also need some check on the quality of what they are publishing, because the staff at publishers are seldom experts in the field in which they work. To accommodate this they put alternative mechanisms in place.

Normally publishers will set up a panel to review your work. These are often people you have nominated, but the publisher may suggest people they have worked with in the past. In my experience the reviewers look mostly at the first few chapters you submit. After a while they fall away, although I'm sure they sometimes stay involved all the way through. Publishers don't pay them very much, so this is understandable.

Publishers may also give you an editor. It is unlikely that the editor will be an expert in your area, but they can read your work, follow your argument and make meaningful suggestions. I've had good editors and poor editors, so you might want to ask in advance what you can expect from an editor.

16. The process

Writing is the least of the problems when writing a book. That I can write a book is without question: I've done it before.

More important questions are *is anyone interested?* and *are they interested enough to buy the book?* However these too I tend to ignore – or at least let my gut feeling make a decision. My motivation for writing is that I have something I want to say, and I know that in the process I will learn something. So while I *should* think about who will buy the book, my desire to write it also plays a part.

I know from past experience that my books will sell some copies. Still, even the successful ones are unlikely to justify the effort I put in financially.

The big problem when creating a book is *editing*. Editing is time-consuming and often boring. Editing is where I'm most likely to lose the will to finish something – right now, editing this book, *I just want it done!*

Editing is largely a 'legwork problem' – it just requires time and energy. While I can outsource the really hard copy-editing, I need discipline to edit. So I can write it, I can get it edited, some people will buy it – no, it doesn't make sense, I'm still writing it for me.

The true problems around marketing are *How do I tell the world the book is here? How to I motivate people to buy?*

Later chapters look at these questions in more detail, but here I want to describe the end-to-end process.

Start writing

Ideas generate ideas, so start writing.

If you don't know where to start, put your thoughts in order first. Think about what you want to say. 'Mind map' if it helps, dictate to a digital recorder, rehearse your prose or just start jotting bullet points down. Start writing some chapters. You can rearrange and edit later – it's digital.

The tools you use don't matter much: I discuss tools in a later chapter. I like plain text and usually work in Markdown, but you can start in Word, Pages or pretty much anything. You can always change formats later on. Get some chapters down so that you feel you have a skeleton and that you want to keep the project going.

Book skeleton and structure

If you have something to say you are probably thinking 'I have to say something about' and 'I should mention'. Feel free to start a file and write your ideas down.

If you feel an idea deserves a whole chapter, start a new file. During development my books have lots of files that contain little more than the chapter title or a few words of an idea.

Occasionally I sit at my computer and create empty files with just the name of the chapter. If I've been thinking about a book in advance this can happen quickly. More often I have a couple of ideas, I write a chapter and as I'm doing that think 'I must say something about...' and create an empty file with the title.

As the chapters appear, I find it helps me to imagine what the book is going to look like and, more importantly, what I need to add. This helps if you also want get sight of the whole rather than simply the parts – the book rather than its chapters.

No two books gain their structures in the same way. Some books, like this one, are 'straight through': the ideas and chapters just come. Other books, like *Continuous Digital*, requires a lot of changes: things move about, chapters split and chapters merge. Either way, eventually a structure emerges.

Rationally I should write the first chapter first, edit it and polish it, then advance to the second chapter and repeat. In fact I'm more likely to work across the whole book, writing a random chapter first because the content is in my head. Only as elements start to appear does the structure emerge.

Working in LeanPub I will add the files for chapters to 'book.txt', the file that specifies the structure of the book. Periodically I will generate a preview to get a feel for the book – not to mention a page and word count to see how much I've created already.

Sometimes ideas obviously belong in a particular chapter, so I just open that chapter's file and write the idea down. If the idea justifies a section, I give it a heading marker (heading style or header symbol) so that when I look at the whole book I can see a table of contents.

I might also start to organize the chapter files in to sections. For example, I've just been through this book and created seven subdirectories:

Pre – this is contains any preamble ('frontmatter' in LeanPub speak) I want to put in. So this would contain the Preface, Foreword, maybe notes to the reader, a note about the book being a beta version and so on.

P1-Scene. The opening chapters of the book, where I prepare the context.

P2-Writing, P3-Production, P4-Publishing and **P5-Writing**. You may see these sections in this book right now, or I may have renamed them, I may have rearranged them (*Production* before *Publishing* or vice versa? What am I going to say in each?) or I may have removed them altogether.

Post. The closing elements ('back matter' in LeanPub), so Epilogue, Appendix, admin like ISBN numbers, links to my website, adverts for my other books and so on.

Creating a book

At some point you need to actually create the book project. Although you can create this before you write anything, I find it helps to have a few files to get started with.

On LeanPub you create a book. This might seem a bit scary, but creating a book does not commit you to publish. The book might be published and onsite, but if you don't tell anyone and share the URL nobody will know it is there.

If you are using Microsoft Word or some other tool you may want to use a 'master document' feature to see the parts together as a whole. However you do it, you need to be able to see a table of contents, to summarize what you have in the book.

Whatever your toolset, I strongly encourage you to look both at individual chapters and at the whole. Being able to see what the whole book looks and feels like is important. Not only do you want to spot missing ideas, you also need to spot duplication. I dread publishing a book with two chapters that make the same point in different words.

Setting up a LeanPub book project or Word master document may seem premature, it might seem like a big step, and you might want to postpone it or do more research on what you need to do and what is needed for a book. However, the easiest way to learn is to do.

Until you see the skeleton of a book you don't really know what you are up against in terms of writing. Equally, you don't know what you are up against in terms of technology. In both cases it is far easier to dive in and learn on the job than it is to discover what you need to know elsewhere.

Really, a 'book' doesn't need that many words or pages. When you see all your work together you may well be surprised.

Equally, once you see how the technology works you will probably be surprised by how easy to use it is. Like the *Wizard of Oz*, behind all the razzmatazz it is really quite straightforward. The easiest way to learn is to do.

The only genuine reason I see to delay the process is a need to use Word's master document feature. It must be ten years since I last used Word to write a book. Back then creating such a big file, especially one with lots of pictures, put a perceptible stress on Word or the PC on which it was running. Everything slowed down and crashes would occur regularly.

If I was lucky Word would recover the master file. If I was unlucky I would need to recreate it. I'm sure Word today – with more powerful PCs and more memory – is much better, but I rarely use Word any more. Markdown and the document format converter Pandoc cover most of my needs.

Write, edit

Once you have a skeleton and a few draft chapters, plus a bunch of ideas yet to be fleshed out, you can get an idea the whole book. You might rush to publish now, but more likely you'll hold back a bit.

From here it's a question of putting flesh on the bones, of writing content under your chapter and section titles. In a traditional publishing model you would have needed to produce those titles before writing many words, which would require you to think through the whole narrative arc of the book. That might require some early research. When you self-publish, or before you have a publisher, however, you can just start and let your book develop organically.

If you prefer you can still do your research, create a book structure, write chapter and section titles. If that way works for you then do it, but working digitally you can let the book grow organically. Once you have the book's skeleton it's a question of writing new chapters, editing existing ones, fitting ideas in and moving text around.

Normally I find that there comes a point at which I'm trying to sideline ideas and decide what to leave out of a book. At that point I create a 'More' or 'Extra' directory to store ideas that I'm not going to use.

Short chapters

Over time, and with Johanna Rothman's encouragement, I've found short chapters are much easier to write and, I believe, easier to read. Although it can be hard to keep a chapter short: it requires discipline.

Frequently I will write a chapter initially as a stream of consciousness, but when I look at it the chapter is long. If I am lucky there is an obvious way to split it into two, otherwise I look for sections to take out during the edit. Maybe fit a section into another chapter, or save it for further expansion as another entire chapter. Sometimes ideas are taken out, parked and ultimately removed, but throwing one's own words away is hard: once created, letting go of them is tough.

The hard bit is not so much the actual writing, it is editing and deciding what to leave behind. Longer chapters can ramble and lose focus, they can repeat themselves and they take longer both to read and to edit.

Publish and start telling people

Even once you've published you could keep your book hidden, although this soon becomes self-defeating. Assuming you are happy to tell people your book is published, then it is time to do just that. From here on every time you publish is an opportunity to tell the world "I've a new version out", "I've published the next version of my masterpiece" or "I've added a new chapter".

'Writing' then becomes a cycle of actual writing – say a new chapter, or perhaps an edit – and a fresh release and blast of social media, Twitter, LinkedIn, Facebook or mailing list that you have an updated book out.

Social media is everything here. Traditionally, you might have mentioned that you were writing a book when you did conference presentations, but the audience is small. With social media you can tell everyone again and again and again. It can be boring to repeatedly tell people 'Hey, I'm writing a book', but every event – publication, update, graphic, sales achievement (first sale! tenth sale! hundredth!), new graphic and so on is a reason to shout about your book again.

Pretty near the end, or when you are actually finished, you may want to do a media blitz. Doing this takes time and energy, which you want for writing. Plus, while many will be happy to buy an early preview or draft, version some will want the final book. Social media needs a lot less time and energy to spread the word.

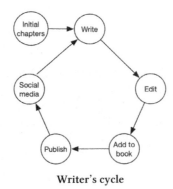

Writer's cycle

That is it, really: write, edit, publish, tell people, repeat.

When are you done?

One of the biggest problems with iterative self-publishing is knowing when you are done. While you may struggle to know what to write at the beginning, if you are anything like me you will eventually find that you can't say everything.

It can be tempting to keep writing. On one hand you want to write a comprehensive book and discuss everything the reader might want or need to know. Such a book will cement your authority. On the other, bigger might not sell more. When I'm buying a book I find smaller books attractive, as I know I will reach the end. For novels that just feels good, while for technical books it implies that the book is focused and to the point.

There comes a point when you just want to finish a book and move on. Perhaps because you have said what you set out to say, perhaps because another project is begging for your attention, or perhaps because you just want closure.

Or perhaps because you have a deadline to meet. Or you want to keep the number of words down – you might decide on a series of smaller books. Or perhaps because the whole looks like a coherent message and any remaining ideas belong somewhere else.

With self-publishing there is no publisher demanding a final manuscript by a given date, or a set number of words. In fact there is nothing to stop you going on forever with a book always in draft.

At some point I start to develop a sense of what I want the whole to say. While I might have additional material I know the what the focus of the book is; adding more will reduce that focus and dilute that message.

I also normally have one eye on the page count because I'm of the opinion that smaller books sell better. Smaller books are certainly cheaper to print, so if you want to keep the retail price down you want to keep an eye on word count. Of course if your book will only ever exist digitally, that is less of a problem.

17. Beginning: Introductions and Forewords

The first few chapters of your book are prime real estate. These are the chapters that will be read most, both by people who buy your book and people who don't. These chapters serve two purposes.

First they set out your argument, your thesis, your purpose in the clearest way possible. They summarize your book in a nutshell. Remember that many people will read nothing else of your book. This is your chance to make your point.

But there is a more important audience for your core argument: you. As author the early chapters are where you explain to yourself what you are talking about. By talking directly to a reader, and even putting yourself into the mind of a reader, you force yourself to compress and condense your key arguments.

If you are writing a reference book (*The Universal Guide to REST API Implementation*, say) this is going to be different to a thesis for world change (*The Need for New Communism*, perhaps). The introduction to the former needs to explain why REST APIs are important and how in 1,000 pages you will reveal all. The latter needs to rally the troops.

Second, the early chapters serve as a hook with which to catch readers. Obviously you need the hook to make them buy: maybe your potential buyer is killing time browsing in a bookshop, perhaps they may have picked up the book from a colleague's desk, or downloaded the free sample from Amazon while looking for a holiday novel.

If you are only interested in making a sale, then the early chapters have done their job when the money changes hands. If, like me, you want to change the world, you need people to read your book – the more they read, the bigger the dent you make in the world. So your early chapters need to persuade people to keep reading. You need to demonstrate in those initial words that you have a thesis that not only interests them, but is worth their time to explore more fully.

When you think about it, persuading someone to buy a book and to read it isn't that different. Both are concerned with persuading the reader to exchange their limited and valuable resources, both money and time, for your words and ideas.

Many beginnings

Fortunately a book has not one beginning, but many. Logically a book begins on page 1, or maybe page i, and readers are expected to proceed sequentially – but they don't, they dip in and out. They may start on page 1 but by page 3 they have skipped ahead. This is especially true if they are browsing in a bookshop or want to find out what you have to say about a particular topic.

Not only does your book have an introductory chapter, but it can also have a Preface, a Prologue, a Foreword and multiple sections. All of these open the book. An introductory chapter might be Chapter 1 and might start on page 1, but it might also be written as 'before you start' frontmatter that occurs before the book formally starts on page 1.

I am sure there are style guides out there that describe what should be on page 1 and what should occur before it, but as an author and especially as a self-publisher you are free to ignore these. Publishers may have their own rules or house style, but so far none of the publishers I've worked with have taken me to task.

Consider *The Art of Agile Product Ownership*. The introductory chapter occurs before the first chapter, while the book also contains a Prologue, a short narrative to set the scene. So this book has three points at which a reader might start: Prologue, Introduction or Chapter 1.

Actually, 'Art' has another 26 possible starting points: 22 chapters divided into four parts. The start of each section and chapter is an opportunity to summarize what is to come and make the big points on which you will expand. In this book each section opens with a quote and two or three pages of summary argument.

Or consider *Succeeding with OKRs in Agile*. The introduction here is Chapter 1, but this time there is a Prologue and a Foreword before the Introduction. There are then 26 chapters and five sections. Each section opens with a quote but nothing more.

The Prologue, Foreword or introductory chapter are the points at which I want to enthuse readers to read more. Each one of these contains more passion and, hopefully, more inspiration.

Ironically perhaps e-books are less likely to be dipped into and read randomly than print editions. While you can browse an e-book, it is much easier to flip through a printed book and stop at random places.

Introductions

Logically, reading begins with the Introduction. Writing seldom does: even if I write an introductory chapter early in the creation process, that chapter seldom stays the course. In fact I'm quite prone to writing several introductions over the course of writing a book.

Sometimes I'm consciously writing an alternative introduction. Sometimes I've got an idea I need to write down and it only becomes clear later that it is an introduction. Sometimes I just plain forget what I've written and feel the need to write it again. At some point they will be edited together and some words will be discarded.

As I've said before, it is the author who learns most from writing a book. You can think of it as peeling an onion layer by layer. Periodically the writing, and the thinking that occurs between writing sessions, unveils a deeper understanding, or perhaps provides a new metaphor that helps to explain the topic. Sometimes its just a sentence or a single line that sums things up brilliantly, but which begs for pages of dissection and analysis.

Sometimes the Introduction is the last chapter I write. More often it is the last chapter I finish. I look at what I've got in the introduction(s) and rework it. Some of it may be cut completely, some moved around within the chapter and some moved elsewhere, to another chapter or section.

Prefaces and Prologues

Sometimes there is just more to say at the start than will fit into an Introduction. Sometimes you want more than one introduction. That is where a Preface or a Prologue can be useful.

But while there might be an editor's manual or style guide somewhere that gives rules on what should be in an Introduction, Preface or Prologue, I've never read it. I'm thinking about what will add to the story, what will flow and where do things fit in logically?

In my mind Prefaces and Prologues are different kinds of starting points. A Preface, as in the case of *Succeeding with OKRs in Agile*, says something about how the book came to be. In that case the Preface starts 'This book is the product of Covid-19'. The Preface describes both how the book came out of lockdown and draws parallels between the way the world reacted to Covid and OKRs.

Prologues on the other hand somehow paint the picture of the problems the world faces. *Xanpan* reprints my well-known *Dear Customer, the truth about IT* letter to describe the dysfunction of technology development. *The Art of Agile Product Ownership* tells a little story about the busy life of a product owner and the challenges they face. Such Prologues are akin to a McGuffin[1] device used by film-makers to set events in motion.

Both Prologues aim to 'warm up' the reader, and both step outside of the factual space. They do something different: they are out and out stories, even fiction.

Forewords

Then there are Forewords. Forewords are normally written by other people. They too attempt to set the scene, to introduce the topic. While you could write the Foreword yourself – there are no rules! – they are normally written by someone else. Which begs the question, *why give prime real estate to someone else?*

Having a Foreword written by someone else lends authority to your work. You may be an unknown author, but if someone with a name, their own brand, endorses your work, then you acquire some credibility. Someone looking at your book cover thinking "Who is this Allan Kelly and what does he know about…?" will be reassured by seeing a better-known name on the cover. Just having someone else endorse your book is good; the bigger and better-known their name, the more authority the Foreword carries.

Linda Rising was good enough to write a Foreword for *Business Patterns* and I feel honoured to have had her involvement. If you are going to ask someone to write a Foreword they should have warning, and preferably have the chance to review the work or contribute in some way. Linda had seen my patterns at several patterns conferences, she knew what I was working on and had contributed in workshop reviews. I think she may even have encouraged me to move to a full book.

For *Succeeding with OKRs in Agile* I asked Mike Burrows. I've known Mike for years and followed his work; he arrived at OKRs about the same time as me and our ideas made a good fit. That is not to say that Mike and I agree on everything, but I wouldn't want a sycophantic contribution.

I asked Mike several months before *Succeeding* was finished if he was interested in writing a Foreword and kept him updated as I moved towards the end. At the very least the Foreword writer needs to have time to read the final draft.

While Forewords don't normally cost – or pay: I've written a few too – they do help with marketing. For a start, there is someone else who has their name on the book and has a vested interest in publicizing it, 'liking' and sharing every tweet, status update or timeline post you make. Especially if you mention them directly: credibility flows both ways.

---

[1]https://en.wikipedia.org/wiki/MacGuffin

On Amazon you can identify the Foreword writer as part of your publishing submission. That looks good to buyers: they see another name next to yours on the page and might even click on the name to see whether they have written books too.

It also means that Amazon's algorithms can make a connection between your book and the Foreword writer's books. I don't know how much weight this carries in the algorithms, but any extra weight is good.

The end: Epilogue

I always find it disappointing when books just end. Quite often you get an inspiring start in the Introduction, followed by chapters of detail and explanation – then it just stops. I want something that pulls it altogether and says "And now you see how it all works..." But most books, including mine, just end. The final chapter ends unceremoniously and that is it. The book is finished.

There is a logic here: most people won't read to the end. If there is some important point to make then make it upfront at the start, don't bury it at the end. Say "When you get to the end of this book you will see how these pieces...", because if you leave it to the end most people won't read it. Hard, I know, but it is rational.

Sometimes however you want to write something to mark the end. *Succeeding with OKRs in Agile* has some closing words. You could have an Epilogue or a 'Finally' chapter. When I'm reading a book I often skip ahead and read these early.

Whether you bill it as a formal 'Finally' chapter or add it as an almost Appendix, Epilogue or *afterword*, you can write a closing chapter. These serve a similar role to an Introduction but at the other end.

In the print world an Epilogue might have been added late in the day after the bulk of the book had been written and produced. In the digital age this doesn't apply – you can change and add material at any time. Hence epilogues can be something a little different. Rather than being information that you can't squeeze in, they are more of a 'Now you've heard everything I have to say' or 'My final learning' statement.

Acknowledgements

I think it important to acknowledge those who have influenced and helped in writing a book, so I usually have an Acknowledgements section. Originally I would put this, as was conventional, at the start of a book, but the first few chapters are prime real estate.

So as much as I love my contributors, my Acknowledgement section now comes at the end. I still acknowledge people, it's just that I can't justify prime real estate – I don't want anything to get in the way of readers getting stuck into my book. Also, if they download an Amazon or LeanPub sample, they don't want to read all my thank-yous just yet.

18. Using quotations

I make extensive use of quotations at the heads of my chapters. Perhaps I make too much use of them. Perhaps using quotations is a little bit vain and self-serving. Still, I like them because they break things up. They also validate my arguments by pointing out that others have similar thoughts, even when they come from a completely different context. Quotations inject humour too, they can be opaque, thought-provoking or reassuring. Hopefully I get the balance right.

It can be a challenge to find the right quotation; although I usually have plenty to draw on, sometimes a chapter has me stumped. The other problem is not duplicating quotations: occasionally I find I've used the same quotation to open more than one chapter.

Not all my books open chapters with quotations, and I should admit I have my doubts over their use at times. *It is my book, why do I need third-party validation?*, but sometimes a quotation is begging to be used. For example, General Huffman just had to be quoted in *Succeeding with OKRs in Agile's* chapter on focus: 'The main thing to remember is, the main thing is the main thing'.

If you are going to use quotations – in chapter openings or elsewhere – please remember two things: make an effort to source appropriate quotations and strive for balance.

Sourcing quotations

I collect quotations from everywhere. Naturally I collect quotations from books and newspapers. As a regular reader of both the *Economist* and *Financial Times* I regularly run across things to capture. I keep a quotes.txt file on my laptop and quickly note them down.

London Zoo, the Science Museum and the Design Museum have provided quotations, as have countless art exhibitions. A phone camera is great for capturing such quotations as they don't need to be in print.

The advent of podcasting and radio and television on demand makes returning to half-heard quotations far easier. If you are really lucky, organizations like PBS have relevant programme transcripts online.

While I own a copy of the *Economist Book of Quotations*, it supplies surprisingly few of those I use. Even a couple of hundred pages of print can only scratch the surface of what is available online. Wikiquote[1] has become my main source and point of reference. However, Wikiquote also debunks many quotations: at the bottom of every page is a list of misquotes and misattributions: sometimes the quote you want to use isn't what you think it is.

One of my favourite quotations, 'Most people fail in life not because they aim too high and miss, but because they aim too low and hit', came from Aristotle. Or at least I was told that originally. Wikiquote lists this quotation as originating from Michelangelo – well, maybe: the quotation is listed on his Wikiquote page as 'disputed'. It might be from American politician Les Brown, but Michelangelo and Aristotle are a lot more impressive sources.

Things can get even more twisted when checking out some of the supposed quotations from the likes of Keynes and Churchill. It can be really disappointing to find that they never said what you have been told they said.

Balance

A few years ago someone pointed out that all my quotations were from men. Since then I've made a big effort to rebalance my sources. However, I'm still a long way from having an equal split between male and female speakers in my quotations file.

While I am sure than women have uttered at least as many quotable lines as men, it seems fewer of these have been captured and shared over the years. Without wishing to excuse myself, I have come to believe the quotations that have been recorded and shared are overwhelmingly from men. Until someone does a gender analysis of the quotations listed on Wikiquote this will remain just a theory.

That is just male-female balance. There are plenty of other criteria I might try to balance. Perhaps, as a mono-lingual English writer, a bias towards English language writers and speakers is understandable – but is it fair?

Then what about quoting the disreputable? And who is to decide who is disreputable? Consider Winston Churchill, a man who sent the British army to fight Liverpool dockers. Should I forget his vile side when using his very funny quotations? Or was it all too long ago to matter?

This may seem trivial, but one editor pulled me up when referencing the 45th President of the United States. Would using a quotation from Hilary Clinton discredit me with many American readers? Or do my American readers vote Democrat? Am I in danger of self-censoring? And is that wrong? I don't know, but I do wonder.

[1]https://en.wikiquote.org/

When working with an editor – or more likely if you are working with a publisher – they may hold you to a higher standard and demand your quotations are attributed and traceable. They may also warn you off using quotations, or even references to some people.

19. The #NoProjects story

Sometime in 2013 Steve Smith, Joshua Arnold and I started talking about the evils of the project model of software development. On Twitter this went by the #NoProjects hashtag and could provoke a lot of heated debate: some tweets went viral.

Interestingly Steve, Josh and I all had a different take on what was wrong with the project model. In 2015, at the invitation of Duarte Vasco, I started to put my ideas into writing for his newsletter. I very quickly had over 8,000 words. Vasco suggested I turn this into an e-book, but I resisted. It was too small, and besides, publishing a book entitled #NoProjects could be career-threatening – *who would hire a consultant who openly doubts the validity of projects to assist project delivery?*

A while later I started expanding the essay into a book. The book grew and grew. Early buyers were getting the original essay plus the new material. The ongoing Twitter fight drove sales, but also meant I wanted to write something more constructive than 'No'.

The name kept changing too. I eventually settled on *Continuous Digital*, or 'CD' as I call it. By the time I'd completed CD it ran to around 80,000 words. I came to realise it was too big, so I split it into two companion volumes.

The first is Project Myopia[1]. This runs to about 23,000 words and is essentially the original essay – the *project model critique*. The second, Continuous Digital[2] runs to nearly 69,000 words and describes the alternatives to projects.

Not all of CD was new material. I had originally written some chapters for another, aborted, book – 'Xanpan 2'. These had appeared in the unfinished Xanpan appendix – Management and team[3].

In retrospect I made multiple mistakes with both books.

First, I should have listened to Vasco and expanded the original essay into a book much sooner. It would have hit the market at the time #NoProjects was at its most active and would have generated more sales. It would also have served to prepare people for the second volume.

---

[1]https://leanpub.com/myopia
[2]https://leanpub.com/cdigital
[3]https://leanpub.com/xanpan2

Second, *Continuous Digital* is too big: at 68,000 words it should have been three or four smaller books. Each section could be a book in its own right, with an omnibus edition at the end.

This might be obvious in retrospect, and clearly I should have listened to Vasco, but *Continuous Digital* would not be the book it is if it had been written as four separate volumes. The sections only emerged with time and chapters moved between them for a while. It was only by conceiving it as a whole that it came together; it would have been hard to write the four parts as four distinct and sequential books.

By the time I was completing CD I really wanted it finished: it had taken up too much time. I didn't think about separating it as I don't think I realised quite how big it was. To have done so would have made more work in publication terms. Although it wouldn't require more copy-editing and I could have used similar cover art – as I did with *Project Myopia* – it would have involved a lot of admin.

Perhaps in retrospect what 'the twins' needed all along was a development editor. Someone to challenge my writing, cajole and nudge me towards publishing and point out that it was not one but two or perhaps even three books. That might have saved a lot of time.

Given that I was slow to accept that #NoProjects should even be a book at all, however, it's debatable how much time could have been saved. Not until I decided it was a book would I have appointed an editor or approached a publisher.

My other question is whether, given the (then) controversial nature of the thesis, an editor might have talked me into diluting the message? I like to think not. If nothing else, *Project Myopia* is a good story.

My books

These days I see my books in two groups. *Changing Software Development, Project Myopia* and *Continuous Digital* are my 'philosophy' books: they provide an alternative interpretation of the modern world. *A Little Book about Requirements and User Stories, Xanpan* and *Succeeding with OKRs in Agile* are much more day-to-day practical what-to-do books.

The second group sell, while the first are masterpieces. The philosophy books put the world to rights, but in financial terms I should have done something else.

Business Patterns is hard to categorise. While I think it does contain day-to-day advice, it never really succeeded in reaching the audience that could use that advice. I suspect most readers find it 'above their pay grade', as the saying goes. The book also contains a lot of philosophy.

The jury is still out on *The Art of Agile Product Ownership*. When writing it I was determined to make it a practical companion to *A Little Book about Requirements and User Stories*. Unfortunately, while one can give hard advice on user stories, the wide variety of product owners makes it hard to give immediate advice to role holders.

In my mind the philosophy books, plus *Xanpan* and *Business Patterns*, form a single narrative and describe *Allan's Universe*.

III Production

20. After the writing

Once you have finished writing the work really begins. Up to this point you might have been able to do everything yourself, but from here on you will benefit from specialist help: a copy-editor, a graphic designer, an indexer, an actor, reviewers and possibly a fan club.

Working with other people introduces delays, because you need to give them time to do their stuff. Those delays aren't necessarily as bad as they might seem, even though waiting always feels like wasted time. The people who support you might be doing things you can't do, or things that would take you longer. Plus, if you get the timing right, they can work in parallel, so waiting for two people needn't take twice the time.

Having said that these processes start after you have finished writing, you might want to start some before you finish, such as copyright checks on third-party material, or commissioning a cover design. The downside is that doing so can distract you from your focus on writing.

If this is the first time you have produced your own book and have never considered any of these things, then this is the time to take stock and decide what needs to be done. Even if this is your fourth or fifth book, you still need to work out what is needed. Think of it as an 'end of writing' checkpoint. If you've been undecided about using a publisher, the end of writing is the logical time to think again and perhaps start shopping your manuscript around.

Of course it isn't really the end of writing: as you control the process you can add extra chapters or change those that are 'completed'. If you are anything like me, though, you will reach a point at which you really want the book to be finished, and as much as you might want to add another chapter, you know that it's time to close this project.

LeanPub Author Services

During the time I have been writing this book LeanPub has launched 'Author services'[a]. As they describe it themselves: 'Your book, for sale on Amazon, in hardcover, paperback and Kindle ebook formats.'

In other words, once you get to 'finished' you can hand the whole thing off to LeanPub to produce and publish. So far I haven't had a chance to try this service, and to be honest, now that I am experienced in doing it, I'm not sure I ever will. Still, I'm sure author services would save me a lot of head-scratching, agonising and time. Whether I would be prepared to hand off that degree of control I don't know.

For a first time author who wants to get their message to the world and not be bothered by things like page size, ISBNs and pricing, author services has a lot to offer. That said, author services doesn't cover everything: you will still need to pay attention to third-party copyright and arrange a copy-edit and index if required.

[a]https://leanpub.com/author_services/buy

Batch activities

In the traditional publishing world activities like copy-editing, indexing and copyright validation had to occur at the end because it didn't make sense to start them earlier – things would change. Hence publishers operated on a big-batch model: complete manuscript comes in, complete manuscript gets copy-edited, complete index created and the complete book typeset and printed. Publishing early and often, by contrast, operates on a small-batch model. So what happens to those processes?

Some of them can be foregone: an early release e-book doesn't need an index, as readers can use the search function. Some processes, like copy-editing, probably remain big-batch. While one could find a copy-editor to work chapter-by-chapter, it will probably push up cost because some chapters would inevitably get copy-edited twice.

Pushing copy-editing back may cause a few smiles, but it is unlikely to get you into big problems. However, copyright infringement could. Third-party copyright gets its own chapter in Part 3.

Blurb

Look inside ↓

🔊 Listen

See all 2 images

Follow the author

Allan
Kelly

Follow

Succeeding with OKRs in Agile: How to create & deliver objectives & key results for teams Paperback – 15 Feb. 2021

by Allan Kelly ˅ (Author), Mike Burrows (Foreword)

★★★★☆ ˅   39 ratings

See all formats and editions

Kindle Edition	Paperback
£7.45	£9.63
Read with Our **Free App**	1 Used from £6.32
	3 New from £9.63

Note: This item is eligible for **FREE Click and Collect** without a minimum order subject to availability. Details
OKR's are about goals bigger than the next story.

OKR's prioritise purpose and strategy over backlogs. Objectives are big goals; key results are smaller goals that build towards the objective.

Does your agile team get lead astray by burning fires?Do you struggle to keep your agile team focused?
Do you feel the need for more than just doing the top of the backlog every two weeks?
Are you using, or want to use, OKR's with an agile team?

Blurb for *Succeeding with OKRs in Agile*

When you post your book online you will include a description. To keep things simple you can use the same text for the description on the back cover of print editions. This is the *blurb*. I know that sounds like a slang expression, but according to the dictionary it is an accepted term.

Often blurbs are written to sound as if a third party is recommending the book; when I first wrote a book I expected the publisher to write the blurb. But no – it is the author who is responsible for it. I had to blow my own trumpet.

While there is no rule that says you have to write the blurb in the third person, it does lend a bit of authority – it sounds as if some learned person is praising the book. Of course if you wanted to be more personal you could write it that way too.

On LeanPub I usually create a quick blurb when I first publish the book. Later, when the book is nearing completion, I revisit the blurb and improve it. Sometimes I even recycle text from the Preface or Introduction. In other words, for me the blurb is always a bit of an afterthought. It shouldn't be that way: the blurb is your opportunity to hook the buyer in: you want the blurb to attract people, make it sound as if your book can help them with their challenges, and convince them that the book is both readable and worth reading.

I expect there is lots of advice out there on writing blurb, but I haven't looked at it. I honestly don't know what makes a reader move from browsing a book to buying it. I should have, but I haven't.

It can be helpful, if only for your own focus, to pose questions to attract a buyer's interest. Your blurb might start with something like 'Do you struggle to know when work will be done?'. The rest of the blurb should then hint that the book contains the required answers – I use a similar approach when writing conference talk synopsis.

The blurb on the back of a printed book is limited by the available space. While you might be tempted to reduce the font size and squeeze more in, I'd advise against this: the reader can always open the book and read some of the contents if they really want to know what's in the book.

So for a printed book I'd rather reduce the number of words and increase the font size. After all, if someone is reading the back cover in a bookshop or while standing at someone else's desk, they probably have plenty of distractions around them already.

The blurb is also the place where you can put some endorsements: 'The best book on stain removal I've ever read'. This does of course mean you need some endorsements to start with. This isn't such a big problem for digital books and descriptions on Amazon, but it is if you are having your books printed.

Publishers usually solve this problem by having the author nominate readers who can have advance copies, or at least e-books. This requires a little more planning to make sure you give people time to read the book. Having a 'fan club' of regular readers, perhaps people who regularly attend your presentations, can help here.

Of course, more endorsements means less space for your own text. Online, on Amazon at least, space is not the issue. In fact I find it difficult to come up with even half the volume of text that Amazon allows.

Fortunately, Amazon also allows the inclusion of endorsements here, so I can recycle review excerpts to add to a book's description. You can also use a few elements of HTML styling in the description, for example to make **some text bold** and other *in italics.*

Unlike the rear cover of printed books, you can also change the Amazon blurb after you have published. With some of my books I've revised the blurb to include quotes from online Amazon reviews.

I don't bother contacting the writer when using Amazon reviews as endorsements. Often I can't, as I don't have their contact details, but as the writer has already made their name and comments available on Amazon I'm just quoting them, so I think I'm safe. Nor do I ask permission if I use comments from volunteer reviewers. Such people have normally already agreed to either give me early feedback on the text or to write a review, so I feel they have already given their permission to be quoted.

If however someone emails me with comments, I usually ask if I can use their words in the online description or back cover.

Indexes

When I buy a non-fiction printed book I've always considered an index essential. I hate the experience of reading it, then thinking 'Where is the bit where they said *that*?' and not being able to find it without an index.

However, creating an index is a lot of work, and at least partially specialized. I know it looks easy, but there are professional indexers with their own professional body, so I assume there is a lot I don't know.

When I work with publishers they employ a dedicated indexer. First I have to work through the text and pick out terms I want included in the index. The indexer then uses these term as a starting point, but also adds to them.

While part of an index can be created in advance – key terms, for example – it cannot be completed until the page layout is stable, as only then do you know on which page(s) the terms will appear. Thus indexing must come at the very end of the publication process.

All of this means that indexes, while essential, are a pain.

In an e-book the whole idea goes away. In theory at least, you can forget about the index; every book reading software application has search functionality, so e-books are, on the face of it, far easier to search. This is another argument in favour of digital publishing. However even the best search feature doesn't know about abbreviations, acronyms and aliases, nor can a search suggest *see also* links for related concepts.

However I am guilty – I have sinned. I love indexes, but I have failed to have any of my self-published books indexed. I should have done, and I should do in future, but my original target was e-books, so I felt able to skip the index. The extra steps and cost of indexing mean I've continued to do so.

I should change my ways.

Xanpan 2 – an abandoned book

Unfortunately the post-writing production phase can drag on. It may well take longer than writing the book in the first place, as I expect to happen with this book. Occasionally I give up: the will to finish the project runs out. *Xanpan 2* was never finished. After finishing *Xanpan* I had lots of ideas, some complete chapters and some half-written text. The text was there but the unifying theme was lacking.

Eventually I accepted that fact that I lacked the motivation to finish the job, but I still published *Xanpan 2* as *Xanpan Appendix – Management and Team*. It was never copy-edited and has no cover or print version. I don't market or promote the book: it sells a few copies of its own accord and helps sweeten a LeanPub bundle, so it brings in a very small amount – $272 as of today.

21. Copy-edit

I keep mentioning copy-editing without explaining what it is. Copy-editing is the process of going through the text, finding and correcting spelling, punctuation, grammatical (SPAG) and other lexical nonconformities.

In my mind copy-editing and proofreading are the same thing. However, I suspect publishers and printers differentiate between them: a proofread occurs later in the process, after typesetting probably.

Copy-editing is not about fact-checking your work or reviewing the quality or the soundness of your arguments. You copy-editor might raise some point but I wouldn't guarantee it: it would depend on your copy-editor.

Many copy-editors work freelance – type 'hire copyeditor' into Google and you will find copy-editors and websites like Upwork that will help you hire a copy-editor. There even industry standards for copy-editor charges, such as the US Editorial Freelances Association[1]. Your copy-editor may charge more or less than these rates.

If you work with a publisher they will arrange the copy-editor. In my experience this is frequently offshored and the quality is poor.

When writing *Business Patterns* my publisher contracted Steve to do the copy-edit. Steve had copy-edited several pattern books before so he was familiar with the conventions in use. Subsequently, for my self-published efforts I usually hire Steve directly, and I'm happy to recommend him to others.

Copy-editing doesn't happen overnight, so you need to allow some time for it. Exactly how long it takes is going to be dependent on the number of words and how your editor works, among other things. It is probably best to ask your prospective editor how long they expect the process to take.

You may also find that your chosen copy-editor is busy and can't do the edit immediately, so you want to open discussion with them before you are ready in case you have to wait for them to become available.

During the process the copy-editor may want to ask you questions – sometimes my sentences can be ambiguous. This is a sign of a good copy-editor. One of the problems I've had with

---

[1]https://www.the-efa.org/rates/

weak editors is they don't ask questions, they just assume. However this question-and-answer process will also take time.

When the copy-edit is finished you should read through the text. The final work will bear your name, so you should make sure you are happy with the result. I say 'should' because, having worked with Steve multiple times, I increasingly trust him and don't feel the need to read everything, even if I should. A good copy-editor might be able to give you chapters to read as they work, to allow you to spread the work out.

Bad copy-edit

My worst copy-edit experience occurred with a big publisher who sent my book offshore for editing. When the results came back I had to use a truly awful website to review each change, and I only had a week to do the work.

Reading the text, even I could see SPAG errors. I requested a few changes but I was embarrassed by the text. However, I didn't feel I had the power reject it.

I assume that if I had asked for another copy-edit the work would have gone to the same place, but I should have asked, even if the cost had come out of my royalties.

To this day I'm a little embarrassed by the book. I'm also resolved to ask for Steve to copy-edit any book I might do with a publisher in future.

Copy-editing illustrations

Any illustration that contains text needs copy-editing too. This is so easy to forget that I do so in every book. Luckily Steve doesn't. Consequently you want to ensure that you keep the original source files for any illustrations you draw or manipulate, as you may need to return to them.

You therefore also need to retain the ability to open and edit the files, which means that you need access to the same editing software. I wrote *Changing Software Development* on a PC with Microsoft Word and Visio for diagrams. I switched to an Apple Mac shortly before the end of the work, which caused a few problems, but as I still had the PC I could return to it.

Microsoft doesn't offer Visio for Mac; I use OmniGraffle[2] for diagrams, which does the same

---

[2]https://www.omnigroup.com/omnigraffle

job and is very good – although it can cause extra work if the copy-editor can't edit the files directly themselves.

Keeping editing access to diagrams is not usually a problem, but can be. I also use mind-mapping software such as Inspiration, but when Inspiration Software closed a couple of years ago I lost the ability to open old files. The PC version of the software has since reappeared, but the files on my Mac are now inaccessible.

Copy-editing for dyslexics

When producing early release versions it makes sense to forego copy-editing. For authors who have mastered SPAG that is probably no big deal: their pre-copy-edit text will be quite good. A copy-edit might make sense, but the raw text is quite passable.

For dyslexics and others who are SPAG-challenged, this is harder. I keep meaning to talk to my copy-editor about interim copy-edits. Are they possible? What would it cost? But also know I chop and change the book so much that I would still need a final end-to-end copy-edit.

So I go ahead and publish anyway, although I now include a note at the front of the book – not really a disclaimer, more an expectation-setting exercise. I'm not asking for special treatment, I just want to say "I know the SPAG is a mess, that's me, I'll sort it out later.".

My copy-editor tells me he has, over years of editing my books, noticed I make different mistakes to others. Some are all my own! That is another reason for working with the same editor again and again: he is used to my style and the changes I need.

Even so not everything gets caught. Some of my Amazon reviews note my poor SPAG, some even mark my book down because of it. It probably costs me lost revenue. While I'm embarrassed and wish those mistakes weren't there, I have to let the water roll off my back.

Being dyslexic brings me many gifts, but in a society that values the written word so highly it also brings weaknesses. Dyslexia is a sociologically constructed disability: in a society that didn't use the written word it would never be considered a disability.

Dyslexia allows me to see the world differently, to understand the world differently and to communicate differently. That also means that I relate to words differently: they are two sides of the same coin.

Years ago when researching my dyslexia one author said something like "Dyslexics can't learn the way others learn, but it is not a symmetrical problem. What works for dyslexics is normally better for non-dyslexics too.".

I don't consider dyslexia a disability; rather, I consider it a superpower. If you want my ideas and my explanations, then a few spelling, punctuation and grammar alternatives are the price you pay. You don't get one without the other.

22. Third-party copyright

International copyright image

If every word and picture[1] in your book is your own creation, you probably don't have to worry about third-party copyright, because you already own the copyright to everything. Copyright exists whether you put a (c) mark on your work or not.

I say probably, because you might have signed away some of your own work. This might happen, for example, if you publish a journal article which you then decide to recycle into your book. Some publications, usually print journals and those who pay, will ask you to sign an agreement before publication. In that agreement you turn over copyright to the publisher, or possibly agree an exclusive licence.

When that happens you still own the ideas. You can write another article expressing the same thoughts, but you signed away those actual words and their sequence to the publisher. I have no idea how different your new article needs to be to the old one, or who checks this.

I know that my original patterns are all available for free download from my website. I also know that versions of most of my patterns have been published by John Wiley and Addison-Wesley. I also notice that many academics make pre-print versions of learned articles available to download from their websites, while the final versions are published in journals from Springer, Blackwells and others.

Just because something is copyright does not mean you cannot use it, but you have to be careful.

---

[1]Opening image by 'McDutchie' Martijn Dekker, from WikiCommons

If you are going to publish early versions of your book, you need to keep copyright in mind all the way through rather than leaving it untill the end. Traditional publishers don't publish until the end, so they can delay thinking about copyright to a late stage: publishing early means you need to think about copyright sooner.

Fair use

The fair use[2] provisions allow the use of quotation and short excerpts of text from other authors, especially if you are going to credit those authors. Indeed, given that many academics are judged on how often their publications are cited, they will probably be very happy for you use some of their text providing that you credit them.

Having said that, there are limits to how much you can use. If I recall correctly you are allowed to quote up to 10% of a text before you need to apply for copyright permission. That is actually quite a big chunk of text if you think about it, 10% of a 400 book would be 40 pages, but 10% of a song might be just one line.

Before you get anywhere near this mark I strongly recommend you check the rules yourself: don't take my word for it. Things might also be different where you live. Luckily much copyright information is available online, for example the UK Government has many webpages on copyright[3].

Basically, if you quote a paragraph and credit it, you should be safe. If you take anything more or don't credit it you are on shaky ground, and also run the risk of being accused of plagiarism.

Ask

If you do want to use larger extracts of a work you can always ask. Get in touch with the author or publisher, tell them what you want to use and why. They might ask for payment but they might just say "OK, use it". They might see it as a marketing opportunity: if your book contains one of their chapters then all your readers will be introduced to their work and might buy their book.

Since ideas can't be copyrighted, you could always write your own summary of their work: 'In their classic book Smith and Jones argue the case for... they suggest that because... and...

---

[2]https://en.wikipedia.org/wiki/Fair_use
[3]https://www.gov.uk/topic/intellectual-property/copyright

the result...' Of course this makes more work for you and might reduce the authority that comes from another's words, but you might actually do a better job at explaining their ideas.

If you are publishing incrementally you need to stay on top of these issues as you go. If you publish an early version of your work with a copyright infringement you may well upset the copyright owner and make your life more difficult when you do ask for permission.

Given that, you probably want to ask for copyright release sooner rather than later. Since copyright holders can ask for a fee, you want to stay on their right side.

Copyright cuts both ways

The rules I've outlined here apply to your work too, so you might find people asking for permission to use your material. Provided you haven't signed away the copyright to a publisher you might even make a little money.

I've had a few universities ask for permission to reproduce my work for their students. To be honest I don't know why, because the material in question is free to download: they could just give the students the URL and tell them to access it like anyone else.

The first few times this happened I just said "Yes, sure, permission given", but when the institutes came back the next year I asked them to pay. Not a lot ($100), and in return I sent them an email granting them unlimited rights to copy and distribute my downloadable work.

Copyright on images

Things get more complicated with images. Fair use becomes more debatable. As a general rule, if you want to use anyone else's images you need permission, and they might charge a fee.

To sidestep this problem I either draw my own diagrams or buy them from istockphoto.com. iStock is part of Getty Images and I find their prices reasonable, but there are lots of other image providers: depositphotos.com, agefotostock.com and dreamstime.com, to name a few. Many creators list their images on multiple sites, so the selection is not quite as massive as you may think. I find it helps to stay with one provider because I don't have to navigate multiple licences, or visit multiple sites, each with its own log-in, to find images I've paid for or similar ones.

The images provided by iStock and similar sites are royalty free, which means that you pay for them once and can then use them as many times as you want. When you read the licence, however, you will find it is royalty free up to, say, 100,000 uses. So unless you are planning to write the next Harry Potter you are probably all right.

If by chance you do get into these sorts of sales you will have funds to pay for any image you want. Your biggest problem will be remembering that the image on page 123 is only licenced for 100,000 copies. Which is another reason for limiting the number of licences you use. Since each licence and clipart site has their own conditions, you make more work for yourself checking licences and remembering what you can and can't do with images.

The other option is to use open images, that is to say images which are public domain, Creative Commons License, GNU licence (GPL) or one of the other open-source licences. Such images are available free of charge, but you need to check what you are agreeing to and whether the licence contains any clauses that might cause you problems.

Seen that image before?

There is one more catch with clipart: everyone else can get the same pictures. This means that you might end up looking too generic. After you've spent any time on clipart sites you start to spot their images everywhere.

iStock orders pictures by popularity. So if you want a less common picture, don't choose the first ones that appear – search lower in the list. I suspect the same is true of other clipart sites.

This might be less of a problem with public-domain and open-source images on sites like Wikimedia Commons[4]. Many of these images are subject to Creative Commons and similar licences, so come with some restrictions. Such restrictions may mean they are not so widely used.

Licences and sites

I'm no licence expert but I have some experience and some views. Before you use any images, make sure you understand what the copyright means. I might advise reading the licence agreement, but they are written in such legal mumbo-jumbo that I lose the will to live. Instead I usually search for a licence FAQ.

The other way of handling licence complexities is to avoid them and restrict yourself to material that is in the public domain. Failing that, stick to a limited number of licences that you have checked out.

---

[4]https://commons.wikimedia.org

Public domain

Public domain images don't have a catch. Since all work funded by the US Government must be put in the public domain, there is a rich stock of photos from NASA, the US Air Force, Navy, the Centres for Diseases Control and elsewhere to draw on. You can find these on the relevant websites and on WikiCommons[5].

The bad news about public domain is that outside of US Government-funded images the quality is often too poor to be usable. A lot of very old images are in the public domain simply because they are too old to be within copyright, but again quality can be poor. (And because Disney keeps having copyright law extended, many images that should be in the public domain by now aren't.)

CCL, GPL and other licences

As well as public domain works you will find a lot of WikiCommons images are either Creative Commons License (CCL) or GNU Public License (GPL). There are other open source licences, but these are the main ones: whatever licence you use, remember to read it. I may fail to mention something that is important, so don't rely on me for the details.

CCL licences come in several versions, but the basic idea is that you are free to use an image as long as you credit the creator. This isn't too onerous in an article or book, so such images are useful.

The GPL is more problematic. The danger with using GNU-licenced material is that you might accidentally make your own work GPL too. GPL embodies a concept called *copyleft*, which means that work that builds on a GPL product must also be GPL. This might be less of a problem with writing than with program code, but I tend to avoid GPL for this reason.

Wikipedia contains entries for over 100 free, open-source, permissive and copyleft licences, so I'm going to stop here. Understanding the licences is hard enough: if you uses images with different licences in your work you are making your admin task harder.

Public domain is always my first preference, and I usually start with Wikimedia Commons. After that I'll consider CCL images, but I'm more likely to go to iStock. It may cost me, but I know I'm on safe ground, and iStock has a good selection of images, so I don't need to dredge open-source sites.

---

[5]https://commons.wikimedia.org

Royalty free images?

If you go looking for images it won't be long before you come across websites advertising royalty free images. There seem to be millions of these sites. On the whole I ignore them.

The catch is that such sites need to make money. While a few make money from advertising, most do so by getting you to buy images. They may advertise royalty free images, and even have some public domain images for download, but most of the images they show are not free. 'Royalty free' is the click-bait that lures you in: once you are in you might find that 'royalty free' images still cost money. As with iStock, 'royalty free' does not necessarily mean 'free'.

Unsplash

One exception to all this is Unsplash[6]. Unsplash was and still is an amazing repository of quality free images. Its contributors post their images to showcase their work. Their hope is that someone will want to commission them or hire them. Unsplash encourages users to link to the Unsplash artist – I guess the hope is that all the links will cause Google to rank the artist and Unsplash highly.

I wrote 'Unsplash was...' In 2021 Getty Images bought Unsplash, and while it has largely kept Unsplash unchanged it has integrated the site with iStock. Consequently you might think you are looking at a free image on Unsplash, but you are actually looking at a paid image from iStock. Personally I find the way the sites are integrated really irritating, but I guess 'free' always has a price.

Flickr

Flickr[7] might not be as popular as it was in the early 2000s, but it still exists and has one very useful feature. As part of its advanced search you can specify the licence you want to search on. So you could for example search for public-domain dog images from the US Government, or CCL cat images.

Images in books

So far I have talked about using text from existing books and articles and images from other sources. But what about images in books?

---

[6]https://unsplash.com/
[7]https://www.flickr.com

Unsurprisingly the publishers or authors hold copyright on these. Fair use is more difficult to claim here, so if you want an image from a book you will need to ask, and you may well end up paying a fee.

Not so highly effective

Changing Software Development contains a few images from other publications and, on my editor's advice, I approached the publishers for permission. In most cases I needed to pay a small fee, $100 or so.

In one case I wanted a really simple image: a circle inside another circle, both circles being labelled. The editor said we needed permission, so I approached the other publisher. The publisher didn't respond to me.

So my publisher wrote to them for permission. Still no reply. The editor decided that, as I had asked twice, we could use the image under fair use. The book proceeded to production.

At this point the other publisher woke up and demanded payment. I forget how much – it was something like $200. My publisher agreed to pay – although the fees would come out of my royalties – so we asked for an invoice. Silence again.

A year or two later the other publisher asked why we hadn't paid. Only then did we get an invoice and pay.

The funny part is this: the images comes from one of the best-selling books about self-organization and personal advancement, *The Seven Habits of Highly Effective People*.

Keeping track of licences

You might have noticed that image copyright is a lot more complicated than that for text. If you work with a publisher you may well be asked to sign something that specifies that you take responsibility for image licences. If I recall correctly, even Amazon KDP has a box you must tick to say you are not using any images for which you do not have copyright or permission. If Amazon finds you have violated copyright they can pull your book.

You therefore need to stay on top of your licences. If you are doing one big publish at the end you could delay thinking about copyright until this stage and then go through every image. I've done this and can report that not only is it boring, but you hit small delays.

The alternative, which you really should do if you are publishing incrementally, is to check the licence on each image as you go. Not only does this allow you to publish as you, go but it also breaks down a big boring task into many small and less boring ones.

Let me suggest two options for keeping track of your images.

Either create a spreadsheet, make a note of every image you use, where it came from, what licence applies to it and, if necessary, how you have permission to use it.

Alternatively, don't ever use an image for which you don't have permission. That is why the vast majority of my images come from iStock. Since they all come from iStock I only have one licence to think about and I have one account with all the images listed.

When I use a third-party image from elsewhere I attach a footnote to say where the image comes from. Few readers will care, but it makes it easier for me to keep track of where the images are from and their copyright status.

Thus all images in my books fall into one of three groups: images I create myself, images I have iStock licences for, or images that have a footnote detailing their source and copyright. For all the latter I have a separate file and copyright statement.

If you don't want lots of footnotes in your book you could keep a table at the back listing images, source and copyright. This involves a bit more effort, though, to ensure you don't put an image in and forget to add it to the table.

I take this one step further: all images I use are in one directory on my laptop. That is divided into *iStock*, *Unsplash*, *Public Domain* and *Open*. Every image I use gets its own subdirectory. For every image I haven't paid for I also make a PDF image that shows the image with its copyright statement and the URL where I found it. (Just printing the Wikimedia Commons page as a PDF is enough).

Hopefully, even if I don't say in the book where the image came from, I have a record. If needs be I can then provide evidence that I believed I had the right to use the image.

Publishers

Some publishers are very hot on third-party copyright and will want to pin everything down in detail. Others are very relaxed by comparison. If you decide to work with a publisher, make sure you understand what your publisher will expect of you and how much help, if any, you can expect from them on copyright issues.

23. Illustrations

Apart from the third-party clipart and pictures I use, almost all the illustrations and graphics in my books are of my own creation. Modern graphics packages such as Visio on PCs and OmniGraffle on Mac are pretty good for this. I've also used mind-mapping software for diagrams, but these – even to my eyes – tend to look less than professional, so I try to avoid them.

Still, my images could be better, and sometimes they really need to be better than what I produce. Here again, as with book covers, I use a graphic designer. This is simple: I pay, he designs, we iterate to get something that explains my ideas.

If you are working with a publisher you may want to find out whether they will use your illustrations or have an artist redraw you images. You should find out what involvement you will have in that processes and whether the publisher is paying, or whether the costs are coming out of your royalties.

I'm sure if I used a graphic artist more often my diagrams would look even better. On the whole the illustrations that appear in my books are my own work created with inexpensive software packages like OmniGraffle or open source Gimp[1].

Assuming you have diagrams that include words, watch out for spelling mistakes and places where you change your own terminology. My copy-editor regularly points out spelling mistakes in my diagrams that even I would fail to spot in the text. On other occasions I find I change my text and neglect to update a diagram, leaving them inconsistent.

Some books, like this one, have few illustrations, while others have many. Images create extra work. In particular, images take you into new questions of copyright and layout.

I discussed copyright in the previous chapter, so much of this chapter will be about the layout implications of images. Make sure you read the chapter about page size first.

Images will also add substantially to the file size of e-books. Not only will that make them slower to download, but it will also make them more expensive. I discuss this in the chapter on file sizes and download costs.

---

[1]https://www.gimp.org/

Image layout

Getting illustrations to appear the right size in your book can be a problem. This is going to depend a lot on how you produce your book. A publisher will handle this as part of layout, but if you are self-publishing and have nobody to help you it can be troublesome. More than once I've found myself up a blind alley with images, wasting hour after hour.

LeanPub gives guidance on how to size images, but I find it's not enough, or perhaps it is enough but the issue is so complicated that I don't understand it. I can set up the 'right' number of pixels, size and resolution, but when the image appears in the book it suddenly takes up the whole page or appears far too small. More frustratingly still, when I use Pandoc to create review files an image might look good, but then LeanPub processes it differently and it appears too big or to small.

I usually find myself iterating: creating an image the size I think it should be, looking at what gets generated, adjusting the size and repeating. This can be very frustrating, because I don't know if it's me missing something, making a mistake or whether it's just the way the world is.

Part of the problem with illustration layout is paper size, coupled with the fact that e-books aren't actually on paper. This is one of the places where changing page size can create problems.

An image that takes up less than half a page of A4 may take up a whole page of A5 because the layout algorithms don't want to put a mere few words by the image. Or the opposite: the image might take a lot of space but there are a few odd-looking words floating around.

One of the chapters in the print version of *Succeeding with OKRs* opens with the chapter title, an image to illustrate my point and then... a big white space, as the text starts at the top of the next page. I missed this and it's embarrassing.

More embarrassing still, I sometimes find that images that are perfectly sized for the print version appear tiny in the e-book version. Or the way an image appears in the ePub version is different to the way the image looks in the Mobi version.

To complicate matters apps render the same file differently. Consider the diagram which opens this book, which is probably page 1. Viewed with the Amazon Kindle App on my Mac the diagram takes up most of the page. The same diagram, in the same ePub file, on the same Mac, uses less than half the page when viewed in Apple Books.

More than once I've simply given up and accepted that in some formats, on some e-book readers, some of my images appear too big or too small.

Fortunately, Amazon announced in 2022 that it would stop using the Mobi format and instead use ePub on Kindle. LeanPub subsequently stopped supporting the generation of Mobi format files, removing one set of combinations to work with. Although it still leaves the question of whether the same ePub file looks ok on a iPhone, iPad and various versions of Kindle.

24. Layout and page size

I am a regular disappointment to my copy-editor because I settle for second best when it comes to layout. In addition to copy-editing he is an expert at book layout – or typesetting as it is also called. To his eye my layouts are less than beautiful and could be better.

From my point of view my layout is good enough: to my eyes it is fine, and to be honest, I wouldn't know a beautiful layout if it slapped me in the face. I'm happy to take 80% of the quality for 10% of the effort offered by automated layout algorithms. In fact I might even argue that when working with e-books you can't get any better.

If you are working in LeanPub and if, like me, you are prepared to accept the layouts that LeanPub offers, you can skip this chapter. Layout isn't completely off the table with LeanPub: it does offer options, but those options are a fraction of what could be done. If you are prepared to devote time to tweaking all the options you can still get fancy.

At the other end of the spectrum, people who really care about layout, and those who know about layout themselves, probably want to skip this chapter, because you already know more than what I'm going to say. For everyone else, read on.

Layout, typeset, camera

In printing circles the terms *layout*, *typeset* and *camera-ready* all refer to the process of turning a manuscript – possibly even one written on a typewriter – into a form that can be mass printed. These terms have their origins in the history of printing.

I tend to use the three terms interchangeably as if they were synonymous. Hopefully this doesn't cause any confusion.

The guts of the problem

Traditionally when a book was typeset or laid out for print the publishers knew the page size. In the digital world page size goes away. Not only are you potentially producing three (or more) file formats – typically PDF, ePub and Mobi[1] – but those files will be rendered on different devices: Kindles and other e-book readers, phones, iPads, desktop PCs and Macs, as well as specialist devices like reMarkable.

When your text and pictures are rendered on these devices the user will be able to change font, font size, line spacing, text density and maybe other factors. The devices have different sized screens and, as new devices are launched and others updated, new screen options will appear. Finally, the software on each of those devices will be different and will render a page differently.

For example, if I am reading on my ten-year-old Kindle, or Kindle software on my iPad, sometimes when I flip forwards a few pages and then flip back the page is different: it might start and end in different places, or adjust the word spacing.

If you are printing a book you can create a great layout that will last, but creating a great layout for an e-book means either catering for an unlimited number of possibilities or targeting your e-book at a limited number of devices. Even then they may change in future. That does not mean you cannot improve an e-book's layout, but it does mean that options are limited.

Page sizes

When working in e-book formats like ePub page size is a minor consideration. The reader software will resize the pages for the display and in the process change where page breaks occur.

Conversely, PDF readers don't do this: the whole point of PDF is that it maintains the layout. So PDF readers maintain page size, which means that PDFs can be difficult to read on a e-book reader like my old Kindle. PDF is great when you are printing, but not when you are using an e-reader.

For a printed book the page size is, obviously, very important. More pages mean the book is more expensive to print and post. So more pages mean your book will make less money for you at any given selling price. This is particularly important if you intend to give your printed books away for free.

If you look at the books on your shelves you will see they are of different sizes. Printers and publishers have standard book sizes, but they have a lot of them. Part of the reason

---

[1]LeanPub always produces PDF and ePub versions, and used to create Mobi too. There are numerous other formats: Kindles have used AZW, AZW3 and KFX. I assume Sony had a proprietary format when they produced e-readers and wouldn't be surprised to hear of others.

I originally chose to work in A5 was because it is widely recognized and supported: Lulu printing supported A5, LeanPub supports A5, and my office printer can print two A5 pages onto one sheet of A4 paper, so less paper needed.

But Amazon KDP (CreateSpace) does not.

The print versions of *Xanpan, A Little Book about Requirements and User Stories, Project Myopia* and *Continuous Digital* were all originally A5 in size. This was because I was initially only working with LeanPub for e-book and Lulu for print. I used Lulu's global distribution system to put the printed books into wider distribution and get them on Amazon.

When I decided to move printing from Lulu to Amazon I found that Amazon did not support A5 printing. It had plenty of other options, but not A5. So the page size had to change. (I discuss why I did this later.)

Now when I start writing I keep things in A4 format – more words per page and easier on the eye. At some stage I switch the books over to A5 format and most of my self-published books appeared in that format.

At a late stage in the production of *Succeeding with OKRs in Agile* I decided I wanted something different, so changed the page size to 7.5x9.25 inch. The larger format looks better and more professional to my eyes, but even without any layout changes it still caused me extra work.

Choosing a new page size was not a trivial matter. When creating camera-ready PDFs LeanPub offers a lot of options for page sizes, but not all of these are available on Amazon. (Naturally Amazon offers sizes LeanPub doesn't, just to complicate things.) To confuse things still further, LeanPub offers a standard page size called 'technical', as well as a 'theme' called *technical* that has a default page size that is not the 'technical' page size!

To add further confusion, the page size and the space used on the page are also different. Some of the LeanPub page sizes just have wider margins and more white space than other options that are almost the same size. This means that choosing a larger page size doesn't put more words on the page, and so doesn't reduce the page count and doesn't reduce printing costs.

If you want your book to look big – perhaps to increase authority – this is good. However, if you want a smaller book that looks less intimidating and takes up less storage space, or a lighter one that is cheaper to post, then including more white space is probably not what you want.

I measured some books on my shelves to decide what page size I wanted. Here I hit two problems. First, page sizes are still normally quoted in inches – *Imperial* or *English* measurements – while I, being a good European, tend to use the metric system.

Second, having measured a lot of books and looked at the page sizes available, I have been forced to conclude that all measurements are approximate. Some books come very close to official sizes – a millimetre or two – but don't quite match them. I also discovered that some of the page sizes I liked are not available on Amazon or LeanPub.

Navigating page sizes

So what should you do?

1. Find a page size you like – look at the books you have and measure them.
2. Check that this size is supported by the system or systems you intend to use. For me this is LeanPub and Amazon.
3. Decide on the size before you get your cover designer involved.
4. Stick with the size and avoid changing it.

Hopefully, like me, once you have found a size you like you can use it for book after book. Having moved away from A5 I'll be sticking with the 7.5x9.25" size I used for *Succeeding with OKRs*. I can then at least copy the settings.

Changing LeanPub layout

Having started by arguing that sticking with LeanPub layouts is good enough, I should point out you do have options, even when working in LeanPub.

You can work with and incrementally publish via LeanPub. Then when you get to the point where you want to make your book's layout better – and I suggest you wait until near the end – you can get hold of the LeanPub file and change it.

LeanPub has the option to export to InDesign files. InDesign is Adobe's professional layout package – the successor of PageMaker, for those of you who remember that. So you, or your layout professional, can take the file and edit to your heart's content and produce new improved camera-ready files for your printer.

LeanPub says of the InDesign export option that 'this feature is fairly early in its lifespan', so results may change over time. Alternatively, my understanding is that InDesign can import PDF files, so you can still produce your files in LeanPub then work with InDesign – or whatever package you decide to work with – but options are severely limited.

If you do decide to put extra effort into the print layout, then make sure you don't change the page size after you've started. Choose a page size you are happy with and that you won't want to change. Indeed, I expect that you won't want to start changing the layout using a tool like InDesign until you have entirely finished writing.

Exporting to InDesign and adjusting page layouts are not things I've ever done, so if layout is important to you and you think you will want to massage what LeanPub produces, then I suggest you check out the options sooner rather than later.

Publisher's problems

Even though publishers can create beautiful layouts for printed books, they still suffer from e-book reader screen and font size variations. I expect layout experts can offset some of these problems, but the solution will never be complete.

To be brutally honest, I've been disappointed with all the publisher-produced e-book versions of my books. This may be a little unfair to Wiley, since it is over ten years since they published one of my books and I expect their capabilities have improved.

In my experience publishers are still print-centric. I'm sure some publishers are more e-book-oriented than others, and even within publishing houses some people will be more e-book savvy than others, but in my experience publishers still think first in terms of print.

This means that the print version of a book may be available before the electronic version, even when you have worked entirely electronically. It may also mean that the time and attention paid to layout is not what you might want.

In fact, even with printed books I have found some publisher's typesetting choices to be questionable. I suspect that in their efforts to economize some have accepted reduced quality as the price of reduced cost.

If layout is important to you, therefore, then the control that comes from self-publishing might be an advantage to you. If you do decide to work with a publisher, you might want to find out about typesetting before you sign any contract.

25. Book cover

One image you most definitely want to invest time and money in is your book's cover. Despite the popular adage, people do *judge a book by its cover.* Unlike the images inside your book, for which black and white might be good enough, you will want a colour image for the cover.

Many more people will see your book's cover than ever read a word of it. Your cover – both in a bookshop and online – is your opportunity to capture readers' interest. Remember that potential buyers will encounter your cover picture as a fairly small image, so detail will be lost.

In addition to pictures the cover will contain the title, your name as author, possibly a subtitle and even some bullet points of what is covered.

Cover of Business Patterns with bullet points

Initial cover

When I start a book I don't do anything for a cover, I just accept the default LeanPub text-only one. When I get to the point of publishing early drafts, however, I create my own cover.

For the initial cover I fire up OmniGraffle on my Mac and set the page size, add the title and name. I might also add a bit of clip-art, some bullet points and 'sticker' saying 'Draft version'. This is fine while the book is being sold in draft and only for sale on LeanPub, but for a final version you want it to look professional, you want it to be eye-catching and you want the cover to help sell the book in a wider market.

Initial book cover for this book

Graphic artist

Unless you are yourself a talented artist and have the time, I strongly suggest you get a professional designer to create your cover. This need not be expensive, and websites like Upwork or Fiverr allow you to find artists easily.

All the covers for my self-published books have been designed by Anton Fimaier[1]. Anton isn't expensive and has a knack for coming up with covers I like. I've no idea who designed

---

[1]mailto:a.fimaier@gmail.com

the covers of my publishers' books. While Anton and I may iterate over the cover, I've rarely done that with a publisher.

For *Changing Software Development* I suggested something abstract in the style of Piet Mondrian, Ben Nicholas or Ellsworth Kelly. In return I got a picture of the sky with a jet fighter – I hazard a guess that someone typed 'agile' into an image search engine.

Business Patterns was better because it stayed closer to the existing Wiley 'POSA' (Pattern Oriented Software Architecture) series style. This dictated that there would be a picture of buildings on the cover. I suggested the 'Three Graces' of the Liverpool waterfront I grew up with. These buildings symbolise the strength of Liverpool business in the early twentieth century. Wiley's designer then offered several possible layouts.

I have no recollection at all of how *The Art of Agile Product Ownership* got its cover. While on LeanPub it had one of my functional covers. I seem to recall Apress just sending over the finished version.

Many covers

While the cover art and the basic text will be common, you may well need three or more versions of your book cover. The need for multiple versions in different sizes is another reason for working with a professional designer.

Obviously you will need a cover for your e-book. This is fairly straightforward because it is a single image. Since e-books don't sit on bookshelves, your purchasers will rarely see the cover. However, potential buyers will see it while scrolling on Amazon or another online site. It may take as little as the title or your name that encourages them to click and read more about the book.

You will need a cover for the print version of your book. This has three parts. The first part is for the front of the book. This will be the same as the e-book, although probably a different size. The second part of the cover is for the back of the book. This could be a continuation of the image on the front, but you probably want to add some blurb – a couple of paragraphs about why the book is great, maybe a bio of yourself, perhaps even your photo, and finally the ISBN barcode.

The third part is the spine. Looking at my books I see that the publisher-produced covers are the same background colour as the front and carry the book's title, my name and the publisher's name and logo – that's it. For my self-published books Anton has continued the illustration onto the spine to make it more interesting.

You may well want two versions of the printed book's cover, one for paperback and one for any hardback version. Amazon has only recently introduced hardback print-on-demand books, so I haven't had a chance to try out this feature. Still, it is obvious that while the same design can be used, the measurements and ISBN will differ between hardback and paperback versions.

On-line print services may provide a cover designer or allow you to upload a cover. I advise you to use a professional graphic designer to design yours. You will need to provide one image that contains all three parts, which introduces an extra complication.

Your third cover is for the audio version if you are producing one. Audible ACX expects you to provide an image of the size of a CD box inlay. The main consumers of this image will be potential buyers scrolling through options online.

The spine

The front and back covers of your book are the same size every time, but the spine size changes. The more pages your book has, the more space the spine will need, and the weight (thickness) of the paper to be used is also a factor here. While the odd page here or there doesn't matter, if the spine is too narrow you will have problems.

Some online services will refuse to accept a book cover that is the wrong size. Others may allow an incorrectly sized spine, but it will steal or donate space from the front or back covers. Since you won't know exactly how many pages you will have until you are very nearly finished, you need to iterate here.

Sequence

Once the end is in sight for a book I have my designer create an e-book cover. This might need to be adjusted before the end, for example to add the name of a foreword author. This cover is usually in place on the final draft copies available on LeanPub.

At some stage – perhaps while the manuscript is in copy-edit, or perhaps after the e-book is on Amazon and I'm waiting for reviews, I'll create a print file on LeanPub and see how many pages the print version of the book will need. I can then get a book cover template from Amazon[2] and give this to the designer to work on the print cover and spine. If you are working with another printer they will either have a similar template or be able to give you the measurements to use.

---

[2]https://kdp.amazon.com/en_US/cover-templates

Most likely the blurb that goes on the book's back cover is going to be the same blurb that is used on Amazon as the book's description. The back blurb will need to be shorter than on Amazon however, as Amazon allows a lot of space, and I might make some other small changes.

By this stage I will also know the relevant ISBN number, so this, together with a barcode, can go to the designer for inclusion on the back cover.

It is possible that the copy-edit will result in a different number of pages in the book. This is unlikely to differ by very many pages – two or three perhaps – but that might be enough to resize the spine and require a new template, so this needs to be double-checked and repeated if necessary.

Now I can think about getting a test print of the book. Authors can buy test copies at cost, but they come with a 'Not for resale' banner added to the cover. I can get a test print before the copy-edit is finished, which might speed things up a little by revealing problems. But I'm generally prepared to wait a little longer just in case any spine changes propagate to the cover.

Other uses

When you engage a designer you should check who will own the copyright for a cover design. While I tend to assume that commissioning the work means I get the copyright, it is not always the case. Years ago I came across a logo design company that retained the copyright – in the small print of the contract you only received a licence to use the images they created. This gave them an opportunity to sell you the copyright for an extra fee once you were using the logo.

Similarly, you might want to obtain any original graphics files, in case you subsequently want another artist to modify your images, you fall out with your designer or you fear losing the contact.

Once you have a cover and its copyright you can choose to use the cover for other activities. You could also use any illustrations in blog posts, online tutorials or flyers for the book.

If you are doing a presentation you will want to include a picture of your book and remind people to buy it. You could also use the graphics from the cover to illustrate a presentation.

One of the advantages of owning the cover copyright is that you can reuse its images and create more images in the same style. This allows you to build more of a brand identity – something I've failed at, as I'm always looking towards something new.

If you are working with a publisher you have a problem: they own the copyright for the cover design. Ideally your publisher will be cooperative and allow you to repurpose the cover images, and perhaps connect you with the artist to create more, but that has not been my experience.

26. File size and download costs

When you buy a printed book there is usually a charge for postage and packing, although this is sometimes waived by the seller. When you download a book there is no delivery charge, but someone somewhere still needs to pay for the bandwidth. As a buyer your download costs are set in the contact with your ISP, but as an author you might be expected to pay some of the download costs incurred by the seller.

LeanPub doesn't impose download charges, nor does Amazon on the lower royalty rate (currently 35%). I recall Amazon limiting download sizes to 5Mb, but I can no longer find that limitation, so I either imagined it or it has gone away. I expect there is a file size limit, but it doesn't seem to be an issue Amazon feels the need to highlight.

If you want the higher Amazon royalty rate of 70% there are download charges. The 70% royalty rate is paid after download costs are deducted from the sale revenue, so every megabyte of a book's file costs you. Conversely, the 35% rate is calculated from the sale price without any deduction. So its either 70% of a smaller number or 35% of a bigger number. (I discuss multiple royalty rates in the chapter on Amazon in Part IV.)

Currently in the UK Amazon downloads cost the author 10p/Mb, in the US 15¢/Mb. While the author pays for the download, the download costs (and maybe price) vary by country. It doesn't matter which country the author is in: download costs depend on the country the buyer is in.

A 5Mb book sold today in England would costs 50p to download. The same book would cost 60c to download in most (if not all) Euro countries, ¥5 in Japan, 75¢ in the US and 75¢ in Canada. Which, since the loonie is worth less than the greenback, means that downloads are cheaper north of the US-Canada border even while the nominal 'dollar price' is greater.

All these are reasons for keeping your book's file size down.

The good news is that text – which usually constitutes most of a book – is cheap, because it is small in byte terms. If you have written an all-text work such as a novel, it is entirely possible your book will not be much more than one megabyte.

The bad news is that images take up space: the more images you have, and the higher their resolution, the larger your file size. The larger your file size, the higher the download costs, and thus the lower your revenue.

Do the math(s)

Putting lots of images in your book will increase its file size. At some point it is better to settle for a lower royalty rate without download costs than a higher royalty rate with them.

Consider a 5Mb book selling for £5 in the UK. At a 35% royalty rate the author would make £1.75 per sale. On a 70% royalty rate the download charge would be 50p, so the author would make 70% of £4.50, which is £3.15. So it still makes sense to be on a 70% royalty rate.

On a 35% rate it doesn't matter how big the book gets – the author still makes £1.75 per sale. If the book grows to 25Mb, however, then it will incur £2 of download charges per sale, so the author makes 70% of £3 (£5 less £2 of download charges), which is £1.75, the same as for the lower royalty rate.

The maths for a 5Mb book selling for $5 in the US or Canada looks similar. The 15c download fee means that the author makes $3.40 per sale for a 1Mb book, but the trade-off point comes sooner. Selling a 16Mb book in the US makes the author 7¢ more on the 70% royalty rate. If the book's file size reaches 17Mb, the author would make 3.8¢ more on the 35% rate.

If your book has many fantastic pictures you may well want to charge more than just $5 for it. A book selling for $20 at the 70% royalty rate will make the author more than the same book selling at the 30% rate as long as the file size is below 66Mb. After the $9.90 download fee (for a US buyer) the author would receive $7.07 at 70%, but only $7 on 35% and no download fee. If the same book grows to 67Mb then a 35% rate still earns $7 but the 70% rate makes $6.96.

So unless you are writing a graphic novel you probably don't need to worry about these issues. For everyone else the decision is pretty simple: take the higher rate and pay the download charges. Although that doesn't mean that you can forget about file size. You still need to monitor size because it makes a difference to your revenue. It only takes one or two byte-heavy images to push up your download charges and push down your revenues.

Image sizes

In a book such as this with few images I'm probably not going to have a problem[1], but images can surprise you. Most self-drawn digital diagrams aren't going to be a problem unless you save them at an incredibly high resolution, but clipart can be. Almost every time I've been surprised by file size it has been because some third-party art work is of a far higher resolution than I expected.

---

[1] At the time of writing the most recent draft is 1.7Mb in PDF and 2.2Mb in ePub format.

If you are writing on LeanPub all your images are probably in an 'images' directory, so you can just look at the file sizes and find any bloat. If your images are scatted around multiple directories, finding any guilty parties means looking in many different places. However, if you have written in Word or something similar and embedded the images as you go, then you might have a problem finding any large images.

The lesson here is to take care with your images. If you embed images, always keep track of the original files. This advice is good for managing copyright issues too.

I keep all my clipart in one directory, divided into licences, pubic domain, own creation and other subdirectories. I keep copies of any images I get online, together with a note of their source and copyright. When I use one of those images in a book I save a copy with the book's files. Observant readers will notice that some images appear in several of my books.

Once you've found an oversized file (by which I mean a file that has more bytes than is justified), you can attempt to reduce its size. You can reduce the size and/or reduce its resolution, but remember to check the image's appearance and its size after editing it. Simple drawings usually reduce without too much trouble, but if you are reducing a picture then things can be more troublesome.

If an image doesn't render well at a lower resolution you might want to replace it with another that illustrates the same thing. Alternatively you could ask yourself if you really need it, and maybe remove it all together.

Black and white

One way of reducing image size is to convert an image from colour to black and white. For some images or simple diagrams that can be trivial. For other images greyscale might be just fine. If the image is a simple diagram, then removing all the colour may not change the message the diagram is trying to convey. Other images might benefit from being rendered in greyscale.

Converting images to black and white comes with a print versus e-book caveat: what works in one format might not work so well in another. For a printed edition you might want to convert images inside the book to black and white, to reduce printing costs or because it will happen during the printing process anyway.

To add to the possibilities, some e-book readers, such as my old Kindle, have screens made of 'electronic paper' – 'e-paper' or 'e-ink'. These aren't very good at rendering pictures at the best of times. However, since e-paper is generally black and white only, black and white images tend to work better.

You might decide to convert all your images to black and white to keep things consistent. Since some Kindles and most print processes will do this anyway, you might prefer to make sure the images look the way you want in just two colours.

Image formats

Another way to reduce image file size can be to change the file format. Take the image of the writing cycle in Chapter 16. The original image using PNG format (recommend by LeanPub) was 126Kb, while the JPEG was 148Kb and the TIFF 132kb. For that fairly simple picture the format shouldn't make a big difference, although it might. However when I exported the TIFF from Preview my Mac estimated the file size would be 8Mb.

After really minor edits the writing cycle image changed size. The JPEG is now 62Kb, PNG 126Kb and TIFF 21Kb. In theory one might expect PNG and TIFF to always deliver bigger files because they are lossless formats (data is preserved), while JPEG is lossy (some data may be lost) but as these figures show that is not always true. In general, JPEGs are better for photos (and similar) but best avoided for line art. Not being an expert here I don't know what other factors are at work: sometimes which format I use comes down to simple experimentation.

Most obviously, formats like JPEG allow the resolution and quality to be adjusted. A higher resolution and/or a higher quality image will result in a larger file.

While two software packages may implement the same algorithm, there may well be small differences when exporting the same image at the same resolution. When added up these differences become noticeable. Other differences could come from the operating system and even the CPU.

Now consider the screenshot showing *Succeeding with OKRs in Agile* at number one in project management. The PNG used in this book is 359Kb, while the TIFF image is 2.2Mb. Generally TIFF is a larger format, so I avoid it.

As a JPEG the same image reduces to 139Kb, so I will probably swap it soon. I also have the option of reducing the image at a lower resolution: doing this reduces it to 39Kb. On my big screen monitor this smaller image looks fuzzy in places, but it might be acceptable on a tablet or e-reader screen.

Cover

The largest image in your book is likely to be the cover art. You may well have specifically designed full colour artwork that you want to reproduce at high resolution. Reducing the size of this would seem questionable.

Remember though that you upload your book cover to KDP separately from the manuscript. The cover contained in your e-book file is not the same as potential customers see on the website. If you really want to minimize the cover's file size you could use low-resolution cover art in the e-book while using a higher-resolution image for the Amazon listing.

Don't forget print

Unfortunately there is a catch here. Sometimes you can reduce the resolution of an image and it works acceptably in an e-book, but when the same image is used in a printed book it looks poor.

On one or two occasions I've had to produce two version of a book. I produce the book on LeanPub with low-resolution images and upload them for the e-book. I then change the source files in LeanPub to use higher-resolution images, recreate the print-ready file on LeanPub, and then use that file for the printed book.

This is a fiddly hassle at best, and if you need to update a book at a later date – it shouldn't happen, but it does – you need to repeat the process. You really want to avoid doing this if at all possible. Having one set of source files from which you can generate all versions of a book keeps things simple.

Other formats

To complicate the file-size discussion further there is the issue of e-book formats. E-book file sizes can differ massively between formats: the PDF version of Xanpan is 3.9Mb, in ePub format this reduced to 3Mb, while the same book in Mobi format was 7.2Mb.

Sometimes reducing file size while maintain good image size and appearance can feel like a whack-a-mole game. You reduce the resolution of an image to reduce size, the Mobi size shrinks and it looks fine, but in ePub the image is too small; you change the image, rebuild the book and the image looks good in all formats, but the Mobi file size has gone up[2].

You can shortcut this process a bit. Amazon doesn't sell e-books in PDF format. If someone really wants a PDF they can get it from LeanPub, where there are no download charges. Alternatively, just don't offer PDF.

---

[2]The retirement of Mobi format simplifies this issue, but it is probably only a matter of time before another format appears.

As I've not been uploading to Apple I've largely ignored the ePub format used by the Books app on iPhones, iPads and Macs. This may not be the case in future. KDP used to ask for Mobi-format files, so I used to upload the Mobi files from LeanPub. In 2021 KDP started requesting uploads in ePub, Docx or KPF format, and in 2022 retired Mobi. (KPF – Kindle Package Format – is new to me; I believe it is an Amazon proprietary format.) So here in late 2022 it now makes sense to put effort into getting the ePub file nicely formatted and small in size.

The whack-a-mole game isn't necessarily over, however. According to Polgarus Studio[3] Amazon now converts the uploaded file to KPF format, which seems to have replaced Mobi as the preferred format. (Amazon's Kindle Create[4] and other third-party software can create KPF, but LeanPub currently does not.) So while you may strive to keep your file size down and image quality up, it is difficult to future-proof yourself.

Finally

As you can see the options are pretty much endless, and that's before you consider what might happen inside your chosen publishing system. It is entirely possible that you upload your file to Amazon or elsewhere and their system then converts the format you have supplied to another format for users to download. Images may also be reformatted during such a conversion.

My advice is to keep writing, use the images you want to use, don't worry too much about file size, but keep an eye on it. Prefer smaller and lighter-weigh images if you can.

Only start looking seriously at file size near the end of the process, unless of course it becomes an issue for you or your early readers before then. At that point work on the larger images as described: try different file formats, reducing resolution, reducing size, switching to black and white. Iterate.

Choose a single target format; right now I'd recommend ePub. Make sure your images look good there and work to reduce the file size until you are happy with size versus quality trade-offs.

Having done your best, don't worry too much about what happens when you upload the book or what might happen in future. Your ability to do much about it is limited anyway.

---

[3]https://www.polgarusstudio.com/faq/
[4]https://www.amazon.com/Kindle-Create

Overweight?

This book does not contain many images and I have always expected it to be a couple of megabytes, but I've noticed late in the day that the PDF and ePub books are about 4.5Mb. There are over 10Mb of files in the images directory, so I need to slim things down. Almost all the images over 100Kb are screen shots, so I need to start playing with their resolution.

27. ISBN

Once upon a time the *International Standard Book Number* was a good way of getting hold of a book: give a library or bookshop the ISBN and they would get the book. You can still use ISBN numbers like that, but modern search technology means it's easier to search for 'Allan Kelly Continuous Digital' than '978-0-9933250-9-0' – and certainly easier to remember the former.

While you don't need an ISBN to sell your book on LeanPub or Amazon, you will need one to register it in international databases. You may well need one to sell a book in other places, but if Amazon is your main target the ASIN (Amazon Standard Identification Number) that Amazon issues is probably enough.

Having said that, I feel that having an ISBN is an essential part of making a book a book. Having an ISBN for your book is professional; every publisher will ensure a book has an ISBN, so if I want to be considered a publisher I need one too.

It is not just one ISBN number, however. According to the ISBN rules every edition of your book should have a unique ISBN. Print and e-book constitute separate editions, and each e-book format counts as an edition. As a result most of my books have four ISBNs, for the print edition, PDF edition, ePub edition and Mobi edition. Some of my printed books in fact have two ISBNs, because when I moved printing from Lulu to Amazon the paper size changed, so that counts as another edition.

If you have an audio version of your book you can assign an ISBN to that too. A hardback edition adds another, so thats is six – but maybe I don't need an Mobi number any more, so five.

How to get an ISBN

Getting an ISBN can be fiddly and might cost a bit, but it can also be easy and free. Each country issues its own ISBN numbers – the first three digits identify the country that issued the code. 000 to 019 are the US, 500 to 509 are the UK, 590 is Poland – search Google for 'GS1 country codes' to find other international codes.

Lulu, and I assume other print-on-demand services, will issue you an ISBN free of charge if you select that option during the production processes. I've never had a problem with the

ISBN Lulu issued for Xanpan, but I've read warnings that accepting a free ISBN might in some way surrender some of your rights, so be careful.

Amazon recently (in early 2022 I think) introduced free ISBN numbers[1], so there really is no reason to not acquire an ISBN for your book.

Once I realized that I was producing more books I decided to buy a block of ISBN numbers. Initially I bought ten in 2015 for £144. I quickly used these up and bought a further 100 for £300 in 2018.

Using four or more numbers per book quickly uses them up. While you could save some numbers (why give a PDF a number if you don't intend to sell it?), once you've bought 100 a few here and there doesn't matter. I'd rather do it properly than save a few pounds.

Where you buy your ISBN numbers is going to depend on where you live – or perhaps where you want people to believe you live. As each country runs its own ISBN system, they get to nominate their own ISBN agency, or even agencies: multilingual countries like Canada can have separate agencies for each language.

In the UK the ISBN agency is not a government entity, as in some countries, but the commercial Nielsen book services[2]. Even writing the name 'Nielsen' makes my heart sink: they have one of the worse websites I have ever used[3]. Obtaining ISBNs requires you to register, and registration is itself a bureaucratic pain. Once you have registered you can buy some ISBNs.

I say Nielsen's website is awful, but in fact the website is split into two or three different sites, which further confuses things. I hope by the time you read this Nielsen have sorted the websites out but, as they are the exclusive issuer of ISBNs in the UK, I don't see them having any motivation to do so.

If you are unlucky to be in the UK you just have to force yourself through the Neilsen system. Hopefully those of you in other countries will have more friendly agencies with better online services.

ISBN barcode

For printed editions you will want to put the ISBN number and matching barcode on the back cover. Amazon now has an option to generate a barcode and add it to your back cover

---

[1] https://kdp.amazon.com/en_US/help/topic/G201834170
[2] https://nielsenbook.co.uk/
[3] To add to my woes, I always confuse *Nielsen* with *Neilson*, the specialist ski holiday agency.

for you. If you want to control exactly where the barcode goes, however, you will want to get your own barcode and incorporate it into your cover design.

Getting a ISBN barcode is surprisingly simple to do: search 'ISBN barcode generator' and take your pick. While some generators charge a fee, many are free. I was surprised to find free generators and assumed there must be a catch, but they do genuinely seem to be free. I can only assume they make their money either from advertising or selling additional services. For this book I used the generator on Kindlepreneur[4] where Dave Chesson, like me, offers advice to writers and self-publishers.

Once you have your barcode, send it to your cover designer if you are using one and have them integrate it into the design.

Registering ISBNs

When your book is done, or when you are happy that nothing will change, it is time to register the book with the 'great book database in the sky'. In the UK this means returning to Nielsen and doing battle with the interface again to register your book. I assume ISBN agencies in other countries also handle both ISBN issuing and catalogue data.

Finally

As every edition of your book should have its own unique ISBN number, then strictly speaking you should assign every fresh book publication its own number. I may publish a dozen draft editions of a book on LeanPub before I get to 'finished', so I don't do this: I only assign the ISBN(s) when I reach the end, the final publication.

While I may have decided on the ISBN numbers to be used during the production process, and even had them incorporated into the cover graphics, I don't add them to the book until the very end.

I leave adding the book to the Nielsen catalogue for even longer. Once a book appears on Amazon the world knows it exists and can find it with modern technology. Still, in the name of professionalism and maximizing the places where my words can be found, I want the book to be registered.

---

[4]https://kindlepreneur.com/isbn-bar-code-generator/

28. Audio books

Once you have finished your book it is time to think about an audio version. Like copy-editing and printing, this is best left until the contents has stabilized – you don't want to have to go back and make audio changes every time you edit a chapter.

There are two key reasons for considering an audio version of your book. Firstly, to get your message out – if you are writing to share you knowledge with others, then you can reach more people in this way. Secondly, because audio books drive sales. From the evidence I've seen I'm convinced that making an audio version available increases the sales of the underlying book.

Some people will listen to an audio book rather than read a print or electronic edition, and some will do both. I'm not a big audio book listener, but I'm the exception: in recent years the market for audio books has grown faster than the market for text-based books. I have only bought a few audio books myself, but in most cases I've also bought the actual book too, usually the e-book version.

You can't highlight an audio book – although you can't highlight anything if you are listening to a book while driving. Nor can you search an audio book; maybe you will be able to in future, but when you want to say "That bit where they talk about…" you are currently a bit stuck. Nor can you cut and paste a bit of the book into your own work.

For all these reasons and probably more, people who buy an audio version may well buy a physical or e-book version too. When I released the audio version of *A Little Book about Requirements and User Stories* I could see a clear jump in sales of the e-book and print versions shortly afterwards. I continue to believe that having an audio book boosts e-book and print edition sales.

Finally, having a book recorded isn't that expensive. From past experience (2019–2021) it costs less than $1,000 to have someone record and produce a 25,000-word book. In terms of audio sales alone that may take a year or two to recoup, but if you factor in increased book sales it is quicker.

An audio book is also another give-away product that you can share with people, and one that might result in a book sale. You might give the book away outright, or bundle it with another product such as an online course.

In 2019 the Agile on the Beach conference team decided to give mailing list subscribers a Christmas present. I offered the files for *Little Book*: February and March showed noticeably higher sales as a result. More recently I repeated the give-away with *Succeeding with OKRs* and saw an immediate uptick in sales.

How to create an audio book

The first big decision is *should you record the book yourself, or have someone else do it?*

Next, *who will edit and produce the audio book?* To date I have had Stacy Gonzalez record, edit and produce all my audio books and I have been very happy with the results.

As with writing, you could do it all yourself. That would certainly keep costs low and further your understanding and control. You will also gain from deepening the connection with your listeners. Listeners will hear you as the voice, so your voice will be the 'voice of authority'.

Don't underestimate how much work you are taking on, though. I've been told 'never again' by people who have recorded and edited their own audio. If you feel like doing it this way, perhaps try recording and editing the first chapter before you finally decide.

Since it typically costs around $1000 to have a book narrated, edited and produced I don't even ask myself this question: the producer-narrator takes the whole thing away from me. All I have to do is listen to the final recording, perhaps ask for a few minor changes, then make it live.

The downside is that this means that *my* voice is not on the recording. I lose both the authority enhancement that comes from narrating the book and the opportunity to get closer to my readers. At least one listener has told me of their disappointment that I had not voiced one of my audio books.

Making an audio book

There is now a large industry of voice actors, editors and producers who will create your audio book for you. Google any of these and you will find so many that the problem quickly becomes 'How do I choose between them?'.

As you might expect, Amazon have commoditized the process, which both aids the self-publishing author and pulls you further into their ecosystem. This time authors need to step out of KDP and into ACX.

Audible ACX

Basically ACX is Audible: Audible is the customer side of the operation, ACX is the author and producer side. The whole thing was bought by Amazon back in 2008. While Amazon offers Audible products through Amazon sites, Audible still operates its own website.

Audible would rather customers subscribe. For a regular monthly fee subscribers can choose a number of audio books each month from the Audible library. However you can also buy their audio books outright, either on the Audible website or on Amazon.

To get your book onto Audible you need to go into ACX. You register your book with ACX, and if you get it right ACX will pick up most of the book's details from Amazon. Of course that assumes your book is already listed on Amazon: if you are kicking off a recording before the book is listed it can't do that and you have more work to do.

Recording

If you have recorded the book yourself you can upload your own files. ACX has some rules about what files are called and what files it expects, but as I use a producer I don't know all the details.

Remember that if you chose to record your book yourself there is still production work to do. Your audio is going to need editing, the recordings set up as ACX wants them and the files uploaded. Personally I find editing audio (and video) files annoying and fiddly, so even if I did record my own voice I'd pay someone to edit it.

If you decide to hire a narrator there is little reason to then produce the audio book yourself. I assume most narrators will handle production too, so there is only one person to deal with. ACX has made choosing a narrator easy. You could find a narrator outside ACX, but ACX operates a narrator market to make things simple. You list your book, put up a sample for narrators to audition and wait for the replies.

When I did this I had over 20 people audition; I was amazed. Perhaps I got so many because I was very open about who I would accept: male or female, UK or US accent, little experience or lots, high price or low price – ACX gives you a lot of options.

Most of them were very good and it was hard to choose between them. Choosing on price is the rational thing to do, but one always feels a bit cheap just choosing the lowest price. While I am British and have a slight Liverpudlian accent I didn't want people mistaking the narrator for me, so I had a slight preference for an American accent.

The big decision was: male or female? Rationally I should probably have gone with a male narrator, but I wanted to be obvious that the narrator was not me. That led me to decide on a female narrator, which immediately cut the number of candidates from about twenty to about three.

There is one more decision to be made over your narrator: how are they to be paid?

ACX offers two options: royalties or fee. I've always used the fee option and paid my narrator outright. By my calculations, even my best-sellers would have paid a narrator less in royalties than the outright fee. Since most books don't sell even that number my guess is that the best narrators will always prefer a fee. (Remember that I care less about Audible revenue because I'm selling more books.)

Finally, the recording process I've described assumes that you stay within the ACX system for production: you use the ACX narrator audition process and you use the ACX production process. Alternatively, you can find a narrator and produce books outside ACX, then just upload the files. Judging by the number of audio actors and producers I come across at business meet-ups, this would seem to be a booming market. It might even result in a better product, lower production costs and a happier narrator.

In my experience using the ACX process, choosing a producer-narrator familiar with ACX and going with the flow is relatively easy and financially worthwhile. While I might be able to save money by stepping outside the process, it probably isn't enough for me to justify the extra work that would be required. Besides, I find Stacy great to work with, so why change?

Pricing

With ACX Audible pricing is easy: you have no control, they decide.

Since ACX's real aim is to get people to take subscriptions rather than buy titles one at a time, that probably makes sense. It does leave one wondering, though: if it was cheaper, would more people buy it? It also means I have no advice to give on pricing audio books.

Royalties

At the time of writing you have two decisions to make here: whether to be ACX-exclusive or pay the producer-narrator yourself.

Currently ACX offers two royalty options: 70% and 30%. Obviously the 70% rate has a catch: as with KDP Select, ACX wants exclusivity for the higher rate. This means that you can't upload the audio book to Apple iTunes or any other site. Probably – and I'd have to read the small print to be sure – it also prohibits you from giving away free versions.

Unlike KDP Select the higher royalty rate is harder to get away from. With Select you can give notice and 90 days later you are free. With ACX the lock-in period is several years.

I've never taken the higher rate, so I can't tell you how much difference it makes. While I've given away many audio copies, and included them in some online courses, I have never got around to putting the audio book on another service. Arguably I've missed out financially, but I value keeping my options open.

Timing

If you are planning to launch your books with the biggest splash possible, it probably makes sense to have the audio book available at the same time as you reveal your e-book and printed book, to offer potential purchasers all the options for acquiring your work.

While I aim to make an initial splash, I'm happy to let the audio book trail a few weeks behind. Exactly how long depends on how long it takes my producer-narrator to read the book and for me to check it. I reason that the release of the e-book is an opportunity to make a bit more marketing noise, even if I lose a few initial sales.

So I typically finish the e-book and get my reviewers to work, begin work on the printed book and then work on the audio book. If time allows (and I remember), I'll contact my narrator and let her know there is a book coming and ask about her availability. Once the e-book is finalized she can start work while I finish off the printed book.

Most of the time preparing print and audio books involves waiting. I wait for the graphic artist to adjust the sleeve for the exact number of pages, wait for the test prints, wait for the audio producer to record and so on. It is more an act of preparation and managing mental workload than actually doing things. Given that ACX apply some quality control to books and review them, you can't know exactly when the book will be live, so I don't worry about it.

With the e-book and printed book selling, I see the audio book release as an opportunity to make further marketing noise on social media. Shouting "Audio book now available!" is another reason to remind people that I have a new book out.

Caveat

It probably doesn't need to be said, but there are some books that will not work as an audio book: photography, for example, in fact any picture- or diagram-heavy book that relies on people interpreting visual material. Nor can I imagine a book with lots of code examples working either.

One solution to this is to avoid using diagrams and pictures. This also has the advantage that you avoid image rights issues. However, as they say, a picture is worth a thousand words; sometimes you need a diagram to illustrate a point or a picture to demonstrate an example.

As a dyslexic I know that pictures speak in ways that words can't – but I also know that other people's pictures fail to carry as much information as those I create myself, so the loss of pictures in an audio book need not be a showstopper. In most of my audio books I simply ignore the pictures. After all, the ability to see the pictures adds to the incentive to buy the physical or e-book versions.

I suppose one could ask a narrator to describe the pictures. This might work for simple images or where there is a well-known example. However, as anyone who has played the 'blind drawing' parlour game in which one person describes a picture and another draws what they hear will know, that might not work out too well.

Where diagrams or code form a large part of a book and the message, an audio book could be billed as an abridged version, for which you own up to the fact that the audio version contains less than the actual book. An abridged version could drop entire chapters that are heavy with pictures and/or code, or even just contain a few chapters that don't depend so much on images.

This might require a little bit of marketing gymnastics to ensure that people see the two versions as the same thing. It might also require some extra work with Amazon/ACX customer services to ensure the two products are associated with each other. I haven't tried this strategy, so this is merely an idea. However, as my aim is not so much to replace the book as to use the audio version to drive book sales, it makes sense.

Other audio services

There are other audio book services, Apple iTunes being the most visible. I should probably have made my books and audio books available there, but it turns out that ACS supplies audio books to Apple, so all my audio versions are there already. (While you can't buy any of my self-published books on Apple, the three books I've done with publishers are there.)

Is it worthwhile? How many extra readers and sales would I accrue from other platforms? I might get a few, but with Amazon, Audible and Apple already covered there can't be many. At best I would merely be shifting buyers from one platform to another.

I also know that Amazon's algorithms favour titles that sell. So if half my sales were elsewhere I would have fewer sales on Audible, which would mean that my titles would drop down the rankings and fewer potential buyers would be made aware of them.

Amazon don't operate a 'walled garden', but it is very good at encouraging you never to leave their garden. I should probably experiment with other services, but that requires time and effort.

IV Publication

"Publish and be damned!"

Attributed to Arthur Wellesley, 1st Duke of Wellington, 1824

29. Amazon

KDP (Kindle Direct Publishing) is Amazon's self-publishing platform. As its name suggests, KDP started as a platform for publishing e-books. Although KDP began in 2007, two years after Amazon acquired CreateSpace, the two were separate until fairly recently. Today KDP offers book, Kindle and print publishing, while CreateSpace has disappeared almost entirely inside KDP.

While LeanPub is a great place for writing and selling an early version of your book once you have completed it, you really want to be on Amazon. Amazon has more customers, more book browsers, more data and better algorithms for matching buyers and books. People are far more likely to find your book on Amazon than on LeanPub, simply because Amazon reaps an order of magnitude more eyeballs than LeanPub.

If you have written your book on LeanPub you have already done most of the work. You can use the same pricing, the same blurb, the same keywords and, importantly, the same file. LeanPub-created ePub files are perfect for uploading to Amazon, because that is what LeanPub expect authors to do.

Having said that, each copy sold on Amazon earns less than on LeanPub, as the royalty rate is lower and there are download costs. However every month I see more of my books selling on Amazon. As most buyers don't even know that LeanPub exists, you will need to create an account and then transfer their purchase into Kindle or Apple Books, so there are more obstacles for buyers. It is not a question of *how do you make the most money per book?*, but *where are buyers most likely to buy?*

Amazon's algorithms create a virtuous circle, so the more books you sell on Amazon the more likely you are to sell more books on Amazon. Once my book is on Amazon I don't really want people to buy it on LeanPub, so I direct buyers to Amazon rather than LeanPub.

Amazon account

The chances are you already have an Amazon account. You can use this to start publishing books on KDP: go to https://kdp.amazon.com/[1].

---

[1]https://kdp.amazon.com/

You might however prefer to create an account on Amazon just for publishing. If like me you operate a business and intend to put revenues through your business account, such a financial separation makes life easier.

If you want to collaborate with anyone on KDP – say having a co-author do book uploads, or a marketing assistant finesse your book details or download sales reports – you will need to share your KDP email account.

Normally sharing an account, which means sharing an email id and password, is not a good thing. However, Amazon KDP is intended for self-publishers and has no support for small teams, so the only way to share details is by sharing the account. I believe that somewhere in Amazon's terms and conditions this is disallowed, so if you do want to share your account you would be advised to read the small print. This also creates a problem if you want help with your publishing account.

Uploading

Once you are logged into KDP you will find a great big 'Create' button. Once you click this you will have the choice of Kindle, paperback, hardback or a series page.

Start with the Kindle option – although the other book types are pretty much the same. You will see three screens to input information about the book's *details*, *contents* (including the all-important upload) and *pricing*.

Don't worry about getting the details exactly right – it will probably take you a couple of goes to get everything in place, but that is not a problem. As creating a book is free you may well want to do a dummy run to educate yourself – just don't click on the final 'Publish' button at the end.

KDP details – part

At the end of the sequence of screens you have the option to publish, but you don't have to do so: you can just get everything set up and wait until later. In fact I'd recommend doing this if you haven't created a book before.

You can return and change this information at any time because it is all digital, even after publication. However some fields – including most of the data on the details page – cannot be changed once a book has been published. The other catch is that once you have created a book you can't delete it: it stays on your account for ever. The only time I created a book and then wanted to delete it I replaced the book's image with a picture of a big red cross, X. I have no problem remembering which book to ignore.

KDP content

As the screenshots for *Succeeding with OKRs in Agile* here show, most of the fields are self-explanatory, although a few of them do require more thought. Note that you must upload a cover graphic separately from the manuscript, as Amazon will not extract the cover picture directly from your manuscript.

The categories and keywords section is more involved and requires some thought, so I have given them their own chapter later in this book. If you haven't thought about these when you first add your book, make a note to return to them after you have had a chance to read that chapter and think them through. Similarly, if you haven't thought about DRM – digital rights management – then read the DRM chapter and decide what you want to do.

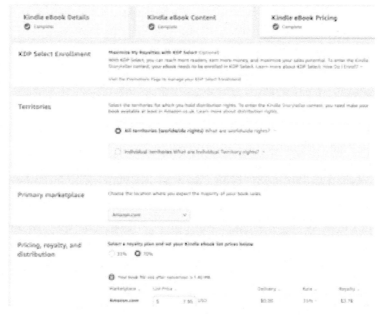

KDP pricing

The final screen in the KDP process is pricing, another screen that requires some thought and its own chapter. The easy option is to decide the price you want to sell for in the US (in US dollars) and let Amazon suggest an equivalent price in other markets. Just because that is easy, though, does not mean that it is the best option.

Pricing is a complex subject, hence it also has its own chapter. Suffice to say for now that a book that sells for $9.95 might be better priced £9.95 than £7.97, and at €9.95 rather than €9.37.

KDP prerelease

Amazon allows you to list your book as a prerelease, complete with cover picture and blurb, before you make it available. Potential readers can preorder the book, so that when you do publish they receive it immediately.

The prerelease option is simply a tick box and date when setting up your book on Amazon. This allows you to do useful work while waiting for the copy-edit and, more importantly, gives you the URL to include in your publicity material. However, a pre-publication book can't receive reviews, which is a shame. Ideally you want your book to appear complete with reviews on day one. While I suspect publishers can do this, KDP self-publishers can't.

This creates a small problem: the more pre-sales you have, the higher your new book will appear in the charts when first published. That itself will drive sales, and also provide opportunities for you to publicise your book. Ideally you could tweet '12 hours after release my book is #1 on Amazon', but charting before reviews are in place is suboptimal. I talk about reviews in another chapter, but when it comes to prerelease there are two reasons to be careful.

First, without reviews potential buyers are less likely to buy. People seeing your book's page without reviews hold back on buying – it is risky to buy a book that nobody has reviewed. Entering the sales charts before reviews are in place may be peaking too soon. It therefore makes sense to keep you powder dry and save your marking drive until you have received some reviews.

Second, you run the risk that someone will buy your book and quickly post a less than glowing review. As I describe in the chapter on reviews, the anchoring effect means that good reviews beget good reviews, while poor reviews beget poor reviews. You want your first few reviews to have as many stars as you can muster.

So by all means use the prerelease feature and get early orders, but until your reviews are in place you want to hold off publicizing the book.

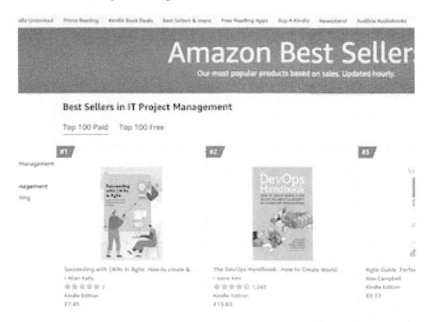

Succeeding with OKRs in Agile at number one in the IT Project Management category

Royalty rates

Amazon royalty rates can change, so things might change between my writing this and you reading it. The general policies are likely to remain the same although the numbers may change. If these things are important to you, check the current rates on Amazon yourself[2].

At the time of writing, in the UK I have the choice of two Amazon royalty rates: 35% or 70%. Obviously one will choose the 70% option, so why does Amazon have a 35% rate?

First you may not have a choice: in some countries Amazon only offers the lower rate. So if someone in India buys one of my e-books I will get the 35% rate irrespective of the fact that I have selected the 70% rate.

Second, Amazon insists that if your book is mostly public domain content, you use the lower rate. So, for example, if you are publishing your own annotated version of Shakespeare's Macbeth, Amazon insists you use 35% because approximately half the book is a public-domain text.

Assuming you can select the 70% rate you might still prefer the 35% rate, because download costs are included in the lower rate. Royalty rates and download costs are discussed and analyzed in the chapter on pricing later.

Amazon versus LeanPub

The maximum 70% royalty rate that Amazon pays is less than the 80% that LeanPub pays. The difference is actually bigger than that, as Amazon charges for delivery while LeanPub doesn't. So if you have captive buyers you might want to coerce them to buy on LeanPub by not listing your book on Amazon.

While I can imagine cases in which you might be able to insist that readers buy your book, such as required reading material for a course, I can't imagine it occurring very often. Even here there is a question of fairness, as getting a book bought from Amazon onto a Kindle or iPad is a lot easier than getting the same book from LeanPub onto the device.

Early on I viewed this royalty difference as justifying a discount for LeanPub buyers. After all, I can make the same return at a lower price on LeanPub, but as Amazon algorithms incentivize you to put all sales through Amazon this doesn't make sense. In fact there is a logic to making a LeanPub book more expensive to encourage people to buy from Amazon: when a book sells on Amazon it boosts your book in the rankings, which makes another sale more likely.

---

[2]https://kdp.amazon.com/en_US/help/topic/G200634500

30. Printing

Although print-on-demand services were my entry point into the world of self-publishing, it took me a while to realize the importance of printed books. Today the print versions of my books substantially outsell the e-book versions. Nor am I alone: I hear from other authors that print sales often exceed e-book sales.

Perhaps my personal preferences coloured my view of printed books. Since buying my first Kindle over ten years ago I've much preferred reading electronic books to printed ones. For me the ability to change font size, search a book, see all my highlights in one place and carry several dozen books onto a long-haul flight are game-changers. I certainly like the texture and look of printed books on my shelves, but I also like the shelf space I reclaim when I dispose of old books. While I regard e-books as more practical, I also recognize that my preferences are far from universal.

Although printed books cost more to produce and ship than e-books, they can command a higher price, which means that they can be more profitable. That said, printed books lack the flexibility of e-books: you can't publish a printed book incrementally, or correct a mistake after delivery. So my advice is to write your book electronically, publish early versions electronically, and move to print only when you are sure that you are finished.

Digital technology has made print-on-demand publishing economically viable. No longer do you need to commit to a print run of several thousand copies, no longer do you need to store hundred of copies in stock, and most important of all, no longer do you need the capital to finance such printing and storage. For the self-publisher the economics and logistics of print-on-demand changes everything.

The self-publisher today has a myriad of printing options. Over the years I've tried several and looked at several more. What follows are my experiences with these services, but for all I know there might be an even better service out there I haven't heard of.

Samples

With all printing services I've tried the cover imagery is the main pain point. Whether you are using Amazon or another printer, make sure you order some print samples before you tell the world your book is ready. It is all too easy to make a mistake with a print version, but much harder to fix.

Print samples cost, so there is always an incentive to save money and time by skipping them. However, discovering a mistake when you've seen a dozen copies and readers are buying the book can be wasteful and embarrassing. Even if a sample comes with the caveat 'Sample copy – not for resale' printed in big letters on the cover, you can still give it away, making any errors very public.

A little book of OKRs

When writing *Succeeding with OKRs in Agile* my working title was *Little Book of OKRs and Agile* – I was hoping to emulate the successes of *A Little Book about Requirements and User Stories*. Close to the end I changed the name.

I had already had Anton design the cover for the printed edition as *Little Book of OKRs and Agile*, so had to have him change it when I changed the title. We both reviewed the changes, I uploaded the new cover and published.

Only when the first ten copies arrived and I looked at the stacked up books did I realize that we had both missed the book title on the spine, which still read *Little Book of OKR and Agile*.

As I recall I had ordered a sample but had overlooked the spine. It was only when seeing a stack of copies did I realize the mistake. Since I was planning to give these copies away – to reviewers and at publicity give-aways – the mistake wasn't a big issue. In fact I fessed up to the mistake and told recipients they had a collector's copy.

Amazon CreateSpace

Amazon's print services are now my preferred printers for two reasons. First, the print and distribution costs are lower than Lulu. Second, once you have your e-book published with KDP, creating a printed book is quite straightforward. Having both fully within the Amazon system also makes it simpler to associate the two books, share reviews and ratings and add the audio book.

Books printed by Amazon services are – obviously – available for sale on Amazon. The company also offers 'expanded distribution', which injects your book into the global distribution systems used by other booksellers and libraries. However your share of revenue will then be lower because of distribution costs.

Amazon only offers expanded distribution in the US and UK. This is fine for me, as that is where most of my readers are, but readers elsewhere may still be able to buy my printed book via these networks. How often this happens I don't know, neither do I know if, for example, a bookshop in Munich faces additional costs or problems ordering my book from a UK distributor.

Books are only eligible for expanded distribution if they meet certain criteria[1]. Foremost among these criteria is the need for the book to have an ISBN number and conform to a recognized size format. If these are met then expanded distribution needs to be switched on for each market.

Amazon print royalties

Throughout this book I refer to Amazon royalties of 70% or 35%. However those figures only apply to e-books. Printed books are different.

First, printing costs are deducted from the selling price, so you will only get royalties on $7 of a book that sells for $10 but costs $3 to print. Second, for printed books royalties are currently 60%, so you will earn $4.20 per book. Before you rush to increase your sale price, remember that buyers may well be paying VAT or sales tax plus postage on top of your price.

To complicate matters, printing prices differ by country – I assume Amazon has local printers to save on postage costs. So what costs $3 to print in the US my cost more in the UK or less in Germany. There is also one more twist: if you opt for extended distribution, the royalty rate falls to 40%. So the $10 spent in a bookshop will only earn you $2.80.

Bear in mind that these are the figures as I write in autumn 2022. Amazon can change the royalty rates or printing costs at any time and they can vary by location. So before you start counting your money, check the latest rates where you are.

Lulu

My first experience with print-on-demand, round about 2008, was with Lulu[2]. For many years I was a Lulu regular, both creating mini-books and ordering them to support my

---

[1]https://kdp.amazon.com/en_US/help/topic/GQTT4W3T5AYK7L45#eligibility
[2]http://www.lulu.com

training courses. As I've taken self-publishing more seriously, however, I've moved away from Lulu.

Lulu is good value for money when sales are made through the Lulu online shop. I used to have clients buy books by the dozen to accompany my training courses, which gave me a small additional revenue stream. But the Lulu shop is much smaller than the Amazon shop, there are fewer books, fewer browsers and fewer buyers.

To make the most of Lulu or any other specialist shop you need to spend time making your books attractive, getting reviews and driving sales to the shop. When you do this you are duplicating the effort you put into Amazon, yet the effort-to-return ratio there is higher than for Lulu. Effort-wise it makes more sense to get all the reviews you can on Amazon and drive all sales there. Add in the fact that Amazon algorithms reward success with success and it is a no-brainer, so I've moved away from Lulu.

While I haven't sold a book through Lulu for years, I still make sales there via Global Distribution System channels. In fact, my GDS sales from Lulu dwarf those via Amazon expanded distribution. Not only do I get sales in countries like Germany and India, where Amazon expanded distribution does not operate, but I get sales in the UK or US. It seems that some shops are still ordering via Lulu.

I'm not about to close Lulu down, but I'm not putting any more effort into Lulu and not using it for new books. As you might have guessed, having sales through multiple channels makes it harder to know how many copies you are selling.

While Lulu is book-focused – it can provide ISBN numbers and offers a simple cover design tool – it can also be useful for things that aren't books but nevertheless need to be printed. I used it to create a family calendar one year. That said, Lulu's options for things other than books aren't particularly impressive: Lulu is a book printer.

Mimeo[3] is another service which, like Lulu, allows you to create your own print runs and sell them through an online shop. However Mimeo isn't focused on books, so it lacks ISBN numbers, GDS links and a book cover designer. Mimeo is more suited to specialist publications such as course handouts.

Lulu and Mimeo, therefore, are both print-on-demand printers with online sales, but while Lulu is a book printer that can print other things, Mimeo is a speciality printer that can print books. Bear this difference in mind when you are looking at other print-on-demand providers.

---

[3]https://www.mimeo.com/

IngramSpark

I'm grouping IngramSpark[4] with other printers but really that is unfair. IngramSpark is far more than a printer, more of an alternative to Amazon or even LeanPub. While I know self-publishers who use IngramSpark regularly, I've not used it myself, so my comments are somewhat limited.

Ingram[5] is a long-standing supplier of services to the publishing industry. Ingram operates a global distribution system that is largely used by publishing houses, in addition to print, distribution, marketing and other services. Publishers can offload a lot of their work to Ingram.

IngramSpark, meanwhile, offers Ingram's traditional services to self-publishers. You can write your masterpiece using whatever tools you wish – you could even use LeanPub but not publish there. You are responsible for copy-edit, indexing and everything else, as with LeanPub or KDP. You then deliver a print-ready PDF file to IngramSpark created using whatever layout tools you like: InDesign, LaTeX, Word and so on. You will need to supply your own cover graphics, but unlike Amazon and LeanPub you will also need to create your own ePub file.

When you are happy with your files it is time to publish. Publishing e-book and print-on-demand versions through IngramSpark injects them into their global distribution system so that booksellers (including Amazon) can sell them.

Unlike Amazon, Ingram charges a fee to publish a book or e-book – currently $49 and $25 respectively. There may be additional fees depending the options you choose, plus a per-book printing fee.

The upside is that Ingram returns a higher percentage of a book's sale price to the self-publisher. This is currently listed as 85% of revenue for e-books. However, IngramSpark differentiates between revenue and royalties. So if your self-publishing grows to the point of publishing other people's work, you could have IngramSpark pay both author royalties and a publisher revenue.

All in all IngramSpark provides a fuller service with more options than either LeanPub or Amazon. However, that level of sophistication also means that there is more work to do in understanding and setting up your publications. Whether this is worth the effort is a question you need to answer for yourself.

---

[4]https://www.ingramspark.com/
[5]https://www.ingramcontent.com/

Unlike Amazon and LeanPub, Ingram provides access to hired help. The experts resource[6] allows self-publishers to find editors, designers, marketeers and so on who can be hired to help with all aspects of writing, publishing and marketing. Most of these seem to be independent of Ingram; I would assume many of them work with other publishers as well. (Lulu has a similar 'hire a pro' feature to connect you with hired help.)

The promise of IngramSpark seems to be that it allows the self-publisher to access the same capabilities as dedicated publishers and inject your book into distributions systems on the same terms. In theory this increases the customers you can reach. The downside is that it makes extra work for you.

Multiple printers

As a self-publisher you own your own copyright, so you can use multiple printing services. My early self-published books, like *Xanpan* and *A Little Book about Requirements and User Stories*, can be bought either via Amazon or Lulu and are offered by both for global distribution. Most of my Lulu sales come from India and Germany, where Amazon's extended distribution doesn't apply.

However, as the copies are slightly different (page size mainly), they have different ISBN numbers. The rules around ISBN numbers demand that if there are any noticeable differences between versions a new ISBN number should be used. Arguably I should create a Lulu version of *Succeeding with OKRs in Agile* so that buyers in Germany, India and elsewhere can buy the book in bookshops. But that requires extra work – Lulu offers slight different paper sizes, so the cover needs reformatting, ISBNs need assigning and registering, and more – while the sales probably don't justify it.

---

[6]https://www.ingramspark.com/resources/experts

31. Pricing

Publishers often have predetermined price scales based on the number of pages in a book. I suspect this is less to do with how much it costs to print the book and more to do with the buyers' perceptions: 'More pages, more information, more useful therefore more valuable'.

Unless you are aiming to maximize sales with the lowest possible prices, Walmart-style, you don't want to set price based on production costs: price should be set based on what people will pay. If they won't pay more than a book's production costs, don't sell it.

Cost-based pricing is almost always a bad idea. Do Burberry price their high-fashion coats by the cost of production? Or Porsche their cars based on the cost of manufacturing? If the sales price is not enough to cover costs, plus some profit, then it is not a business to be in. Price is about what the market will pay, not the cost of production.

This is obvious if you think about iPhones and the premium they command over Android phones – but then what is the cost of creating an iPhone? It is not the cost of assembly in a Chinese factory, nor the cost of components which, following Moore's Law, fall in price. Neither can it be the cost of Californian design, as many iPhone models are indistinguishable from the previous one. How do you work out the cost of a new version of iOS when it shares so much with iPadOS and even MacOS?

In a few markets with lots of competition – which implies similar products – the lowest price wins. In these markets price will be cost plus a tiny profit margin. These are not good markets to be in – as an author your book is probably not in one of these markets. Books are unique: if you are the only writer on a particular topic you have no competition. In reality, while your sequence of words is unique, you are almost always competing with books on the same topic.

For the vast majority of authors the time spent writing a book is sunk cost that will never pay back in book sales. If I added up all the hours I have spent writing any of my books and had instead sold those hours to my clients as a consultant, I would have made a lot more. Quite possibly I would even have made more if I'd used those hours to flip burgers on minimum wage.

The time I spend writing a book is irrelevant. The only place cost has a role to play is when considering the marginal cost of selling one more book and ensuring the revenue from that book covers the cost of its sale.

Back to objectives

Setting prices is hard. While it is easy to pluck a price from thin air, it is difficult to know which price will maximize your objectives. To start with one needs to know what the objective is. So before you think about price, ask yourself "What am I hoping to achieve with this book?".

My objective is multifaceted. First, I'd like to make money. While I can still dream of producing a best-seller that frees me from financial worries, I know it is very unlikely. So I don't write books to get rich.

Second, I want to express myself and share my thoughts with others. This may be little self-indulgent, but I believe my ideas can help people. So my third objective is that I want to help people – and by implication their employers – to work better, enjoy work more and have more success in business.

Those objectives conflict, a conflict that I will probably never resolve. If I want to be heard and help people I should probably price my books really cheaply to maximize buyers. *But how many will buy a cheap book and not read it?*

Price elasticity

One way of putting the question is to think about price points: would you rather sell ten books at $100 each or 1,000 books at $1 each? 100 at $10 each? or 50 at $20 each?

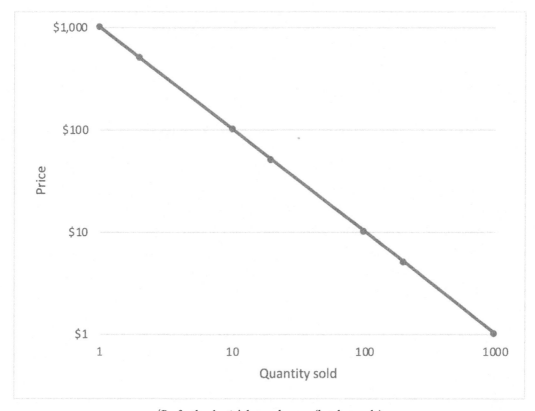

'Perfectly elastic' demand curve (log-log scale)

While each of these options will bring in $1,000, the real world is not like that. A $1 price may well sell more than 1,000 copies; a $100 price might not sell one.

Economists – and I consider myself an amateur economist – call this 'price elasticity'. The hypothetical example given here is said to be 'perfectly elastic', because any price change results in a change in sales that generates exactly the same revenue.

In terms of returns, perfectly elasticity doesn't happen in real life. The question you need to ask yourself is *Will I make more money by selling fewer expensive books or more cheap books?*

This is the age-old question economists and business people have struggled with forever. In theory, LeanPub and Amazon make it possible to conduct experiments to understand your elasticity. In practice no experiment is perfect. There is more about experiments and playing with price in a subsequent chapter.

More importantly, the question you need to ask yourself is *How do I want my book and myself to be seen?* Price is information – unreliable information, but information all the same – and, as I'll discuss in a moment, people infer things about a book and its author from the price.

Ten, $10, €10, £10

Amazon has strong views on e-book pricing: they should be under 'ten', whether that be $10, €10 or £10. It is the psychology of staying on three digits, $9.99, €9.95, £9.90. Sometimes Amazon doesn't even allow you to publish an e-book at a price below ten-somethings.

This breaks down in countries with light currencies, such as the Rupee in India and the Yen in Japan – I'm not quite sure what rules Amazon imposes there. I'm not even sure how it plays out with Australian dollars, which are noticeably weaker than US dollars and Sterling.

I read, five or more years ago, that Amazon had analyzed sales and conducted experiments that concluded that 'ten' is a magic number: books priced below 'ten' earn more. To some degree you already know this: we are used to companies charging a few pence below a price boundary, whether it be $4.95, £9.99 or €19.95.

This boundary simplifies your e-book pricing. If you really want your book to reach a wide audience and minimize barriers to buying, then settle for something like $2.99, 99¢, or even free.

Amazon see 'free' differently, of which more later. To my mind below $5 is a thoughtless throwaway market. Above $5 is a different market, one that requires a little thought. Above $10 and you are in a different market again, one that requires buyers to think more. Above $10 you must be sure that people really want your book and need to buy it.

I price my e-books in the $5 to $9.99 space. This feels to me as if I'm positioning them as something more than an impulse purchase, but not a purchase that requires a lot of thought. It works for me but, of course, I don't know how much better a higher or lower price would work. With UK and US inflation at their highest levels for decades at the time of writing I don't know how long this pricing scheme will last.

That's e-books. The price of an e-book forms a basis for pricing the physical book. These can justify a higher price, although not everyone exercises the option, and Amazon seems to be less concerned about print prices. The next chapter discusses print pricing in detail.

The other thing to note here is currency: there is no reason why a book that sells for $10 in the US should sell locally at the current exchange rate. At the time of writing that would be £8.11, €9.50 and C$12.96, tomorrow it will probably be different. Pricing is about psychology: a $9.95 book is probably a €9.90 and £9.50 book.

VAT and sales tax

All the example calculations I'm giving here ignore the UK and Europe's *value added tax* (VAT). For example, an e-book selling at £10 from Amazon UK to a UK buyer will be subject to approximately £2 VAT, which means you will not get 70% of £10, but 70% of £8: £5.60.

More about VAT later.

Price and credibility

Price is not only about revenue: higher prices can mean more sales. Think about all those 99¢ books on Amazon – I've even bought a few myself.

What do you think when you see that a book is priced at 99¢?. It's cheap, it's throwaway, perhaps – or that you can afford to buy it and if it's rubbish you've lost nothing. But what if it's good – how does a price of 99¢ reflect on the author?

A cheap book may lack credibility – indeed most books I've bought for 99¢ can be read in a few hours and contain little real content. They also reflect badly on the author: I seldom come away thinking 'Here is an expert'.

Of course you might manage your expectations. Try to write a 99¢ book titled 'One hour starter's guide to Python programming'. Saying 'this is a short book' and pricing it at 99¢ might be a good combination, because buyers' expectations match. On the other hand, what does it say if an author can command $25 for a book?

Price implies value, price gives credibility. If you, like me, are making a living as a jobbing consultant, that might be more important to you.

Revenue versus costs

While price should not be set based on cost, one nevertheless has to remember cost. The cost of sales on LeanPub is zero, as LeanPub doesn't charge for bandwidth – but Amazon does.

Consider the example of a 5Mb e-book selling in the UK for £5 with a 50p download charge. On the 70% royalty rate that would make you £3.15, so selling 100 copies would earn you £315.

Suppose you sold 50 copies at £10. Each book would still cost 50p to download, but you would only be paying for half as many books. Each book would earn £6.65, so selling 50 copies would earn slightly more, £332. Going in the other direction, selling 200 copies at £2.50 would reduce revenue to £200, a significant drop.

The bigger a book is, the less sense it makes to sell a lot of copies at a low price. This is perhaps obvious, but worth bearing in mind. This also means that if you decide to go for a low price point you will want to put more effort into reducing file size, perhaps by limiting your images.

International pricing

Living in London, I like to think I have a good understanding of book prices in the UK. Perhaps naively I believe that understanding extends to Europe, North America and even Australia. When it comes to Brazil, India and Japan, and indeed most of the rest of the world, I have neither an understanding of book prices nor a feel for what their currencies are worth.

Outside my comfort zone I am reduced to little more than following the exchange rate. I tend to tweak prices a little. For example, at today's exchange rate a book selling for £9.95 would sell in India for ⊠948. I might go with that because it seems psychologically just below price breaks at ⊠950 and ⊠1,000.

I don't sell many copies in India[1], however. That could be an argument for going lower – ⊠895, ⊠750 maybe – since I wouldn't lose much money and I could build a following. Conversely, I could think that a higher price wouldn't lose many sales, so go higher – ⊠995, ⊠1,200.

An Indian reader once wrote to me and suggested to a price for a book. He said "I would expect to pay…". Great advice that I immediately put into action. Unfortunately I've now lost the email. I should take the time to survey local markets, look at the prices other authors are selling at, perhaps even find out what the best-selling titles are and the price at which they retail. All that all takes time.

If I put more effort into India, Brazil and so on I could make more, perhaps even build a following. This might be another reason for working with a publisher, if they were prepared to make that effort for you.

---

[1]It is possible that on your e-book reader the Rupee symbol I'm using here doesn't show correctly. To understand why see the note in the postscript about symbols.

Fairness

I sometimes agonize about book pricing because I want to be fair to my readers. If I price a book at $9.95 in the US and C$9.95 north of the border to stay below the magic 'ten' boundary, then Canadians will get the book for less. Is that fair? Probably.

But if a book sells for $9.95 USD, is it also fair if I charge C$13 in Canada? Now, as I've broken the 'ten' ceiling, maybe I should charge C$15? It probably doesn't make a big difference to the buyer, but neither will it make a big difference to my income. Am I now being fair? I worry about this: sometimes my conscience wins, but not always.

More troublingly, is it fair to launch a book at £20 then, a few weeks later, reduce it to £10? Is that not being unfair to my most enthusiastic readers?

One could argue that by buying a book early readers have benefitted more from my ideas and have had more time to put them into action. What if my buyers start to notice that I reduce my prices after a few weeks, though? Might that not motivate them to postpone buying my book? And if they postpone today, do I have any guarantee they will actually buy next week?

I don't know the answer to these questions, but that doesn't stop me agonizing about them while trying to be fair.

More pricing

There is far more to pricing than I can say in this or the following chapters. I don't claim to know everything about the subject; in this chapter – like the rest of this book – I'm merely sharing my own experiences and my logic. In places I've probably got it wrong – if you think so, please tell me.

If you really want to get into this topic, search the internet on 'How should I price my e-book'; you will find a great many posts on the subject. In the meantime this chapter should help you get started. As with almost everything else in the digital publishing world, you can change things later.

Writing these chapters on pricing has made me think again about the topic. I think I should be charging more. Especially now, in mid-2022, when inflation is on the rise.

32. Print pricing

Printed books cost more to produce and ship than e-books, so production costs are a bigger consideration in pricing. Selling price still needs to be based on what the market will pay, however, rather than on the production costs.

Printed books can command a premium over e-books. Buyers' price expectations are anchored by the e-book price. As it is almost certainly more than the cost of printing, the lowest price for your printed book is not the cost of printing, but the price of your e-book. So decide on your e-book price first.

You don't need to price your printed book higher, but most publishers do. If your aim is to spread your message you might want to sell it at the same price as your e-book, but if your aim is to maximize your reach you could give away the e-book and charge for the printed book at its cost to print.

How much higher should you price the print version? You can do your own survey: look at similar books on Amazon and see what others are doing. In general I add between £2 and £5 to the price of a printed (soft back) book. However, having done some research for this chapter I suspect I should be charging a higher premium. Simply putting '1' in front of the e-book price seems quite common, so £7.50 becomes £17.50 and $9.99 becomes $19.99.

Hardback books

The discussion so far has been about paperback books. Amazon has only recently made hardback self-published versions available. In traditional publishing hardback versions are generally released first and command a premium over paperback versions.

I can see why one would charge a premium for a hardback book over a paperback version, but I'm not sure I would want to stagger their releases. Part of the hardback premium is due to hardback versions being available before paperback versions, but I am not sure I would want to lose a sale because only a hardback version was available. I would happily accept a lower-priced sale than no sale at all.

I don't know the answer to this conundrum. I've yet to create a hardback version of any of my books, so I have yet to think through the pricing and timing questions in detail, but I am sure the printing costs would be higher.

Printing costs

I'm told that when books are printed in bulk there is little difference between printing a 100-page, a 200-page or a 400-page book. Printing is only one of the costs, to which one needs to add shipping, from the printer to the publisher's warehouse and from there to shops. That all entails handling – usually by humans. Once there is a need to move a pallet of books with a forklift truck it matters little if the book has 100 or 400 pages: the fact that a human being and a forklift truck are involved is the major cost.

In the world of print-on-demand and self-publishing, shipping and logistics is less of an issue: most of the warehouses, storage and handling issues go away. I imagine a machine printing, wrapping and posting a book to the customer without any human intervention.

How much paper and time is required is a bigger factor; in this case there is a cost difference between printing a 100-page and a 200-page book. You will therefore want to keep an eye on how many pages are in your book, and you might want to cost-engineer it if you intend to give many copies away, as I did with my *Agile Reader* series. A shorter book with fewer pages leads to lower costs and more profit. Likewise, fewer diagrams leads to a smaller download, lower costs and more profit.

Distribution services

Being physical, printed books need to move from printer to seller to customer. This is where global distribution services enter the picture, specifically printed book GDSs rather than airline or other global distribution services.

There are printers, publishers and booksellers. Clearly, when a bookseller wants to sell a book they need a copy of it. Big publishers will have direct relationships with big booksellers: Barnes & Noble shops can probably call someone at Pearson and order a book directly. Pearson's probably have a warehouse somewhere that will then dispatch the book to the seller.

But that model won't scale: if Mrs Miggins' Corner Bookshop wants to sell a copy of one of my books they won't know who call. Instead they call a book distributor, which holds a catalogue of books and will know where to buy each from, whether that be a publisher, a warehouse or a printers.

Distribution costs

Everyone in Mrs Miggins' supply chain will want a cut of the sale. Say your book sells for £10 and costs £4 to print, the seller might expect 20% of the sale and the distributor another 20%, which leaves you just £2. Disappointing, isn't it? Suddenly that 10% royalty paid by a publisher doesn't look so quite bad.

When comparing prices for printing your book you also need to consider the costs of distribution. Firstly, does your chosen printer have an online book store? Direct sales from the printer will cut your distribution costs and leave you with a better return. Although, as LeanPub and Lulu demonstrate, how many people will use the direct sales channel?

So even if readers can buy your book directly from the printer, you will still want it to be in a global distribution system. Thus you need a printer that can inject your book into such a system. At that point you need to consider how much you are paying for global distribution.

Consider my *Xanpan* book. The list price on Lulu is £12.95 and it costs £5.06 to print. If the book sells from the Lulu website my revenue is £6.31. Don't ask me where the other £1.58 goes – it must be a Lulu fee. If the same Lulu-printed book sells via a GDS I make £1.13. I can offer discounts on the Lulu website and still make money, but because the GDS costs are so high I don't have much margin on the same book printed and distributed from Lulu. Lulu won't allow me to sell at a loss.

The same book is available via Amazon's print-on-demand service (formerly CreateSpace) and made available via 'expanded distribution'. Here the book costs £3.03 to print. Amazon's print costs differ by region, while Lulu has one price for printing even though I believe that books are printed in multiple locations.

As a result I can price the book lower on Amazon: I currently list *Xanpan* at £9.99. Books sold on Amazon make me £2.96. Sold via expanded distribution I make £0.97, so I charge £3 less but make just 17p less on each sale.

For comparison, the *Xanpan* e-book has been selling for £3.99 on Amazon UK – in the budget space – but makes me £2.65, 31p less than the print version.

Price comparisons

Scrum in Easy Steps, 2017, by my friend David Morris, sells for £7.69 on Amazon UK in both Kindle and print. But on Amazon.com the Kindle version is $9.99 (about the same as the UK), while the print version commands a $4.49 premium.

Another friend and self-publisher, Dave Farley, published *Continuous Delivery Pipelines* himself at $9.99 and $27, a $17 premium for print.

The print version of Christina Wodtke's *Radical Focus*, published by Cucina in 2021, sells at $29.99, a whopping $20.75 premium. Both Dave and Christina sell expensive printed books while keeping the e-book below Amazon's magic 'ten' metric.

Outside the world of technology, Little, Brown and Company price humorist David Sedaris' *Calypso* at $12 (Kindle) and $14 (print) on Amazon.com, compared to £5.49 and £6.66 on the UK site.

I recently read Fiona Hill's big seller *There Is Nothing For You Here*. This book on US politics is more expensive on Kindle than in paperback. The hardback version is £22, reduced to £17.75, while the Kindle version is £20. At Amazon US the situation is reversed, with $20 for the hardback and $17 for Kindle. Which just goes to show that there are no hard and fast rules: if you have good content, why not make e-book buyers pay the same or even more?

Looking at this data – and assuming publishers know what they are doing – leads me to conclude they don't see the Kindle, paperback and hardback editions as selling to different markets.

Amazon is changing

In surveying book prices I found a few odd things and noticed some new behaviour from Amazon and other publishers. Here are two examples, but it's possible this chapter will be out of date before you get to read it.

On Amazon UK Jeff Sutherland's *Scrum: The Art of Doing Twice the Work in Half the Time* is £3.99 for the Kindle version and £8.09 for the print version – a £4 difference, but with the print version double the price. On Amazon Germany you will pay €9.08 for the Kindle version and a €1.01 premium for the print version. Oddly, though, on Amazon US right now the Kindle version is $16.99 and the print version is only available secondhand.

Don't ask me how Jeff's publisher, Random House, decides prices – maybe that's why they are called 'Random'. There are several possible explanations. Maybe this is very cunning price scheme, or maybe the price setters don't really understand online pricing. Or Random House might price for the US market, the print version is out of print and nobody has paid much attention to the rest of the world. The final possibility is that this is a mistake. The first option shows how much more publishers know than I do, the other three demonstrate how publishers are imperfect.

Mark Lutz's *Learning Python* costs $56 to buy new in paperback, but the first edition on my bookshelf, dated 2000, cost me just $30 in a San José bookshop. The Kindle version is also expensive at $35, but Amazon offer a rental option for $16. While I know about Amazon's 'Kindle Unlimited' library, I've not seen rental options before. It looks as if these are only available in the US, however.

33. Playing with price

As a self-publisher using digital tools you have much more control over pricing than when you work with a publisher. With a publisher they set the price – end of story.

On LeanPub any price change is effective immediately, while on Amazon there may be a few days lag. If you are using another system such as Lulu there may be a longer lag, but you can still change prices.

The fact that you might change the price in future is one reason not to put a price on your book's cover. Most of the older books on my bookshelves have a recommended price printed on the back near the ISBN number, but newer books don't.

Countries such as the UK once had laws about book pricing, and discounting was frowned on. Most countries have relaxed their laws in recent years, although I believe France is an exception here. Consequently the need to have an indelible price on the cover has largely gone away.

Digital publishing allows prices to be changed, which creates a number of opportunities. If you are working through a publisher these options are probably not available to you, even if the publisher can use them. One of the reasons for working with a publisher is to relieve yourself of decisions such as 'How much should this book sell for?'.

Price discovery

During prerelease LeanPub allows potential buyers to suggest the price they would expect to pay for your book. After publication it allows you to set a minimum price and a suggested price. LeanPub also allows buyers to pay more if they so wish. Potential and actual buyers use all these options, so in theory LeanPub gives you many more data points to work with, but what LeanPub cannot tell you is why buyers chose to pay what they did.

The other issue is that over-payers on LeanPub represent a rather small number of people. LeanPub buyers are by their nature not representative of the wider market, because they are usually people who have come to LeanPub specifically to buy your book and not, as on Amazon, those who have stumbled on your book while shopping for another.

Amazon doesn't support any of the options LeanPub has for 'price discovery', but Amazon does allow you to change the price at any time you wish. This is even easier if you sign up to KDP Select. In theory you could conduct experiments: one price this week, a higher price next week, an even higher one the week after. However, as with LeanPub, Amazon cannot tell you the thought process of someone buying your book. Has someone bought *A Little Book about Requirements and User Stories* because it is inexpensive and will take a chance on it? Or has it been highly recommended by a colleague?

A bigger problem affecting experimental pricing is that buyers are often prompted to buy your book by other events. I once saw a big spike in sales of *Succeeding with OKRs in Agile* after a podcast I recorded went live. Had that happened during a pricing experiment I'd have had to start all over again.

While I tend to know about big events like a podcast going live and might plan around them, I don't known when someone on LinkedIn or Twitter is going to post about the wonders of my books. In a couple of cases people have read a book and created an infographic. This is wonderful and gets lots of exposure in social media, but it would distort any experiment.

So if you are going to run experiments you will want to pace or suspend your marketing efforts, as a blog post, newsletter or tweet about your book during a pricing experiment could distort the sales. Likewise, if you go public about your pricing experiments, you might distort sales, as people are likely hold off buying if they believe the price will go down, or rush to buy if they think the price will go up.

A sales surge

There may be other processes at work that can also distort sales. Looking at the annual reports for *Business Patterns* for one year I saw a big surge in sales in October.

I hypothesized that *Business Patterns* had been included in a college reading list and students had rushed out to buy the book one autumn. If that theory was true then I should have seen another spike 12 months later when the next year started the same course. It never happened, so I will probably never know.

My two best-sellers, *A Little Book about Requirements and User Stories* and *Succeeding with OKRs in Agile*, also see occasional sales spikes at random times. Last week *Succeeding* sold more than six times more in one day than normal, while for *Little Book* there are occasional days when it sells three or four times more than normal. These are one-off events rather than a gradual increase or decrease: I conclude that someone has bought a batch for their company.

Publisher pricing

At least with Amazon and LeanPub you can conduct experiments and you can see the results almost in real time. With the publishers I've worked with sales data is either not available or comes in months later. If you decide to work with a publisher you might want to ask about this in advance.

To be fair to publishers it can be hard to know how many books they have sold, because they sell through channels. They may know how many physical units they have shipped to a specific bookshop, but they often ship on a sale-or-return basis. You may see a sales report with 100 copies going out, only to see 90 of them return over the months ahead. Of course the time delay makes things harder.

Pricing over time

Sales apart, there are other reasons why you might change a book's price over time. One popular technique is to release a book on Amazon at a very low price, say 99¢. The aim is to make a big splash, get a lot of sales logged, drive the book high in the charts and spread the word. After a few days or weeks it then increases to full price. Indeed, you probably want to tell people: 'Introductory price of 99¢ for the first week'.

However, if you think your book is in great demand and people are waiting for it, you might take the opposite approach: launch at full price and only reduce the price after the initial demand is serviced.

I've observed this with novels and children's books where an author is well-known and has a big following. A lot of publicity leads up to the launch, which is at full price, but a few weeks later the book is half price in many bookshops.

This approach can work well if the book is linked to a particular time. Consider the *Guinness Book of Records*: a new one with next year's number appended appears in early November each year. So in a few months time I expect to see the full-price *Guinness Book of Records 2023* on sale.

Most of these books will sell as Christmas presents. Some shops will discount the book a few weeks before Christmas, while some will hold it at full price. However, everywhere will cut the price as soon as Christmas has passed and you will find it at half price in the January sales. By the end of January it will be in the discount bin and in February in the bargain bookshops.

I'm guessing your book will not be so time-dependent, but it might be. Jon Jagger was commissioned by Microsoft to write a book coinciding with the launch of the programming language C#. Initially Jon's was one of the few books available on the new language, but not for long: it quickly became dated. Jon sensibly took a fee rather than royalties from Microsoft.

I was originally surprised by how sales tailed off within months of a book being published, although I should not have been. I suppose some books build sales over time, but my early books sold a lot in the first few months and then slowed. You might reason that reducing price will help drive more sales, or the reverse: once sales have slowed it is only enthusiastic buyers buying, so increase the price.

Traditionally secondhand booksellers would sell books at a discount compared to new copies. Over time, as books went out of print, prices would increase as copies became limited and only available on the secondhand market. Digital books and print-on-demand books, in contrast, need never go out of print. Perhaps secondhand booksellers need a new model.

Looking more generous

Despite being one of my favourite books, and setting out a manifesto for the future of business, *Continuous Digital* doesn't sell. Four years after finishing the book there is just a trickle of sales.

'CD' is still useful to me: it is currently the free download when people subscribe to my newsletter, and it still serves as a useful give-away on courses and elsewhere.

Would reducing the price increase sales? I suspect not: a five-year-old book that was never a big seller isn't going to be an impulse buy.

Would increasing the price change anything? While it is possible that a higher price would increase credibility, I doubt that would drive sales now. But neither would a higher price deter many buyers – I suspect the trickle would continue much the same, so I'd probably make a little extra.

However, if I were to raise the price say from $9.95 to $19.95 then it would allow me to make my free download offer more valuable to subscribers. Rather than boasting 'Subscribe and download Continuous Digital for free, worth $9.95', I could say 'Subscribe and... worth $19.95'.

34. KDP Select and Kindle Unlimited

Amazon would really like you to enrol your e-book in *KDP Select*. Joining is free and there are two big advantages, but there is also one noticeable downside, although it may not be an issue to you.

The first advantage is that Select allows you to run special offers and do free book give-aways. You can do these without Select, but it requires work, you don't have much control over timing and it doesn't leverage any of Amazon's marketing tools. Given these hinderances, I've never gone to the effort of running a discount.

Second, Select makes your book available in the Kindle library system, Kindle Unlimited. Subscribers to Kindle Unlimited can 'borrow' books from the library at no charge apart from their regular subscription. Authors get a payment based on the number of pages read, so you might expect sales revenue to go down but a new rental revenue stream to appear. (Select has top-up payment schemes such as 'All Star Bonus', but these require more effort to understand and then further effort to participate in. I've not been convinced they are worth the effort.)

Being in Select and Kindle Unlimited provides one more advantage: pages read. Among the reports Amazon provides is one of how many pages readers have read. This data is interesting and might even tell you something useful.

The sad truth is though that you will find a high drop-out rate, that most people who start reading your book stop before they get to the end. The early chapters are more likely to be read than the later chapters.

I think this is true of all books, but without data on how far readers get in other books I'm not sure what value it is to me. Since your book will already be published at this stage you can't change it, although the information might influence future books.

Select downside

The downside of Select is that you must give Amazon exclusivity. You cannot sell your book elsewhere – on LeanPub, Apple or any other digital platforms. Print issues are not restricted.

I have only ever enrolled one book in Select, *A Little Book of Requirements and User Stories*. After a few months I removed it. I find it hard to know whether Select is worth it.

The only other place I sell my e-books is LeanPub, so I'm not missing out on much. Even there I don't really want them to sell, because I want all sales to be through Amazon. Giving exclusivity to Amazon shouldn't be an issue for me, but I feel a duty to the people at LeanPub to leave my books for sale there. I love LeanPub as a writing and early sales platform. I want it to succeed, to grow and prosper, so I want to support them. I just don't want LeanPub to sell too many of my books.

Leaving my books on LeanPub has one more advantage: I can use LeanPub to give targeted free books and discounts. For example, if I am teaching a class I can give everyone a free copy or a discount code. As far as I know Amazon does not have that option.

I could, in practice, give away free e-books without LeanPub, by just sharing a secret download link. I think giving away is within the rules of Select because it is not selling, although Amazon might argue even that breaks exclusivity. Discount codes present more of a challenge because that is effectively selling.

During the months I had *Little Book* in Select I never collected enough evidence to convince me that it was a good or a bad move. Perhaps if I had made more use of the marketing tools I would have seen it differently.

Select has other benefits, such as the 'Amazon Literary Contest' – no, I don't know either. I don't find any of the benefits compelling. As I understand it some Select benefits are only available in the US, so as a European author the offer is less than compelling.

Leaving KDP

Books are enrolled individually in KDP Select, so you could enrol one book and leave others generally available. If you decide to leave though it requires a 90-day notice period, so you are stuck if you suddenly find you want to sell elsewhere.

When I removed *Little Book* from Select the 90-day period was irritating but nothing more. If I had a specific reason to remove it I might have been in a hurry, but I find it hard to imagine such a reason.

Select is another example of how the Amazon ecosystem seeks to pull you in. Already it makes sense to put all your sales effort into Amazon: Select doubles down on that proposition. For me there comes a point where enough is enough: I am sure that I am not the only person who has a love–hate relationship with Amazon. Whatever their flaws they do what they do very well, usually far better than their competitors. Maybe if I put my misgivings to one side I could make even more money from my books.

35. Categories and keywords

Let me admit – I've been putting off writing this chapter, because while book categories are important I also feel they are something of a black art. Or perhaps just a black art on Amazon. For while I think I understand them, but they never quite work out as I expect.

Book categories tell bookshops and libraries where to place a book – on which shelf, in which section. Should it be in fiction or history? Romantic fiction or science fiction?

Some readers may remember searching libraries using *Dewey Decimal* and *BIC codes*. I say 'remember' because digital books and search engines mean that hunting through library shelves is a becoming a thing of the past. Indeed, the BIC (Book Industry Communication) Standard Subject Categories scheme is itself due to be retired in 2024[1].

While having your book in the right section of a bookshop is essential if you want to catch browsing buyers, I honestly wonder how many people browse by category on Amazon. Certainly I normally start with a search term, either the title of a book I want to buy or a topic I want to find a book about. However, categories are still important at Amazon, because they influence what books are shown and where, such as the titles that sell best in a specific category. Categories also influence the contents of 'You may also like' or 'Products related to this item' sections.

Setting your categories

When you register your book on KDP or log details in book databases like Nielsen, you will need to specify a category – or rather two categories, as shown here for *Succeeding with OKRs in Agile* – together with the keywords.

---

[1]https://www.bic.org.uk/files/pdfs/Press%20Releases/Press%20Release_BIC%20Codes%20obsolete%202024_FINAL%20v.1.1.pdf

Keywords   Enter up to 7 search keywords that describe your book. To enter the Kindle Storyteller contest, you need to add the keyword
                    StorytellerUK2022. How do I choose keywords? ⌄

                    Your Keywords (Optional)

agile	okrs
Objectives	Key results
teams	MBO
Value	

Categories   **Choose up to two browse categories.** Why are categories important? ⌄

                    Nonfiction > Computers > Software Development & Engineering > Project Management
                    Nonfiction > Business & Economics > Management

                    [Set Categories]

Categories and keywords on Amazon for *Succeeding with OKRs in Agile*

Nielsen's title editor also asks you to specify two categories. Nielsen[2] complicates matters by working in BIC codes, which you have to look up. Notice in my two screen shots that I've not specified the same categories, that is a little bit foxy of me, but the world hasn't ended.

Nielsen BIC Subject & Qualifiers :	Management & management techniques (KJM)
Publisher BIC Subject & Qualifiers :	KJM
	UMF
BookScan Product Class Code :	T17.1
BookScan Product Class Text :	Careers & Success
BISAC Subject :	BUSINESS & ECONOMICS / Management (BUS041000)
	BUSINESS & ECONOMICS / Management (BUS041000)
Readership Level :	Professional & Vocational

Categories on Nielsen for *Succeeding with OKRs in Agile*

So far so good? The book categories have fiddly interfaces and are time-consuming but manageable. However from here on it gets complicated.

---

[2]Nielsen companies play various roles in the book industry. In the UK they are the administrators of the ISBN system, which is why I'm referring to them here. You will need to check who the authority is in your country. In the US it is R R Bowker, while in New Zealand it is the National Library.

More categories

While Amazon allows you to specify two categories that apply to all global markets, these aren't necessarily the categories buyers will see. Look at the screen shots for *Succeeding with OKRs* from Amazon US and Amazon UK and play 'spot the difference'.

Product details

ASIN : B08S3DHJJW

Publisher : Software Strategy Ltd. (February 9, 2021)

Publication date : February 9, 2021

Language : English

File size : 3670 KB

Simultaneous device usage : Unlimited

Text-to-Speech : Enabled

Screen Reader : Supported

Enhanced typesetting : Enabled

X-Ray : Not Enabled

Word Wise : Enabled

Print length : 211 pages

Page numbers source ISBN : 1912832062

Lending : Not Enabled

Best Sellers Rank: #359,793 in Kindle Store (See Top 100 in Kindle Store)
#61 in IT Project Management
#73 in Software Project Management
#266 in Computers & Technology (Kindle Store)

Customer Reviews: ★ ★ ★ ★ ☆ ˅   49 ratings

Succeeding with OKRs in Agile (Kindle edition) categories on Amazon USA

Product details

Publisher : Software Strategy Ltd. (15 Feb. 2021)

Language : English

Paperback : 209 pages

ISBN-10 : 1912832062

ISBN-13 : 978-1912832064

Dimensions : 19.05 x 1.22 x 23.5 cm

Best Sellers Rank: 328,654 in Books (See Top 100 in Books)
  1,094 in Software Design, Testing & Engineering

  11,975 in Business Management (Books)

Customer reviews: ★★★★☆ ˅   51 ratings

Succeeding with OKRs in Agile (print edition) categories on Amazon UK

You should have spotted several differences: the US Kindle edition is listed in three categories plus an overall rank in the Kindle store. The UK Kindle edition also has three categories, but not only do the categories differ between Kindle and printed editions, but they also differ by country. Amazon UK lists the Kindle edition against *IT Project Management, Computer Programming* and *Software Design, Testing and Engineering.* While the first appears in both the UK and US entries, the other categories are different.

If you start browsing the Amazon category tree – this is displayed on the left-hand side when looking at books, although not necessarily by default – you find that Amazon UK and Amazon US don't even have the same categories. Indeed there are separate trees entirely for print and Kindle editions, which are also different again for audio books and different for all the other Amazon sites as well.

< Any Department
  < Books
    < Computers & Internet
      Programming
        APIs
        Algorithms
        Compilers
        Database Design & Theory
        Device Drivers
        Games
        Graphics & Multimedia
        Interface Design
        Introduction
        Introduction to Programming
        Languages
        Languages & Tools
        Linux & Unix
        Mac OS X
        Microsoft Windows
        Mobile Phone Programming
        Network Programming
        Software Design, Testing & Engineering

Section of the Amazon book category tree from Amazon UK

Before you ask "Where are all these categories coming from?", go back and look at the screen shots. Hopefully you will notice that while the categories I specified in KDP and Nielsen have some relationship to the categories on the product details pages, they aren't the same. In fact you can't specify the categories that appear on your book page – most of them don't exist in the category list. The categories you specify don't seem to appear on the Amazon site.

Now do you see why I think of this as a black art?

Attentive readers will remember that you get to specify two categories when you set up a book online, but as you can see from these screen shots buyers might see three. Occasionally you see just two categories, and I am sure I have seen books with four categories on rare occasions.

You can think of the categories you specify in KDP or Nielsen as 'official categories' that conform to the international standards, but Amazon operates unofficial categories of its own design. While you can influence where your book goes in the unofficial categories, you don't have complete control.

So bizarre

If you want to delve into the details and understand what is really going on, please do. Ultimately, it seems to boil down to Amazon believing their algorithms can do a better job for you and your book than you can. Sometimes this can lead to seemingly bizarre classifications: consider Bill Gates's *How to Avoid a Climate Disaster*.

Product details

Publisher : Penguin; 1st edition (23 Aug. 2022)

Language : English

Paperback : 272 pages

ISBN-10 : 0141993014

ISBN-13 : 978-0141993010

Dimensions : 12.9 x 1.5 x 19.8 cm

Best Sellers Rank: 12,418 in Books (See Top 100 in Books)
  6 in Alternative Energy

  14 in Natural Resources Management

  15 in Introduction to Programming

Customer reviews: ★★★★☆ ⌄   9,675 ratings

How to Avoid a Climate Disaster printed edition

It is hardly surprising to see Gates' printed edition listed in *Alternative Energy* and *Natural Resources Management*, but *Introduction to Programming*? I suppose the energy consumption of different languages should be a consideration for new programmers, but more surprising still is that the book is fifteenth in that category, lower than the first two categories.

Product details

ASIN : B07YTNGRCY

Publisher : Penguin; 1st edition (16 Feb. 2021)

Language : English

File size : 18171 KB

Text-to-Speech : Enabled

Screen Reader : Supported

Enhanced typesetting : Enabled

X-Ray : Enabled

Word Wise : Enabled

Print length : 256 pages

Best Sellers Rank: 21,026 in Kindle Store (See Top 100 in Kindle Store)

  1 in Environmental Technology & Engineering

  3 in Software Development (Kindle Store)

  13 in Functional Programming

Customer reviews: ★★★★☆ ∨   9,675 ratings

How to Avoid a Climate Disaster Kindle edition

Now consider the Kindle edition. *Environmental Technology & Engineering* makes sense, *Software Development (Kindle Store)* is odd, but perhaps more appropriate than *Introduction to Programming*, but what is it doing in *Functional Programming*? Does this imply that functional programming languages use less energy than procedural or object-oriented ones?

While this may make you laugh, it also hints at what is going on behind the scenes. It also tells you that programming books outsell alternative energy books.

What is going on?

You can read about categories on the Amazon help pages, in blogs and in books by other authors. However, I've never found any of these descriptions to completely explain what is going on. I think that is partly because things have changed over the years that my books have been listed on Amazon.

Basically, Amazon is turning over categorization to algorithms. Amazon is reasoning that their algorithms can categorize your book more appropriately than you can. For Amazon the test of 'more appropriate' is *does it sell more?*

The algorithms – and I hesitate to describe them as 'artificial intelligence' – take multiple inputs. Your categorization is but one: the categories you request are closely tied to the BIC Standard Subject Categories I mentioned before. That scheme is closing, and I think I now understand why.

The algorithms take many more inputs, another being the keywords you specify with your book, as shown for *Succeeding with OKRs in Agile* earlier. Amazon describes some of this in the KDP help pages[3].

The Bill Gates example shows that another input is going to be the author and any other works with which the author is associated. Not only has Gates written several books of his own, he is also the subject of many books. These books are overwhelmingly to do with technology and, a little further out, programming. Therefore when the algorithms crunch in all the data, Gates is closely associated with programming topics, so his books get included there. Lots of programmers buy his books.

---

[3]https://kdp.amazon.com/en_US/help/topic/G201298500

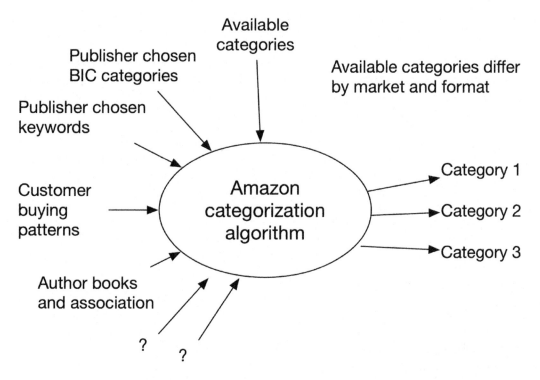

Reverse-engineered understanding of the categorization algorithm

Adding to this is Amazon's desire to sell more books. Amazon is also noticing 'Customers who viewed items in your browsing history also viewed' and what books *you* buy. Budding programmers, often young, will buy books on beginning at programming. Many of them will have been inspired by Gates' success and use Microsoft products; additionally they may share the environmental concerns of many of their generation. When browsing for a new programming book they can maybe be tempted to buy a book on climate change from one of their heroes. It doesn't take many such purchases before the algorithms start to see data that suggest that people buying books from the *Introduction to Programming* category also buy books by Bill Gates.

Another input to the categorization algorithms seems to be the other books that buyers buy. The algorithms will start to add Gates' book to the *Introduction to Programming* category because the same people buy both. When other Amazon algorithms are working out which books to recommend as an add-on purchase ('Frequently bought together') the categories are one of the data sources examined.

Another consideration for the algorithms is how well a book sells. So if it is going to recommend a book from, say, *Functional Programming*, it is more likely to recommend the best-seller in that category than the hundredth.

Possibly some of these algorithms end up being circular: because a book sells well it is recommended more, and because it is recommended more it sells more. Just how clever the algorithms are I don't know, but it wouldn't be the first time Amazon's logic favours the winners.

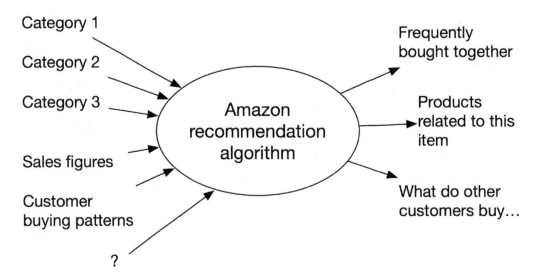

Reverse-engineered understanding of the recommendation algorithm

What to do about it?

While you might argue with my description of the algorithms, and you might believe that I have misunderstood the way they work, what you cannot argue with is the algorithm itself. So if next year the algorithm changes, the best way to keep up your sales is to change your approach to marketing.

As I understand it now you will want your book to be high in a category: the higher the better, preferably number one. In fact on my current understanding it is more important to be high in a category than it is to be in the right category.

It therefore makes more sense for Bill Gates' book to be number 15 in *Introduction to Programming* than to be number 99 in *Introduction to planet saving*. When it comes to ranking a book in a category what is important is not how many people buy the book because it is in that category, but simply how many people buy the book.

Let's stick with Bill's book. Suppose it is selling 100 copies a day on Amazon UK. That means that there are five books in *Alternative Energy* that sell more than 100 copies a day and there are 14 books in *Introduction to Programming* that sell more than 100 copies a day. If the book sold 200 copies today it might earn first place in *Alternative Energy*, but still be ranked tenth in *Introduction to Programming*.

Now what I don't know – and which Amazon might describe somewhere – is over what period sales are counted when ranking a book. That is to say, is Bill's book sixth in *Alternative Energy* because it sold more than all but five others in *Alternative Energy* in the last 24 hours? Or are sales considered over a week? Or a month?

You can experiment a little: make a note of a book's position, then buy it. If the book was ranked number two an extra sale might make no difference, if it was ranked 7631st then one extra sale may jump it up by 1000 positions.

With a little thought you can tell which categories sell most books. On one hand you want to be in those categories, because people are interested in those subjects, but on the other you don't want to be there because there is a lot of competition.

I'm sure we would all like to see our books ranked in first place in any category. It's good for the ego, but there are also two commercial reasons why first place has an advantage.

Firstly, being number one in a category is going to get you recommended more often. Secondly, you can use it for publicity: screen shot it and tweet it out, 'Look at me, my new book is #1 in *Introduction to Potato Growing*'. Based on that you might even like to claim you are 'The #1 best-seller' even if the position only lasts for ten minutes.

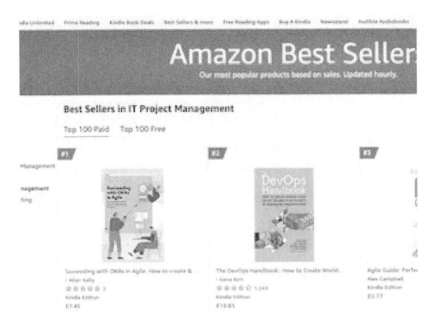

Succeeding with OKRs in Agile made it to #1

Keywords

I haven't mentioned keywords yet. As you might expect, keywords are important for the Amazon search engine, but they are also important for categories. So far you have probably been wondering how you get your book into a category like *Introduction to Programming*. The answer is that you can't just put it there, but you can nudge it there. One way to do this is through keywords.

The keywords you choose when registering your book in KDP are another input to the algorithm that Amazon uses to determine in which category your book should be listed. In fact as far as I can tell they are the most significant mechanism you can use, but they don't guarantee anything.

So the next question has to be *how do I choose my keywords?* I don't think I have cracked this – it's still a black art to me. Amazon has guidance online about keywords[4] so I won't say much here.

The important thing is to use keywords that will help people find your book. So think about

---

[4]https://kdp.amazon.com/en_US/help/topic/G201298500

the subjects your book is associated with, what topics your book covers, what questions your book might answer, and, of course, what categories you would like to see your book in.

At the moment Amazon allows seven specific keywords in addition to the title and subtitle, so you should use keywords that do not already appear in the title or subtitle. You can even put in different words for print and e-book versions. Given that there are different category lists for printed books and for e-books, you might want to try and steer them towards different categories in each.

I have read other authors who recommend getting your book into lesser related categories because, while the category is 'wrong', your book can be ranked highly, a bit like Bill Gates charting in *Functional Programming*. I'm not sure if I believe that author's advice or if I want to adopt such Machiavellian tactics.

Still a black art

There you have it, or at least my understanding of what is happening. Maybe you see why I think of it as a black art?

Hopefully this chapter has given you enough information to get started. However I am acutely aware there is a lot more to categories and keywords than I have covered. If you have the time and the motivation I'm sure more research would reveal insights I have overlooked.

36. Digital rights management

Digital right management (DRM) is both boring and controversial. If as a reader you stay within one ecosystem, such as Amazon's Kindle e-book system, you might not even notice that it exits. But if you want to lend someone a book, or move materials between ecosystems, perhaps to read a book bought from Google Books in the Apple Books app, then you start to notice it.

As an e-book author and self-publisher you have a big decision to make: *will you best meet your goals by applying DRM to your book?* or *will your goals be better met by leaving your book DRM-free?*

If your goal is to make money from your book and you believe that some people will borrow or steal copies of it rather than pay for it, and that if they can't steal the book they will pay for it, you will want DRM. The promise of DRM is that it will ensure that only those who paid for it will be allowed to read your book. As is often the case with antitheft systems of any sort, however, DRM does not prevent theft, it only stops the less determined.

Almost all DRM systems can be broken if someone is determined enough. A quick search on the web ('remove drm from book') and you will find instructions and tools for removing DRM. Before you rush to do this, though, let me point out that in some countries, notably the US, removing DRM is illegal.

Alternatively, if your goal is to share your message, if don't mind some people reading your words for free, and maybe you believe that people will naturally prefer to be honest and buy your book, then being DRM-free is just good marketing. I tend towards the view that I want to share my message, and that people who read free today are more likely to buy in future. If your goal is to get your message to as many people as possible, or to drum up business for your paid advice business, then does it matter if someone gets a free book?

LeanPub does not support any form of DRM: anyone who buys your book on LeanPub can share it with as many people as they like. If you only want paying customers to read your work, then you don't want to publish with LeanPub. Use their tools by all means, just don't click the 'publish' button.

All publishers I know of put DRM on everything. This means that when you buy an e-book directly from a publisher your choice of e-book reader is limited to those that support the publisher's chosen DRM system. This also means that your phone or tablet becomes full of e-reader apps and you have to remember which book is in which app. My iPad currently has Amazon Kindle, Google Books, Apple Books and one called Bookshelf from VitalSource, which is pretty awful and will be deleted soon.

e-book sellers like Amazon are in a position to impose their own DRM. Books bought from Amazon work on Amazon Kindle readers and Kindle apps. I buy most of my e-books from Amazon, but inevitably when I can't locate an e-book it is because it's one of the few books I've bought from Google or Apple and so is in their app on my iPad.

When it comes to e-books, especially e-books with DRM, the relationships between reader, seller, publisher and even publishing technology provider become more complex. Consequently it becomes more attractive to the reader to stay with one system, although that itself has knock-on implications for competition. Witness the disputes between Amazon and publishers, or the failure of e-book readers from the likes of Sony.

When you publish with Amazon KDP you are given a choice, *DRM or DRM-free* – Amazon lets you decide. I always choose DRM-free, as I want my words to reach a wide audience. I also believe that while a few people may get hold of my book free, most will pay. The few who don't either wouldn't have bought it anyway, or maybe they will be impressed enough to buy the book or something else from me.

If you decide to work with a publisher but have strong views on DRM or the quality of e-reader software, then you should talk to them before you sign the contract. Find out if their views on DRM match your own goals.

Cassette tapes

A lot of the music downloads and CDs in my collection are from bands I listened to as a teenager. Back then I couldn't afford to buy as much of their music as I wanted, so my friends and I would buy blank cassette tapes and copy music from each other.

This was illegal but it allowed us to listen to more music. It also generated sales, because my friends introduced me to artists and sometimes I would buy an album they didn't have and share it back. A record company would say that my friend should have bought that new album too, but if they had not shared with me previously then I would never have bought the album.

Decades later, as an adult with funds, I've been back and bought many of those albums. I cheated Jean-Michel Jarre out of money in the 1980s, but by 2022 I'd bought almost all his recordings.

37. Tax

It has been said that only death and taxes are inevitable. Although anyone who has observed the tax-efficient strategies of Amazon, Meta and friends may wonder if tax is really inevitable. However, for the self-publisher, tax needs to be paid.

Royalties from book sales are income and so will be subject to tax. Print-on-demand and e-books make life easier here. Were you to have 100 books printed and sell them out of your spare room, you would have to declare the income from selling them all and argue with your tax authorities about reclaiming the printing costs. Since Amazon and LeanPub only pay royalties, e-books and print-on-demand is much simpler.

Details will vary by jurisdiction, but in general if you are publishing as an individual you will need to declare royalties and any book advances from a publisher on your tax return. Since I operate a private limited company for my consulting business I make the company, Software Strategy Ltd, the publisher, and have all monies paid to it.

While tax is coupled to geography, there are two taxes that may catch you wherever you live. Almost uniquely, the US levies taxes on citizens internationally, which means even if you are not a US citizen or Green Card holder you might still be required to prove it. Meanwhile, the European Value Added Tax system is based on the location of the *buyer* for digital products. So buying an e-book in France from a self-publisher in Montana can be subject to VAT.

US withholding tax

KDP publishing is based in the US. This means that it is subject to US tax law, which in turn means they default to treating everyone as a US taxpayer. So they withhold a portion of your revenue for tax – the so-called *withholding tax*. This can be 30% of the revenue.

For most non-US self-publishers this represents lost income. While you should pay tax on your book sales you should be paying this in your home country, not the US. Indeed, there is every chance you could end up paying in both.

For example, I put all my book sales through my own company. Both my company and I pay UK tax. If Amazon hold 30% for US tax payments then a book sale is effectively taxed both in the US and the UK.

To avoid this Amazon have an online 'tax interview'. This is not actually an interview – more a long and annoying form. The form is littered with the kind of antiquated terms tax authorities love but which are utterly confusing to anyone not familiar with the US tax system.

While painful to complete, it is possible to do the form yourself. When I finally got around to completing it I actually got an extra payment from Amazon – monies previously withheld, I expect – and saw my revenues increase each month.

VAT

If you live in Europe you will be familiar with Value Added Tax (VAT). This is effectively the same as the sales tax that many US states levy, although the behind-the-scene mechanics are very different.

The good news is that many countries exempt books from VAT, but the bad news is that electronic books aren't always exempt. In my case the UK does not apply VAT to printed books, but does apply it to e-books[1].

To complicate things, European VAT rates now depend on where the buyer is, not where the seller or author is. Unfortunately VAT makes the price buyers pay higher and the revenue you make from sales lower.

Fortunately both Amazon and LeanPub are set up to remove this complication from our lives by offering a 'one-stop shop' service. However, you need to be aware that VAT is applicable and that things are happening behind the scenes. You may set your price in Germany at €9.95, but buyers are probably paying more once VAT is added.

---

[1]At the time of writing the UK VAT system has not diverged from the EU's.

38. Legal deposit

In many countries publishers are required to deposit copies of any new book with a national library or libraries of record. This is known as legal deposit[1]. You only need to submit to library(s) in the publisher's own country even if you sell in many.

In the US this means that you need to send one copy to the United States Copyright Office and another to the Library of Congress. For the UK you must send copies to the British Library plus six more, including the Bodleian Library in Oxford and Trinity College in Dublin. And guess what – publishers in the Republic of Ireland also have to send books to the same seven. In the UK you dispatch one copy directly to the British Library and the other six to an address on an Edinburgh industrial estate, from where they are distributed to the other libraries.

The rules vary by country, so have a look for yourself. In particular, in countries like the US and Australia you may find there are additional state requirements. At the moment there is no requirement in the UK to submit digital books, but one can imagine that changing before long.

While you could skip the deposit processes and hope nobody would notice, you might get chased up. Normally I'm pretty good at remembering, but I have received letters on occasion demanding books. In fact the whole process is rather slow in the UK, so I've had letters demanding books months after I sent the books in. Depositing a book isn't necessary for copyright – as far as I know – but it could help reinforce your case if something does happen.

Apart from that, I honestly don't know if anyone ever looks at my books in these libraries. For all I know they could be stored in the warehouse in the scene at the end of *Raiders of the Lost Ark* – certainly that's how I imagine it. Getting the books printed and paying postage adds a little to your costs, but I feel that if I'm claiming to be a publisher then I should do it. In fact I'm proud that copies of my books lie buried somewhere in the vaults of the Bodleian Library in Oxford.

Wherever you are, do a quick search on 'legal deposit' in your country and find out how it works.

---

[1]https://en.wikipedia.org/wiki/Legal_deposit

39. Academic publishing

What can I say that will interest academic writers and publishers? After all, I am not an academic: I come from outside that world and don't understand it in detail. At the same time, because I am an outsider and don't understand the vested interests and vestigial practices, maybe I can offer a new perspective.

There are two reasons this chapter exists. First, while I don't specifically claim to offer any advice to academic writers and publishers, I hope to illustrate how the new world of digital publishing opens new opportunities. Second, for writers and publishers outside the academic world, some understanding of that world can prove useful.

Academic writers – lecturers, professors, researcher and others – write for three audiences: peers, students and what one might call the mass market. Let's talk about them in reverse order.

Mass market

The mass market consists of both professionals in the same field – for example chemists working in forensic labs or biologists working for pharma companies – and the curious general public.

In some fields, such as computing, there is a massive gap between the research undertaken by the academic community and the work done by those in the field. Elsewhere, it is more common for professionals to dip into academic literature and academics to make their research and findings available in a form accessible by professionals.

The true mass market for academics is when they write a 'low-brow' book that explains the more exotic aspect of, say, thermodynamics to the general public. Occasionally one of these books becomes a big seller and the author a media celebrity.

In these markets academics are little different from any other educated writer. Opportunities exist for motivated academics to write their own books to explain their field to a wider audience.

However, academics face an unusual barrier to writing a best-seller. Despite spending much of their working life writing and publishing, many of them are poor writers who struggle to make themselves understood. The world of academic publications is one of captive audiences and a desire to be exact, neither of which contribute to readability. Academic papers tend to follow both standard layouts and section structure. Thus writers don't invest time in thinking about what will make their work more accessible – indeed, why should they? Much of the resulting work is, at best, tedious to read.

Students

Academics write textbooks, often to accompany their own courses. This can be a big money-maker. For a start, they will probably not invest the time to write a book for a course that enrols only a few student – even a market of 100 probably isn't worth the effort.

Once their course is big enough to justify a book then it may be possible to compel students to buy the book. A set course-book may sell several hundred copies every year. A class of 200 isn't just 200 potential buyers, it is 1,000 over five years, as each year provides a new cohort of buyers.

If a textbook is good enough for a course at one university, it may well be good enough to use at another. After all, while details may differ, the courses will cover similar ground and the key tenets will be the same. 200 buyers a year at one institution may be 2,000 if ten other colleges set the book, or 20,000 if 100 colleges use the book.

Publishers know these big numbers. They also know that the marketing of such a book is very targeted: the course conveners who set the reading list, not the students. Rather than mass-market marketing, publisher may employ direct sales.

There is a catch. Students are usually short of money and will sell their books; more importantly, they will buy secondhand books. Publishers and authors don't make money when students buy secondhand books.

To offset this publishers ensure that textbooks are updated by publishing new editions every two to three years. Consider Richard G Lipsey's *Positive Economics*, the textbook I used to study economics over 30 years ago. First published in 1969, over 50 years ago, it was already in its third or fourth edition when I had a copy. Now just called *Economics*, the fourteenth edition was published in 2020 with Alec Crystal joining the original author.

Adding authors in academic publishing is very common. If you are creating a new edition every three years it helps to share the workload. Once you have a hit book you can farm out the work to a junior colleague or someone at another institution who can bring in more readers.

The treadmill of new editions has another effect: it increases the book's size. A new edition has to look different, and the easiest way to do that is to add content. After all, the basic words and core content are still good, so they don't need changing, and textbooks are unlikely to contain ground-breaking insights. How else can publishers deter students from buying a secondhand copy?

The digital world is changing this too. Not only do students want their books in digital form, but there is much more free content available on the internet. Without DRM students can simply share books with one another. Even with DRM a motivated student only needs a quick Google search to find out how to remove it[1].

Publishers have responded by moving to a rental model, otherwise known as a library. Rather than buy a book, students pay a recurring fee to access books. This neatly removes the secondhand book problem.

At the same time, the tools and approaches discussed here mean that it is easier for more academics to publish their own textbooks. Those with smaller classes or those who already share extensive course notes could choose to publish these digitally themselves.

Students' revenge

Students could use the same techniques. As an undergraduate I was the first person at my university to take lecture notes on a laptop. Occasionally other students would ask for a copy of my notes when they missed a class. My reputation spread and at the end of term people were asking for a complete sets of notes. In return I usually received a pint of beer.

Then one day I found another student in the library photocopying a set of my notes she had borrowed from someone else. I laughed but I was cheated out of the beer! Today I could use LeanPub sell my notes with updates after each lecture.

Peers

The vast majority of academic publishing isn't textbooks: most of it is written to report on research and cement the authors' standing and position. In many places, particularly in the UK, academics who don't publish are risking their careers. The mantra is less 'publish and

---

[1] I'm not advocating that students do this: in the US the *Digital Millennium Copyright Act* makes it illegal.

be damned' and more 'don't publish and be damned'. Without publications academics can't advance their careers or research.

Self-publishing isn't going to help here. Making money from book sales is not the aim – it is for publishers, but not for academics. It is even arguable that being widely read isn't the aim.

In this world the credibility of the publisher is vital. The publisher is a guardian of quality and not all publishers are equal in that respect. One of the ways they guard quality is through peer review.

There are out and out books, but also journals that appear periodically: monthly, quarterly or less often. These journals are collections of papers and have editors. In reality, a 'journal' is pretty much a book, and the repeated publications a book series. Each edition uses the same boilerplate – title, style, cover art, editors, reviewers and so on.

Traditionally these journals had very short print runs and were bought by university libraries. They are expensive, as publishers may sell just a few dozen copies.

While journals may still be printed and physically shelved, they are more likely to be accessed online through the database systems that university libraries are compelled to subscribe to. The downside of this model is that academic journals and books are inaccessible to anyone outside academic circles.

Much of the writing is unintelligible, not because it is full of exotic terms, but because it follows a stylized form, in a small font, which makes it boring and more difficult to read than it need be. Fortunately most of us can get away with reading opening summaries and closing conclusions.

Digital technology is slowly changing the academic publishing world. The rise of *open access* publications and new funding models is loosening the big publishers' grip on the market and making research more widely available. However, I've yet to see any evidence that it is making journals any more readable.

Harvard Business Review

One 'academic journal' that does reach the mass market is the *Harvard Business Review* (HBR). This is one of the few journals that manages to straddle the gap between academic credibility and the general market. Academics form the core of HRB writers, but there are a fair few consultants too.

If you look behind the articles in HBR you may well find that the writer has also published an article on the same topic in another academic journal. Yet the writing style is very different: the HBR piece is engaging and readable, while the other publication will likely be dry. HBR succeeds because it makes insights and research accessible.

HBR has a sibling, *Harvard Business Press* (HBP). HBP has published some of the biggest-selling business books; the authors are largely academics. HBP follows a formula: issues are a little over 200 pages long, and like HBR they are written in a readable form and peppered with lots of stories. I have been told that much HBP output is actually ghost-written.

I've noticed that if you do a bit of digging – Google searching – on a HBP book and its authors you frequently find that they wrote an article on the same topic for HBR a year ago. Or if not HBR, then another journal such as my personal favourite, *MIT Sloan Management Review*. The earlier article will be far shorter while conveying the same points, albeit with fewer stories and case studies.

V Marketing

40. Amazon

Amazon is not the only bookseller. It is not even the only digital bookseller. Neither is it the only digital publishing platform. While it may dominate physical book sales, electronic book sales and even, through Audible/ACX, audio books, it does not command even 50% of the market.

The extent of its market share differs from country to county and by book category – fiction, non-fiction, reference, children's book and so on. However it does all this in one place across all countries and categories.

For a self-publishing author or small publisher Amazon offers an unparalleled route to many markets. Once you have a book listed on Amazon you have the book listed in every market in which Amazon operates. Where else can you get that kind of reach?

With Amazon all the markets are in one place – a single interface and web page for the US, UK, Germany, Sweden and elsewhere. Amazon might miss a few countries – until fairly recently it was absent from Australia – but no other seller includes so many.

Bookshop chains, local bookshops and supermarket sales might collectively represent a bigger market than Amazon, but they are not in one place. In general the effort put into Amazon reflects in all Amazon's markets.

So we'll assume that you want to be on Amazon. But Amazon is ruthless in how it sells.

It's a search engine

Start up your web browser, flush cookies and any other identifying data, go to your favourite Amazon site and search for my book 'Xanpan' – just search on 'Xanpan'.

You might see 'Xanpan: Team Centric Agile Software Development, by Allan Kelly' as the first item in the list, but more likely it will be far further down, perhaps even on the third or fourth page. Despite being a unique search term, you will probably get a lot of green tea and health supplements first.

The Amazon search box is not an index onto products Amazon sells. It does not attempt to make the best match between your search term and the products available for sale.

Instead, the Amazon search box is a search engine like Google or DuckDuckGo. Google orders search results using the PageRank algorithm, which regards every web link to a site as a confidence vote. Amazon uses a similar algorithm, but instead of using votes from other websites as Google does, Amazon uses sales. The more a product sells, the higher Amazon will list it.

So, although your search for 'Xanpan' may closely match my book, the book doesn't sell many copies. The Amazon algorithm may reason that the average shopper is more likely to be looking for something else and have mistyped the name when they search for 'Xanpan'. So Amazon is more likely to sell something if they list better-selling products before those with a closer match.

I've just repeated this search and it is not as bad as it used to be. On both Amazon UK and US my book *Xanpan* was featured prominently, while a few months back it was way down the list. However, sponsored products – that is, paid adverts – dominate the higher search results. On Amazon US I'm being shown a lot of adverts for cooking pans with my book, while on Amazon UK gardening tools and health supplements dominate.

While you, like me, may dislike Amazon's logic, there is not much one can do about it. In fact there is more to come.

By the way, if you didn't flush your cookies before you searched, Amazon may well have identified who you are from a past visit. If they did then they may well know that you bought one of my books once, and that therefore you are not a random buyer. Unless you also buy lots of body-building protein drinks from Amazon the algorithm will probably reason that you are quite likely to buy another of my books, and that therefore Xanpan should be top of the search results.

The Amazon feedback loop

Amazon applies the logic of sales in many places: once you know about it you will probably spot it at work. The net effect is that if you have a product that sells, Amazon will help it to sell more. This means that you want to put your efforts into selling on Amazon.

As you will have gathered by now, I love LeanPub and think the product Peter and the good people there have created is great. While I'm writing a book I make money from LeanPub, but once my book is published things change: I want every sale to go through Amazon.

This is unfair, I know, which is why I leave my books on LeanPub even though it costs me. In financial terms I am better off selling one book on LeanPub, because I get 80% of the revenue and no download charges. The most I can get from Amazon is 70%.

But I am not selling one book: I aim to sell many copies of a book. The more copies that sell through Amazon, the higher Amazon will list my book in search results. The higher the book is in search results, the more likely it is to sell another copy.

The more my book sells, the higher is will rate in Amazon's category lists. As I discuss in the chapter on categories, they and the sales rank in the category are inputs Amazon uses when deciding what to put in the 'People who bought this book also bought...' section.

When someone buys one of my books Amazon knows that they like my work – or at least like it enough to buy the book. Thus when it is recommending books it is more likely to recommend another of my books.

Paid twice

When someone buys one of my books on Amazon I get paid twice. First in money, but also in data – the knowledge that someone somewhere bought it. Amazon gets a lot more data than I do, and because it has lots of other data it can combine it and use it to drive more sales.

It's not for nothing that people say 'Data is the new oil'. While that soundbite isn't completely true (oil can only be used once), it does convey a lot about the way the digital economy works.

If I sell a book through another channel – LeanPub, Apple, a local bookshop or anywhere else – I only get paid once. Because Amazon didn't see that sale, my book doesn't rank so highly the next time someone searches. (In actuality if my book sold through a local bookshop it may well have come from Amazon via *extended distribution*. However I do not know whether Amazon uses such sales data in its algorithms.)

How do I know?

I'm sure there are more ways that sales drive sales in Amazon algorithms, but these are just the ones I know about. The algorithms change over time just like Google's, and my information might be out of date. In part I learned the way Amazon works by observing when I use it as both an author and a book buyer. I've also learned from a few queries to the help desk and from reading other people's descriptions of how Amazon works.

I also know this because I've spoken to people who worked at Amazon and read some developer-oriented material they have put out. Being an ex-coder helps, but Amazon could change all of this tomorrow if they find a better way.

Do I like Amazon?

Do I like the fact that Amazon incentivizes me to treat other sellers as second class? *No.*

Do I like the fact that that Amazon has a massive databank? *No.*

Do I like Amazon's employment practices and their anti-union attitude? *No.*

Do I think Amazon is a monopolist? *Yes.*

Do I think Amazon should be broken up? *Yes.*

But I can't affect any of these things. As an author and self-publisher, Amazon is a fact of life.

Fortunately Amazon is very good at what it does and also very helpful. The really annoying thing is that, for all its faults, nobody else comes close to being as good.

41. Reviews

You probably don't need me to tell you how important reviews are to buyers. How often do you buy a product online without looking at its reviews? Unless you are buying something you have bought before I'll bet you read the reviews first.

There is an entire industry devoted to getting and influencing online reviews. In this chapter I'll give you my understanding and explain what has worked for me. I'm also sure that if you look around you will find more advice – some of it will be more up to date than mine and some might even be better.

More reviews is better than fewer, higher ratings are obviously better, but a product with 100 only five-star reviews is suspicious. A few poor reviews destroy credibility, but when the majority give a product three stars or less it might not be the one to buy.

If you intend to charge a higher price for your book you will want to acquire more good reviews; if you are only going to charge $2.99 then maybe it is not so important. I can afford to take a chance on a $2.99 book, but I wouldn't spend $29.99 on a book that only had a few three-star reviews.

Suffice it to say that more reviews and more stars are what you want. But now for the bad news, which might puncture your image of reviews. If you want reviews you are going have to ask people for them. Some people will read your book, decide they like it or hate it, and rush to write a review, but the majority won't spontaneously do so.

There are Amazon rules about reviews[1], so you can't just write 20 five-star reviews for yourself. If you get caught breaking the rules your reviews will be removed, your product delisted and even you yourself banned. (While my focus here is on Amazon, other sites will have similar rules.)

When seeking reviewers you will want to start asking early and cast the net wide. Ask a lot of people and be prepared to give away a lot of books. E-books are obviously cheaper and easier to give away and make it easy to give away early drafts: more about printed books later.

You might consider every book you give away a lost sale. In reality each book you give away is only a potential lost sale: not all of your reviewers would have bought your book anyway. While many will not actually review your book, there may even be a few who still buy it.

---

[1]https://www.amazon.com/gp/help/customer/display.html?nodeId=201929730

More importantly, reviews create sales. No reviews, no sales. So giving books away is an investment in selling more: don't save money by hoarding your books, generate sales by giving them away.

Wait for reviews

As I mentioned when describing Amazon KDP, it is possible to list your book as prerelease. Unfortunately, while publishers seem to be able to get reviews on Amazon during prerelease, self-publishers can't. This creates the quandary I discussed before: *should you start your marketing operation before you have any reviews, and thereby reduce the chances of a sale?* For example, Jill may see your LinkedIn post about your new book and rush over to Amazon to buy it, only to find that it has no reviews. Will Jill trust you?

Alternatively, *should you hold off publicity until you have some reviews?* Jill then sees your LinkedIn post, rushes to Amazon, sees some five-star reviews and buys.

But if nobody knows you have released a book, how will you get reviews?

Five-star first

You really really want your first reviews to be five-star. It appears that the anchoring effect[2] applies to reviewers too: if you have five-star reviews you are more likely to get more five-star reviews.

Suppose that Felicity plans to give you a good review and is thinking in terms of four stars. When she gets to your book's web page she sees that the first reviews are five-star. Consciously or subconsciously she is likely to go with the flow and give you five stars too.

I've read several reports about how existing reviews bias reviewers. What you really want to avoid is a poor initial review. If your first review is five stars you will get more five-star reviews and more good reviews and more sales – and more sales means more potential reviewers.

Conversely, a poor initial review will anchor people the other way. Felicity might be thinking in terms of three stars, but if she sees some one-star reviews she might only give you two stars.

If you have some trusted reviewers, possibly other authors who understand your stuff, then within Amazon guidelines try very hard to get a five-star review up as soon as your book appears.

---

[2]https://en.wikipedia.org/wiki/Anchoring_(cognitive_bias)

Your first reviewers

There is probably some Amazon rule about banning your immediate relatives from reviewing your book, but you will certainly have friends and colleagues for who the book is meaningful. These can be a good start for your reviewer hunt.

They might also be people with whom you share the importance of a five-star review. While you don't want to say "Please write me a five-star review", you might say "It's really important to get a five-star review ASAP. If you think you might give me five stars then I would really appreciate it if you could get it in first".

Once your book is published you should tell those who have offered to review it that it is ready for them. Those who you hope will contribute your first five-star review might even be worth an extra reminder, so text, message or even call them.

Finding reviewers

If you have been selling your book through LeanPub as you write it, you already have a body of readers who are the obvious choice. You can just email these people and ask for a nice review.

However, at the moment LeanPub gives buyers the option of keeping their email address private, so you might not have that many candidates. One way of working around this is to do a special update of the book and in the release notes say 'Book now on Amazon, please review'. Although since LeanPub doesn't force buyers to receive update notifications, your massage may not reach everyone.

(While LeanPub allows readers to provide feedback to authors, it currently lacks a review feature, which I think is a major omission.)

You might also add a page inside your book to remind people. In fact, you probably want to do this anyway. Until the book is live on Amazon, though, you don't have a link and can't accept reviews.

Reviewers normally get a final draft, the pre-copy-edit version. I tell them the final version will change and I promise them a final copy. This allows them to start reading and reviewing early. I also hope it gives me a bit of slack over SPAG.

I normally set up a *reviewer* coupon code on LeanPub that allows me to share a URL from which reviewers can download the book. When the final version is available on LeanPub they automatically receive notification to download the final edition.

The reviewer coupon code also allows me to see how many of my volunteer reviewers do actually download the book. I can't see *who* downloads the book, but I can see how many people do. Even at this stage some people who have offered to review will drop out.

Machine gun or sniper?

Sometime you want a message to reach as many people as possible – you want to spray your message machine-gun style. In these cases personalization will be limited to your mail-merge capabilities.

At other times you want to target a message precisely, sniper-style. In the age of mail shots and mail merge that probably means using a high-touch contact mechanism such as a text message, social-media direct message (DM) or even an old-fashioned telephone call. The number of people you can reach is limited by time, but you have a much higher chance of them acting on your request.

When people feel they are being asked in bulk they are much less likely to act: think of emails you are cc'ed on. It's easy to think 'someone else will respond'. When people know they are being asked personally they may still do nothing, but they are more likely to act on the request.

Ask nicely

I've been known to sit down and write a list of people I think might be up for reviewing one of my books. I look through recent emails, Twitter streams, LinkedIn messages and other media. I make a long list of people. I then send a short note asking if they would like to review. If they are interested I can follow up with a longer message and details of how to get the book.

Sending a long initial message is not good: people are busy and don't need to know the details to start off with. Just sending a download URL is no good if people haven't given some sort of commitment – they are unlikely to read and review. Plus you won't know who to chase up.

Bear in mind that the more channels you use – LinkedIn message, email, Twitter, DM, Facebook – the more places you need to check for messages. The problem is that some people respond on some channels better than on others.

If they agree to review make it as easy as possible for them by sending them an e-book. Usually the e-book will be a late draft or pre-copy-edit version. I also give them a target date and an Amazon link. People are very motivated by deadlines. If someone replies to say that they can't make it by the target date, you can always reply that it's OK, that you need a few reviews in place by that date but if theirs is a little late that is still good.

Once the book is published on Amazon and reviews are open, I follow up and ask them to log a review.

In the weeks, months or even years after a book is published I occasionally get messages, especially on LinkedIn, from people saying how much they enjoyed a book. I reply with 'Thanks, glad you liked the book, an Amazon review is always appreciated'.

Asking loudly

While the personal direct one-on-one approach to reviewers works, you can also make a mass request in public. If you have a mailing list or a following on LinkedIn or Twitter you can put an appeal out for reviewers.

The last time I did this I set up a Google form and asked people to register their interest. After a few days I replied to everyone and sent them a pre-final e-book and a target date. Once I had a URL I sent that too. It doesn't matter much if you send them an Amazon US URL and they are in Germany: Amazon usually prompts people to switch to their local site. The downside is that this is yet another click for people and you might lose a few.

Asking a few targeted people nicely against many people loudly might seem like alternative strategies, but they can be complementary. You can combine both approaches: ask a few people directly and then ask as many as you can loudly. For example you might send a DM saying 'Wendy, did you see my mailshot about a book review? I'm hoping you can be one of the first.'

The aim is simple: get some good reviews in early before the inevitable poor ones. Since most people you ask will not commit to reviewing, and most of those who do will not actually write a review, it's almost impossible to overdo your review efforts.

Follow-up

However you get your reviewers, it helps to have a name and email address: doing everything through mass shout-outs has a much lower return. Unfortunately when people see messages to everyone they often think 'Someone else will do it'.

I hate following up and reminding reviewers to file their reviews. I'll do it once or twice, when the book is first available and maybe a few weeks later. Beyond that I just hate asking. If I asked more I would probably get more reviews, and as I've given them a free book, and they have said they will review, I don't think I'm getting spammy, but I just hate chasing people again and again.

The sad truth is that you will only get one review for about every three potential reviewers – if you are lucky. You lose people at the first ask, at download, at reading the book, at filing the review and at every small step along the way.

Many people will say, not unreasonably, "I'm sorry, I've just been so busy". I usually respond with something like "Please don't feel you need to read every word".

Setting deadlines works: humans are very good at working to deadlines. So too does incentivizing people.

> ## Review feedback
>
> Some reviewers will interpret the request to review your book as a request to give feedback you can use to improve it. Unfortunately, if you are at the stage of asking for Amazon reviews, you are long past the point where such feedback could be incorporated.
>
> If you want early feedback to incorporate in your books, set up a review panel early in the writing process. These people can give you meaningful feedback and go on to become some of your first public reviewers.
>
> I always feel bad when I get content comments late in the process, as I genuinely would like to incorporate them. I usually find myself replying with 'Thanks, you make some good points. Right now I'm focused on getting this book out, so I'll keep your comments for any second edition. If you do feel you could write a positive Amazon review I'd still be grateful.'

Printed books

Production of printed books is one of the last things you do, because so much needs to be fixed before you go to print. When focusing on early reviews for your initial launch, print versions are not going to be available, so reviewers who only want to read printed copies are not going to contribute to the first wave of reviews.

Printed books also have the downside that they cost to print and to be posted. Posting a book adds cost and takes time. As an added complication for fellow UK-based authors post-Brexit, some EU countries will expect import duties to be paid by the recipient. These rules are either inconsistent across countries or inconsistently enforced. I've posted books to several EU countries since Brexit; most have arrived without delay or charges, but not all of them. In one case the charges were higher than the cover price, so the recipient let the post office return the book and then bought it from Amazon.

Given that printed books cost money and take time, and given that some reviewers will not review a book, you want to emphasize reviews on e-books. They are cheaper and quicker: I'm almost tempted to say offer only e-books for review.

Printed copies can help in other ways, though, which leads us to the next topic: incentivization.

Incentivizing reviewers

One way of getting reviews and getting them in a timely fashion is to offer some reward for a review. There are rules about reviews.

Amazon does not allow reviewers to be paid or rewarded. In recent years there have been several controversies about this happening, so Amazon has increased its review monitoring.

The current Amazon UK rules[3] prohibit anyone who will benefit financially from reviewing a book, relatives of the author, a review 'in exchange for monetary reward' or in-game credits, or reciprocal reviews. Obviously you can't review your own products. However there are things you can do legitimately.

Top of the list is to give away review copies of your book – you can't give a book as *payment* for a review, but you can give away review copies – which is essential, really. If you give out unfinished copies for review, such as pre-copy-edited versions, you could suggest to your reviewers 'Email me when you've done your review and I'll send you a final copy as soon as it's ready'. If your reviewers have download your book from LeanPub they will be notified automatically.

You might also offer to give away printed copies, although things could become expensive if 100 reviewers asked for a printed book. You could suggest something like 'If you would like a printed copy to update your review, please send me an email with your address and I'll get one in the post'. It might be a good idea to impose a deadline on this offer, however, so that you aren't putting books in the post for years to come.

---

[3]https://www.amazon.co.uk/gp/help/customer/display.html?nodeId=G3UA5WC5S5UUKB5G

Another approach is to gamify the review process: 'Free printed copies for the first ten reviewers', or 'I'm giving away ten printed copies randomly drawn from the names of all reviewers listed on 1 June.'

Is this payment? Does it break Amazon's rules? I suppose one could argue that it does, but it is a tenuous connection. I don't think Amazon will be coming after me on this.

Bear in mind that these approaches might mean that you are giving free books to people who gave you a poor review. Since Amazon is concerned about fair reviews, excluding these really would break the rules. As you need to contact them somehow to get their address, you could say 'Please send me your address if you would like a printed copy'. If they didn't like your book they may not want a printed copy.

Once you start to gamify things your options really open up: you might offer related content, say a summary or reference sheet, maybe another book or maybe something else. Just be careful that this doesn't become too much like a payment.

Other authors

Once you start writing books you may find you have friends who also write books, especially if you start speaking at conferences. They too will be seeking reviews to help boost their rankings, so if one of them asks you for a review, make sure you write one.

While Amazon prohibits reciprocal rating ('I'll give you a five-star review if you give me one') that does not mean you cannot review other books. Nor does it mean that you can't ask an author who's book you have reviewed to write a review for yours.

If you write a review for José Doe this week and next week José Doe writes a review for your book, the Amazon algorithms might get suspicious. To avoid this, don't just write reviews for others when your book is new, write reviews whenever you are asked. If you manage to be one of the first reviewers, especially one of the first five-star reviewers, then hopefully the author will remember if roles are reversed in the future.

Simply being generous does not mean there is an agreement of reciprocality. If Amazon comes asking, you can point out that you reviewed José's book six months before he reviewed yours. You might add that you have also reviewed books from Abdul, Wolfgang and Maria, while they haven't reviewed yours.

Amazon only

As with so much else in this book I'm focusing on Amazon in this chapter. Of course it's good to have reviews on Apple, Barnes & Noble, Waterstones and all the other places that sell books, but getting reviews on those websites will require effort, even if it is only mailing someone to say 'Thanks for your review on Amazon, could you post the same review on Apple?'.

Unfortunately that might create a problem with Google, because its search engine doesn't like duplicated content . There is however some disagreement in search engine optimization (SEO) circles about the degree to which Google penalizes duplication.

If you are lucky enough to have 100 enthusiastic reviewers you need to decide whether to aim them all at Amazon, or split them between Amazon, Apple, Waterstones, whatever Germany's biggest bookseller is, Australia's and so on. Not only does that make more work for you, but it also detracts from your Amazon reviews, because you only have 25 rather than the 100 you could have had.

It is not just buyers you are trying to impress with reviews, it is Amazon itself, and more specifically the Amazon search engine. The number and quality of the reviews you have are yet more input parameters to the search engine. The more reviews you have, the higher the ranking you can get.

My feeling is that I'd rather have all my reviews on Amazon than scattered around. There probably comes a point where one more review on Amazon is worth less than the first review on Apple, but I don't know what that point is, plus it's more work for me. So I push all my reviewers towards Amazon for simplicity.

International Amazons

There is Amazon US, and for me there is Amazon UK. In many ways the amazon.co.uk site is more important to me because, living in the UK, most of my audience is here, although the US is still a big market for me, while Germany is usually third.

Although Amazon.com, Amazon.co.uk and Amazon.de may all look the same, and although one submission to KDP can get your book on all three, they have different reviews. Normally you would use your local Amazon and you will see the reviews from there and, if you are giving a review, it will go there unless you know how to work the system.

Reviewers are expected to have a record of buying on an Amazon site before they can contribute reviews. So even if you decide you want all your reviews on Amazon US, your reviewers in Germany are probably limited to reviewing on amazon.de.

There are few people who can avoid buying from the 'everything store', but there are people who live in countries in which it does not operate. Amazon only launched in Egypt and Poland in 2021, so I have had potential reviewers there who were unable to post reviews. While I always ask them if there is some other site to which they can post, I just accept this. It would be unfair to refuse someone in, say, Iran because there is no Amazon there. In any case it isn't worth my time checking to see whether every volunteer reviewer has a local Amazon site.

Amazon usually lists reviews from other countries below the local reviews. It didn't always do this, and those reviews are still treated differently, although how differently I don't know. It is even possible to get a duplicate review from the same person if they review your book on different Amazon sites. Not a lot of people will do this, but I have one or two dedicated followers.

Product groups

Now it gets complicated.

Amazon assigns a different *Amazon stock index number* (ASIN) to each product. So your e-book and printed book have different ASINs. Amazon lumps all 'the same but different' products together into a *product group*. Product groups don't always work as they should, and consequently it is possible to get differing reviews against them.

This is not good, because 'search juice' is spread between these different items and customers can become confused. In the worst case your printed and e-book aren't even shown together, or along with your e-book is some second-hand retailer selling your printed edition for five times the price of a new copy while the new copy isn't shown.

This only really caused me problems when I created printed editions with Lulu and e-books with KDP. Because the printed book came from a different source Amazon didn't associate them despite the title and author being the same. Although Amazon says it will match titles automatically, it seems that when the sources are different publishers this doesn't happen.

Amazon customer support for KDP self-publishers is surprisingly good, but in this case they couldn't help me. Because I had the printed book coming from Lulu and Amazon saw Lulu as the publisher, the request needed to come from Lulu. Lulu customer support can be good too, but putting all the requests together took time. So staying inside the Amazon ecosystem is the easiest path.

Fortunately, when product groups are working properly, Amazon will know that a review for your 'Great coffee shops of the world' e-book is also a review for the printed edition. Things are a little different for Audible/ACX, but you should see your audio book listed next to the printed and e-books, together with the long list of reviews.

Publishers and Vine

One might expect reviews to be one area where publishers can really help. Maybe they can, but I have had mixed experiences.

The Amazon Vine programme[4] is open to publishers but not self-publishers. Using Vine, publishers can solicit reviews from a bank of regular Amazon reviewers. The publisher pays Amazon a fee and supplies the books and Vine reviewers review it. In return the reviewer gets to keep the free product, which is by no means confined to books.

Business Patterns went through the Vine programme and got some great reviews. I was really grateful to Wiley for putting the book into the programme. This is one way publishers can do something that self-publishers cannot.

Amazon suspended Vine at the start of the Covid pandemic in April 2020. My understanding is that when it returned its charges had been raised substantially. These may well put Vine beyond the marketing budget of all but books that already anticipate big sales.

Vine aside, one might expect publishers of all people to understand the importance of reviews and know how to get them. Unfortunately that does not seem to be the case.

Publishers appear to view each review copy given away as a lost sale. They obstruct reviewers in two ways. First by using obscure e-reader software for e-books; presumably these readers give them greater DRM abilities. They may also expect people to review a draft copy and provide no access to the final version. They may even time-limit the review copies so they expire after a while, which hardly seems a fair way to reward a reviewer.

Second, publishers hate giving away – let alone posting – printed copies. Publishers don't seem to 'get' the idea that reviews generate sales.

When you sign with a publisher they will typically include ten printed copies of the final book in the deal. When you start asking for physical review copies they may expect those copies to come out of the ten you have been allocated. They may even expect you to pay

---

[4]https://www.amazon.com/vine/about

for post and packaging, or to post them yourself. That sort of attitude delays getting review copies to reviewers, so the reviews arrive on Amazon late.

A long time ago publishers used to print 'trade editions' of books, which were somewhat rough and ready but preceded the final printing. These could be distributed to shops and reviewers to generate interest before actual publications. I suspect that this practice has ceased, as e-books can fill the same role.

An exception to publishers' reluctance to hand out review copies comes with academics. I've found publishers that are happy to give academics review copies if they think the book might end up on a reading list.

More

This fairly long chapter is just advice based on my own experience. I'm sure there is more for me to learn. Do a quick Google on how to get Amazon reviews and you will find plenty of sources. There are even books on Amazon about how to get Amazon reviews.

There are plenty of other places where you can get reviews. Good Reads[5] is one that I hear a lot about, although it is actually owned by Amazon. There are even sites that offer to syndicate reviews. I'm a little cynical about such sites and worry whether they might violate some of Amazon's rules, but that might just be me being too pessimistic.

Journals can be another source of independent reviews. Maybe you subscribe to a professional journal or are a member of an organization that publishes reviews. Even if you are not a member you might know of such organizations or journals. I imagine getting your book reviewed by a prominent journal, let alone a newspaper, would require help from a public relations consultant, but you might find smaller journals approachable.

Amazon is not the only bookshop or even the only online bookshop. If you wanted you could spend a lot of time learning about other bookshops and getting reviews there too. But the sheer reach of Amazon means nowhere else offers the same bang for your buck.

Putting it all together

Once you have finished writing you want to get the final version of your book on sale. So waiting for a copy-editor, KDP approval, print versions and so on is frustrating. However, really do try to hold off official publication and marketing until you have reviews in place.

---

[5]https://www.goodreads.com/

As soon as you have passed your manuscript over for copy-editing, start working on your reviewers. Start gathering them and preparing them. Use the final draft to get them started. Keep in touch with them.

If you can, identify some particularly enthusiastic reviewers who might give you your first five-star reviews, then see what you can do to get those reviews in place. When you have everything ready, and once the book appears on Amazon, *hold fire*. Wait for those first few five-star reviews. Once you have them in place, then and only then let your marketing machine roll.

42. Speaking

Have you ever noticed how many radio talk-show guests have recently published a book? That's not by accident: they want to talk. People who haven't recently published a book aren't so keen to appear on the radio at 6.30 am.

Public appearances are a time-honoured way of promoting a book. The audience might come to the author, such as when an author speaks at bookshop events and signs copies. At other times the author goes to the audience, such as speaking at a conference or visiting a school. The biggest audiences are when an author appears on radio or television, which also brings the kudos of being seen or heard on these platforms.

If you can get on radio or television, do so. Most of us lack the contacts to secure a spot, although that is something you can buy. Public relations consultants exist who do have the contacts and can help you get media attention. I've never hired one, but I've seen their services advertised on IngramSpark and Lulu.

Most of us are more likely to appear in a podcast, at a conference or at a meet-up group. In time you might find that your fame precedes you and people call you up and ask if you'd like to appear in a podcast or speak at a conference. It happens to me regularly, but it wasn't always like that.

Such speaking opportunities are something of a chicken-and-egg problem. Until you have a certain level of recognition people don't know of you or don't see any particular reason to invite you. However, once you have some sort of reputation it can bring you opportunities, and speaking gigs beget speaking gigs. Someone who sees you at a conference might produce a podcast, someone who hears the podcast might be organizing another conference and so on.

It is hardest when you are just starting out, say writing your first book. As your reputation as someone with something to say, as an entertaining speaker or as someone with meaningful advice to impart increases, you will find it gets easier to be invited to speaking engagements.

Whether you are speaking at a conference, on a podcast or elsewhere, you should aim to deliver an engaging talk that has people wanting to know more. While you want them to know you have a book, don't turn your talk into a sales presentation. Selling the book is a secondary issue; let them know you have something interesting to say and entertain them.

I sometimes feel public speaking is a little like being a stand-up comedian. I'm there to entertain: the official reason – business, technical, case study, whatever – is just a pretext. If I manage to smuggle a serious message through then that's great, a bonus.

It's the audience, stupid

You may have something to say but when you are unknown you need an audience to say it to. Setting up your own webinar and speaking online isn't the problem: getting people at the other end is the problem. Over time you can grow your social media followers and mailing list to market yourself, but to start with you won't have an audience. So borrow someone else's.

Conference organizers, podcasters and meet-up group organizers have the reverse problem: they have an audience and need content. Guess what?

In time the situation may reverse. As your fame grows you can bring your own audience. This makes you even more attractive to organizers who want to grow their own audience.

Only when you can bring an audience or reliably deliver 45 minutes of entertainment can you start thinking about asking for speaking fees. Until then, forget about it. Until then the best you can hope for is to sell some books. A few places will pay travel expenses, but even expenses seem to be in decline.

As a rule of thumb regular speaking slots don't pay; keynote slots are far more likely to. A keynote slot is also more prestigious, and your vanity may want it even if there is no financial reward.

Conferences and money

Conferences are probably the most established speaking platform. One advantage of speaking at a reputable conference is that it adds to your reputation: not only have you written a book, but you have spoken at a prestigious conference. That is something worth adding to your bio or book blurb: 'Allan is a regular conference keynote presenter'.

Broadly speaking the conference world divides into two: *commercial conferences* and *community conferences*. Commercial conferences are usually organized by a conference production company and will aim to make a profit. Community conferences are often run on a shoestring by passionate people with regular day jobs.

In general there are far more people wanting to speak at a conference than there are slots for them to do so. Thus conference organizers don't need to offer payment, as they can always find someone who will speak for free. That might not be fair, but that's economics for you.

Commercial conference

- For profit.
- Organized by conference professionals who understand conferences but might not understand their topics.
- Sponsors a major source of revenue.

Community conference

- For community knowledge rather than profit.
- Organized by domain professionals who understand the topics but might not understand conferences.
- Revenue mainly from ticket sales rather than sponsors.
- Speaker selection typically very open.

As your reputation and audience grow the greater the chances are that you can charge a fee. Once you get to be really well-known you can insist on one.

When planning *Agile on the Beach 2020* a popular television science personality asked for £5,000 plus travel expenses. Back in 2011 when everyone was talking about *Lean Start-up* the author's agent quoted me $40,000 plus business class flights for him to speak. A colleague once asked Richard Branson to speak: his fee was $100,000 plus travel expenses for his entourage.

Community conferences may, at best, pay expenses. If you are lucky enough to get a keynote slot you might get a fee – in the world of non-profits this is more likely to be called an 'honorarium'. Commercial conferences are more likely to pay, but the organizers are often trying to keep costs down and can always find someone to fill a spot.

On the other side of the equation, conferences have two major income streams: ticket sales and sponsors. Some conferences make so much from sponsorship that they give away free tickets. That also means they have very high drop-out rates. Another rule of thumb: if tickets are free you can only expect 50% of registered people to attend. Some days it might be even fewer. This rule of thumb applies to free meet-up groups too.

Commercial conferences generally select speakers through a closed-door process and often sell speaker slots as part of the sponsorship package, as they are marketing opportunities for the sponsors. The same conferences may pay one or two big-fee names to deliver a keynote talk.

One London-based conference I know always has a big name, who is probably paid, as keynote speaker. The conference runs a public call for speakers, but many speaking slots are sold to sponsors. Free speakers fill the spots they can't sell. While it is not unusual for commercial conferences to sell speaking slots and then pad the schedule out with free speakers, the public call-for-papers gives a veneer of equitability.

Who pays who largely depends on who has the most audience pulling power. Well-known speakers and authors can attract an audience, so they can take fees from organizers. Sponsors are seeking audiences, which conference organizers can provide, so they pay the organizers. Authors like me will pull in a small audience but also want the audience that they can't otherwise reach, so they end up in the middle.

The second factor determining who gets paid is one's willingness to ask for a fee and to accept a refusal. If I were to ask more often I'm sure I would earn more from speaking, but I would also speak less often, which might become a downward spiral.

In general, conferences that sell speaking slots have weaker speakers than those who have a competitive submission process. As a result community conferences often have the strongest programmes and the weakest finances. At first, especially, community conferences may not have any sponsors – their entire revenue may come from ticket sales.

If like me you are trying to sell consultancy services you may find yourself at a disadvantage. Commercial companies often want consultants to pay: they know consultants want to sell. Audiences too can become cynical about consultants telling them what they should do; audiences tend to prefer non-consultants who are actually 'doing the job'. The problem is that people who are working hard at a job don't have the same time or motivation to speak as do consultants.

Academic conferences

I'm consciously ignoring academic conferences here, mostly because I don't know much about them. I am sure that for the right book exposure at a relevant conference will help sales.

Getting a speaking slot

Conferences organizers typically start planning about six months before a conference. Some will start earlier and some later, but six months is a good rule of thumb. So if you want to speak at a conference in the weeks and months after your book is published, you need to engage with conferences long before you have finished writing.

Community conferences often run a 'call for papers' or 'call for speakers' process, then select speakers from those who apply. There can be a lot of competition for speaking slots. I ran the speaker selection process at *Agile on the Beach* for many years: in some years we had over 300 submissions for 40 speaking slots. While most conference will have many more submissions than available slots, this a 7:1 ratio is exceptional. Even a 3:1 ratio is on the high side.

I have found it helpful to know the people running the conferences, particularly if they are part of the speaker selection process. Increasingly however conferences are using blind review submissions to increase diversity, so knowing the organizers is less of an advantage.

In general the more conferences you speak at, the more your reputation will grow. At the same time you will get more experience as a public speaker and refine your material, so that you become a more attractive prospect. In the beginning just get yourself on as many programmes as you can. As your experience, reputation and presentation skills grow, you will find more opportunities and can become more choosy.

Typically organizers will want a talk synopsis, a biography and a headshot photo. Some may want more details of your expected audience (expert or beginner?), the 'takeaway lessons' and so on. Personally I dislike this level of analysis and detail, but perhaps that is because I see my performances more as entertainment than teaching.

The synopsis is the key thing and it's difficult to get right. You don't want it too long but neither do you want it too short. Too much detail can be as off-putting as too little. Neither do you want to spoil any surprises or tell people your entire thesis.

I've read hundreds if not thousands of synopses when reviewing *Agile on the Beach* submissions and I know they are very difficult to get right. If I read my old submissions I can always see a better way of doing them. Sometimes I have two or more great synopses and I don't know which to use. You want to get people's interest, to pull them in, show you have real knowledge, but keep it short and keep some surprises in store.

Generally I like to start a synopsis by describing a problem, perhaps in the form of a question. Then give some hints about what I'm going to say: 'Allan will describe how to overcome these problems'. I aim for several short paragraphs.

Having said that, I get invited to a lot of conferences now that I've largely given up submitting to open calls for papers. This is a little arrogant of me, but the fact is that I need to filter conferences somehow; I can't go to them all. Submitting to conferences where I am guaranteed a speaking slot is a more effective use of my time.

Meet-ups

These have long been small geographically based events, typically running in the early evening and often free to attend. Generally there is one speaker, and if you are lucky you might get a free glass of wine.

The Meetup.com[1] website has effectively named these groups *meet-ups*. They are still largely volunteer-run and free to attend, but there are far more of them than there used to be. A few groups are sponsored by benevolent employers or recruitment agents seeking to build their contacts list.

While some went into hibernation during Covid, many more switched to online events. For the speaker this is a double-edged sword. While it makes it possible to speak to many more groups, more often and in many more places, it also means that you are competing with more speakers, including some very well-known authors.

Once upon a time I would travel out of London to the likes of Brighton, Milton Keynes or Bristol to do an evening talk. Because these groups lacked money and my time is valuable I would rarely travel much further; there was the odd trip to Edinburgh. This also meant that the people these groups could ask was limited by the same geographical and cost issues.

During the pandemic I spoke to groups in Paris, Toronto and Sydney, in addition to groups closer to home in Cambridge, London and Newbury, all via Zoom or Teams. Pre-pandemic I might speak at one event a week, two would be exceptional. During lockdown speaking at three in one week wasn't uncommon.

As an author I can reach a much wider audience online, but because those groups are no longer limited by geography they can ask anyone from anywhere. This might be an advantage for me because I am established, but it creates a bigger barrier to new authors, because you have more competitors and more prominent ones.

However I'm sick of online events, especially online conferences. I want to see people's faces when I say something, I want to talk in people, not avatars.

I have come to prefer on- and offline meet-up groups to conferences. They are more intimate and better at delivering new audiences. The organizers generally work on a schedule a few

---

[1]https://www.meetup.com/

months out and don't operate competitive calls for speakers, so they don't require the same forward thinking. Almost all list their events on Meetup.com, so you can search the site for groups you think might like to hear you speak and then just knock on their door and suggest a topic.

What to present?

Sometimes I create presentations on topics that interest me and sometimes those topics grow into books. However, if I have a book to promote it makes sense to stay on topic and deliver a presentation about the topic of the book. One option is to give a 'live preview' of the book by talking through some of its content. Another option is to talk about some different aspect of the same thing, perhaps even making it controversial.

In my early days of public speaking I wanted to give every audience something unique. I felt I owed it to the audience to give them something fresh and different. However that requires a lot of work, especially if you start speaking regularly, so it makes sense to recycle presentations.

Today I feel a bit bad when an audience gets a new presentation. Inevitably the timing isn't perfect, the slides contain bugs and I haven't worked out all my jokes. I tend to believe a presentation gets better with a few repeats. That said, there does come a point where one wants to move on to something new.

Other advantages of repeating presentations are that organizers can ask for something they know – you can even give them the slide deck – and that you can offer a menu of ready-to-go presentations. This makes it easier to get passed around from one group to another as word spreads.

Submission systems

Although the world is full of potential speakers, organizers have to find them. Part of the problem is a sheer overload of options. Often it is hard to tell who is good and who is not.

Speaker bureaux maintain registers of speakers who can be hired for events – company talks, conferences, after dinner speeches and so on. They have existed for years and usually charge fees, which means the speakers need be able to command a decent fee to start with. Rightly or wrongly I assume I'm not in that league.

Electronic systems like CyberChair[2] have long operated where there is no money. Such systems have traditionally been rather unfriendly to use and focused on the academic market. Many conference automation systems have some submission functionality, but you still need to find your speakers in the first place. (I even created my own submission system, Mimas[3], for *Agile on the Beach*, which I later released as open source.)

In recent years a few companies have created automated speaker bureaux, companies like PaperCall[4]. These allow conferences and speakers to register their details, then allow conferences to approach speakers and for speakers to browse a catalogue of events and submit to many quickly.

Which is great, except that by making it easier for potential speakers to submit, conference organizers have even more submissions to review. While this might improve quality on the face of it, it can have the opposite effect if organizers are overwhelmed. A typical community conference may have one person in a team of four managing speakers. Faced with 200 submissions they may be very diligent, they may call for help, or they may give each submission a cursory review and fall back on their own preferences and prejudices.

For me the jury is still out on whether PaperCall and the like improve speaker and organizers' lives or make them more problematic. It becomes a numbers game: organizers get more submissions, so reject more speakers, which means speakers need to submit to even more conferences.

What might be good for me as a known speaker and writer might not be what is good for the wider community, or perhaps the reverse. My fear is that, rather than broadening participation, these systems will instead focus more attention on established names.

Podcasts

Podcasts offer another platform to speak to someone else's audience. You might be invited by a podcaster – I was invited by several after publishing *Succeeding with OKRs in Agile* – or you might want to find podcasts you consider relevant to your topic and ask directly.

If you are going to invite yourself to a podcast, check out the content and format in advance. Some podcasters do all their own material, while others interview a series of guests.

Some podcasts will be lined up months in advance and may not appear online for several months after recording. Others are set up days in advance and may be released immediately.

---

[2]http://www.cyberchair.org/
[3]https://github.com/allankellynet/mimas
[4]https://www.papercall.io/

Always make sure you get a link to the podcast, and once it is released push the publicity on your own social media channels.

There is nothing to stop you from establishing your own podcast. My friend Luke Szyrmer[5] who wrote a book, *Managing Remote Teams*, launched a podcast on the same topic. The two go hand in hand and promote both each other and Luke. This is one strategy, but it is also a big commitment. Potentially Luke has two products to promote, a book and a podcast, although it might be one: which promotes the other? Either way, one still needs to build an audience.

In-house talks

As your reputation grows you might find yourself invited to speak at companies. These could be company events where they want someone from outside to speak, they might be an internal company conference, or perhaps a rolling tech-talk programme.

Before the pandemic this was usually an onsite event and I needed to travel to the company's offices. During the pandemic such talks moved online and some seem to be staying there.

The good news is that it is far more common to get paid for such private talks. Not always, but more often. Companies have been known to pay tens of thousands to have named speakers at internal events, but I've yet to reach such giddy heights – scraping into four figures is the best I've managed so far.

While I still sometimes speak at company events I now usually ask for a fee. For some companies this is expected, at other times it comes as a surprise.

Asking for money

Maybe it is because I'm English, maybe because I lack confidence, or maybe I suffer from imposter syndrome, but I find it difficult to say that there is a charge for my speaking time.

The formula I have settled on is to say "I normally speak at public not-for-profit events for free, but for private (or for profit) events I charge a fee. Is that acceptable?". This allows me to grow my audience by speaking at community conferences and events, while also earning some money from commercial entities.

---

[5]https://www.lukeszyrmer.com/

So far most companies say "We quite understand", while most conferences organizers still say "We have no money". For-profit conferences are easy to walk away from: since most speakers are buying their slots the quality is usually lower than non-for-profit conferences.

The problem comes when a company says it cannot pay. The chances are that the audience is going to be small, so it probably isn't worth the effort, but as a consultant I'm also looking for an opportunity to sell my services. So if someone says "We can't pay you but you will get to speak to some people who might be interested in you services", I have to make a decision.

I've let myself be sweet-talked into talking for free a couple of times, but I've learned my lesson: they rarely lead to sales, so I'm getting stricter. Besides, if the company can't pay a few hundred pounds for an hour of speaking, what are the chances they will pay several thousand pounds for a few days' consultancy? Money represents value; if they don't value my talk enough to pay then why would they value my services?

Selling books

I've been to a few talks where the author brings a pile of their books and offers to sell them at the end of the talk – I might even have bought one on occasion. However I've never done this personally, partly because I don't want to carry a pile of books to an event and maybe then carry them all home again.

While I have sold books at events, it is usually by accident. I normally try to have at least one copy of my latest book with me and sometimes people just want to buy it on the spot, so maybe I should make more of an effort.

Another option is to sell an e-book, which can happen even while you are speaking. Sometimes I will set up a LeanPub discount coupon, share the URL and tell people that the link will get them 25% off today and tomorrow, and then seen sales on that code. I've even tweeted the link out publicly: '#ConferenceHashTag attendees at my talk today the half-price book offer is at leanpub.com/'. I don't actually care if someone who wasn't in the talk uses the link mischievously, it's a book sale. The conference gives me a reason to shout about my book.

Capturing audience details

Finally, if you are setting out to grow a mailing list or pick up followers on LinkedIn, Facebook or elsewhere, talks are a great opportunity. At the most basic level, make sure your contact details are on any slides you use, and say something like "Please connect to me on LinkedIn".

Some speakers go further and run a raffle: they will offer a book and ask people to put their business cards in a hat or other receptacle. The hat is passed around and business cards collected. At the end the speaker pulls out a card and present the book.

The speaker then keeps the business cards and later emails everyone inviting them to join their mailing list. Data protection laws permitting, they may even subscribe people directly.

I've always felt this strategy was a bit clichéd and have avoided it, but online things change. For a start you can post your contact details and URLs in a chat window, and of course everyone is online, so connecting to you only requires a simple click.

Now when I announce a book give-away at the start of a talk I invite people to use an online form to enter. My online form collects email addresses but also has a check box to 'subscribe to newsletter'.

I much prefer giving in-person talks, but in terms of reaching more audiences and collecting contact details the online world has proved more effective.

Whot, no TED?

Some readers might find it odd that I don't mention TED or TEDX talks. That is because I've never done one – in fact I've never had the urge to do one or made any effort to do one.

I know some people say that TED talks are the pinnacle of public speaking, and I know I would be in great company, but frankly, while I know there are some excellent TED talks out there, I've never been particularly enamoured by them. So I've never done one and have no experience to share.

43. Promotions, sales, discounts and free books

Everybody loves a discount and the word 'free' has an amazing way of grabbing our attention. Reducing your price on a limited-time basis or to a limited audience can be a very effective way of increasing sales.

The questions you have to answer yourself are *how much extra revenue will you earn from people who would not normally buy your book?*, and *how much revenue will you lose from people who would buy your book (sometime) but will take advantage of the discount?*

Even if a discount brings forward a sale by a few weeks it can be worthwhile. An early sale means you have the money sooner and can earn interest in your bank account. More importantly, the sale is made – nothing can disrupt it. Someone may have every intention of buying your book after their next payday, but if their car needs repair between now and then they may not.

There are some vendors who seem to only ever exist in discount sales mode. In some countries there are legal restrictions on the use of the word 'sale', but this doesn't seem to stop some retailers. Kitchen showrooms spring to mind.

Indeed many books on Amazon seem to be permanently discounted. In these cases I suspect the 'recommended' price only exists to anchor buyers so that the discount seems attractive. At the moment Amazon doesn't offer that feature to self-publishers, but there are many other ways of using price reductions and many reasons for doing so.

Discount sales

Holding a promotional sales[1] event is a time-honoured way of boosting sales. The obvious point is that your product costs less during the promotional period and so one would expect more buyers, but there are two less obvious points that I think are potentially more important.

First, discount sales need deadlines: never tell anyone about a promotion without telling them its end date. People respond to deadlines. With a discount sales event or any other

---

[1]You makes *sales* when you sell a book, you also hold *sales* when you offer a discount promotion. I've confused myself with the word 'sales' on many occasions.

limited-time offer there is the fear of losing out. Without an end date there is no urgency to act, without urgency something else can take potential buyers' attention and the moment – and the sale – is gone.

Second, holding a promotional event is a reason to make marketing noise: send a message to your mailing list, broadcast it on LinkedIn and Facebook, and tweet, tweet, tweet. It is not so much that your book is cheaper, but that you have a reason to remind people to buy your book, and they have a reason to do so soon.

Amazon 'countdown deals' allow you to run a sales promotion, but this is only available if you join KDP Select. If like me you have not joined Select, you can synthesize your own discount event by simply lowering your price, although of course at the end of the period you need to remember to put it back up again.

The catch here is that when you change the price Amazon considers it a publishing event and your book has to go through checks before the change takes effect. The problem is that you don't quite know when the price change will take effect, or when your reversion back to full price will occur.

Consequently you will need to make the changes, then wait for Amazon to put them into effect. Only then can you launch your marketing campaign to support the event. It also means that the end might not be exactly when you want it.

While LeanPub doesn't have any support for promotional sales events, you can still use the same manual process. As LeanPub price changes take effect immediately there is less hassle.

Similarly you can do the same thing manually on Lulu. If you are using Lulu to distribute your book, however, the changes may not take effect for weeks or months, so it is hardly worth doing. In any event, Lulu distribution charges are so high that you would struggle to make much money.

Discount coupons

Another way of whipping up sales is by using discount coupons. These are more targeted than a general sale. Rather than being open to all and time-based, they are targeted. You allow a group of people – say a class you are teaching, a meet-up group you are talking to or your LinkedIn followers – to buy your book more cheaply.

As with a discount sale, you offer a reduced price and set a deadline. While part of me wants to give people plenty of time to take up the offer, I also know to *strike while the iron is hot*: incentivize the audience to act rather than ruminate.

The good news is that LeanPub makes creating and sharing coupons easy. The bad news is that Amazon doesn't offer any support for your own targeted discounts and coupons.

Keeping my books on LeanPub allows me to offer targeted discounts and free offers. However there are two problems in doing this if your book is also on Amazon.

First, if you have signed up to Amazon KDP Select, you have to remove your book from LeanPub. This is because Select demands sales exclusivity, so you lose LeanPub's more targeted coupons.

Second, since the Amazon algorithms reward sales with more prominence and therefore more potential sales, it makes sense to push all sales through Amazon. Directing people to buy from LeanPub means lower Amazon sales, lower prominence in categories and algorithms and potentially lower sales overall.

If you do set up discount coupons on any platform, remember to vary them by distribution channel. For example 'LinkedIn discount', 'Twitter coupon' or 'Facebook 20% off'. Although this makes more work, it allows you to see where your buyers are coming from and where to put your efforts in future.

Random Amazon sales?

At the time of writing Amazon has a feature in beta that allows you to offer a book for inclusion in a 'Kindle Deal' – *Nominate your e-books*. However, this doesn't guarantee that Amazon will include your book in a deal, indicate when your book might be in a deal or what the deal price will be, which complicates marketing.

I recently noticed that the print edition of *Succeeding with OKRs in Agile* had been discounted by 40% on Amazon UK, but not on other Amazons. On one hand I was pleased – I might make more sales – but on the other hand, *what about my royalties*? Mostly I was confused about how this happened.

This was the printed book, not the e-book, so I don't think my nominating the book for a Kindle Deal had anything to do with it. Amazon support told me the book had been selected for a random promotion. They also said my royalties would not be affected, so it seemed like a very good offer.

I'd had no notification of the event, I don't know how long the offer had been running when I saw it, or when it would end. Still, I rushed to social media and told as many people as I could.

Given Amazon's analytical approach to everything I don't believe the discount was entirely random; I just wish I knew how it was triggered.

Free book give-aways

One step beyond sales and targeted discounts is simply to give your book away free. While this obviously won't make you any revenue immediately, there are several scenarios in which you might want to do this. We are talking e-books here, which can be given away cost-free, rather than printed books from printers who expect to be paid.

LeanPub discount coupons allow you to make a book completely free. These are ideal if you want to share the e-book with a class, a sales prospect or a reviewer. Giving someone a code for a site keeps things looking professional, simplifies your life and keeps your transactions all in one place.

Of course you could just put your e-books on a server somewhere – perhaps using DropBox or FTP – and share the download link. However, that would not capture any downloader details, and could run foul of corporate security policies and firewalls, so you might want something more sophisticated.

You could put your file behind a registration page on a website. Once contact details had been collected the potential reader would be redirected to the download. That would work, but would take time to set up. I'm sure if you looked around you would find someone offering a service to do this.

However, all these options means Amazon would not see the 'sale', so it doesn't contribute to your tally or boost you in the rankings. Amazon does however allow you to offer your book completely free to all comers. So you could declare a 'free book day' and set your sale price to zero for a day. I say a day, but as KDP must approve the zero price and also approve the reversion to paid, you don't have detailed control over the timing.

KDP Select does offer specific support for short-term free book promotions. At some point I start to wonder if enrolling in Select would be the sensible thing to do.

Why give away your book?

Why would you offer your book free on Amazon if you want to make money?

First, it may well drive sales. If your book is so brilliant that everyone will want to read it, then making it free will create a cadre of devoted readers who will sing the praises of your book and encourage others to buy it.

I would guess that most people who download a free book won't read it, or at least won't read much of it. Many of those who get the free book were never going to buy it anyway, so you are only foregoing a small portion of your potential revenue.

If those who would never buy your paid-for book download a free version, you may still make money from them. Even if they never read it you have registered on their radar. Maybe they will recommend your book, maybe they will file your name away and later buy another book.

Even if you give the e-book away there are other ways to make money. Someone who downloads a free e-book might read a little and decide they actually want to read a physical book or listen to the audio version. Those versions aren't free, so would generate funds.

Amazon best-sellers in the paid *Open Source programming* category

If you are a consultant or speaker using the book to increase your credibility and market your other services, then a free book could be a very cheap way to generate a sales lead.

Finally, remember Amazon's algorithms: giving a book away gives you lots of 'sales', which will boost your book in the eyes of the algorithms. Well, yes and no. Amazon's algorithms, and even book categories, know about free books. In fact Amazon maintains parallel book categories for paid-for and free books.

Amazon best-sellers in the free *Open Source programming* category

I'm not completely sure how Amazon's algorithms work – perhaps some of my readers know more. From what I hear a book that is only temporarily in the free list gets a boost when it returns to the paid-for list.

This is how I *imagine* it working: each book has a single sales counter. Each paid-for sale adds to the counter and the book is positioned accordingly. Books that are completely free are handled in exactly the same way. When a book moves between the categories, having a single counter means that after a week of being free the book returns to paid-for status at a much higher rank. A higher rank means it gets a boost, which leads to more paid sales, and so on.

It almost certainly doesn't work like this, and even if it did Amazon could change the algorithms tomorrow. It does seem, though, that there is some rationale to making books free for a limited time.

Publishers' tools

I've written all this from my own experience and research as a self-publisher. I know large established publishers have other tools at their disposal. At the very least they have their own websites.

Perhaps more importantly, I strongly suspect Amazon provides them with more tools and options for promotions. One of these is the Vine programme, discussed previously.

44. More Amazon and money

There is a lot to Amazon and it changes all the time. Part of me is nervous that I've written about things here that might have changed by the time you read this book. I'm also conscious that Amazon's offer differs from country to country: I know that outside the US some features are not available. I know that because I've read other authors who describe some feature and when I look it isn't there. A little bit of searching and you may find 'Only available in the US'.

Still, there are some parts of Amazon that do seem to be available globally and can make you a little more – but there is also the thorny issue of tax to think about when talking about money.

Amazon Associates

The Amazon Associates[1] programme allows you to take a small cut of any sale provided the buyer comes via your link. So, for example, if you follow this link to Succeeding with OKRs in Agile[2] Amazon sees me as the referrer, so if you then buy the book I get a small cut of the sale.

It doesn't have to be my book. Let me recommend #noprojects: A Culture of Continuous Value[3] by my friends Evan Leybourn and Shane Hastie. If you buy that book I'll get the same small cut, about 6% I think[4].

Additionally, if you follow one of those links and don't buy the book, but while you are looking at it remember you need a new coffee machine and buy *that* from Amazon, I'll get a small cut of that too, although a smaller rate, 1.5% I believe.

These tiny amounts slowly add up. Once or twice a year I get an Amazon voucher from such referral sales – not enough money to live on, but better than a kick in the teeth.

---

[1] https://affiliate-program.amazon.co.uk/home
[2] https://www.amazon.co.uk/gp/product/B08S3DHJJW/ref=as_li_qf_asin_il_tl?tag=allankelly-21&creative=6738&linkCode=as2&creativeASIN=B08S3DHJJW
[3] https://amzn.to/2QHsBd8
[4] https://affiliate-program.amazon.co.uk/help/node/topic/GRXPHT8U84RAYDXZ

254 More Amazon and money

When I launch a new book I will be sharing the book's Amazon URL again and again, in tweets, LinkedIns, presentations, email footers, classes and elsewhere. By giving an Amazon Associates link rather than the raw book page I can make a little more from sales.

When you create an Amazon Associates link you end up with a very long URL, like the one I gave before for *Succeeding with OKRs in Agile*[5]. Helpfully, Amazon also offers a link shortener, so https://amzn.to/3iWOH9O[6] takes you to the same place. Not only are short links easier to work with – especially if they need typing – they also obscure the fact that you are supplying an affiliate link.

Getting an Amazon Associates link used to be a hassle: log into Associates, find the item, request the link, request the shorter version and then cut-and-paste the link. The new SiteStripe feature makes this easier: you can now quickly get a link to any page you are viewing on Amazon. Once you are registered as an associate you might need to change your preferences to get this bar at the top of your page.

One small catch, which you might have noticed already, is that both those links lead to Amazon UK. While Amazon has recently attempted to improve affiliate links across international sites, it is still rather complex and I have yet to grapple with it.

It would be tiring to look up the Amazon Associates address every time I mention a book, so I keep a file that lists all my books and other books I might recommend together with their Amazon Associates links. I add new books at the top of the file so that it's easy to find the most recent.

Amazon have recently launched a related programme, Amazon Influencers[7], which I haven't yet explored. On first impressions it looks like Amazon Influencers pays higher referral fees, but it will require more study.

Author Central

Whether you are with a publisher or self-publishing, you will want to add Author Central[8] to your Amazon account.

Author Central provides two main features. First, for marketing you can create an author profile, your biography with a picture, and other bits like a blog feed. In the past Amazon

---

[5]https://www.amazon.co.uk/gp/product/B08S3DHJJW/ref=as_li_qf_asin_il_tl?tag=allankelly-21&creative=6738&linkCode= as2&creativeASIN=B08S3DHJJW

[6]https://amzn.to/3iWOH9O

[7]https://affiliate-program.amazon.co.uk/influencers

[8]https://author.amazon.com/

has allowed authors to list events and other details, but these were time-consuming to keep up to date and I seldom bothered.

With an Author Central page, readers looking at your book can click on your name and find out about you and your other books. Author Central also allows you to make your profile more attractive, with pictures and videos to accompany your books.

Second, Author Central also gives access to some admin features, specifically sales numbers. Don't get excited, though – the data isn't that impressive.

One data set shows your printed books' sales figures for previous weeks. You can also see the sales rank position (Kindle, print and Audible versions) for a book. This information is hardly secret, though – you can see it by looking at your book's page on Amazon. However, Author Central allows you to see all your books on one page.

If you are self-publishing KDP will show you sales figures in near real time, but if you are with a publisher sales rank may be the most up-to-date way of judging your success. Websites like SellerApp[9] allow you to back-calculate sales from the sales rank. This can also be useful if you want to know someone else's sales figures. For example, John Doerr's OKR book *Measure what Matters* is ranked at 4,750 on Amazon US according to Amz Scout[10]. This equates to 450 copies a month, which is somewhat higher than my OKR book!

I've long found Author Central disappointing. Amazon recently revamped the site but didn't add any killer features. In fact it removed a feature that allowed you to see US sales by state. You will nevertheless want to create an author page to pull data on all your books together in one place.

Amazon adverts

Amazon has recently started to promote adverts for authors to promote your KDP books[11]. Unnoticed by many of us, Amazon is already the fourth biggest online advertising business[12]

From your Author Central or your KDP account you can access the Ads Console. As I understand it – and I've not yet used this feature – this allows you to buy adverts for your books on Amazon.

Having never used this option I've no idea whether adverts are worth buying: this might be something a publisher can help with. However, as Amazon has set its sights on building

[9]https://www.sellerapp.com/amazon-sales-estimator.html
[10]https://amzscout.net
[11]https://kdp.amazon.com/en_US/help/topic/G201499010
[12]https://www.economist.com/business/2022/07/28/the-online-ad-industry-is-being-shaken-up

an advertising business, one can assume that it will increasingly come to resemble Google's tools and system.

Having dabbled in Google pay-per-click advertising in the past I've become weary of online advertising. By setting advertisers against one another the Google auction process seems designed to transfer as much profit as possible to Google. Getting value from Google adverts at least requires both a good understanding of advertising campaigns: where and when to advertise, how to craft a good advert and how to present the buyer with a compelling proposition.

Since Google provides the advertiser with copious amounts of data on where and when adverts are running, how they are competing in the market, who is viewing them and who is clicking through on them, one needs an almost daily understanding of these factors to keep abreast of them.

My experience with Google leaves me with little interest in advertising on Amazon: the effort–reward ratio isn't promising.

VI Tools

45. Word processors

There is nothing to stop you writing your masterpiece longhand and have someone type it for you. I suppose there are those out there that will do that and have a hit book, but they are in the minority. It also misses the point of digital.

Digital tools give you powers that until recently were reserved for organizations with deep pockets. It is not just that the tools are electronic, but they are cheap, easy to use and accelerate the process to a point at which it changes completely. If you write longhand someone has to transcribe it electronically, which injects delay into the process. This pattern plays out again and again in the digital world: tools give creators the power to do more while removing delays and handovers.

The obvious way to write a book is to power up Microsoft Word and start writing. When you are ready to publish on Amazon or LeanPub, you upload the .doc(x) file and publish that. If you prefer you could write in another application, perhaps use LaTeX, produce a PDF and upload that. Amazon or LeanPub will convert your file to other e-book formats and you are in business.

Amazon prefers you not to submit PDF files, claiming that most PDF files do not produce great results in an automated conversion process. I've never tried giving Amazon a PDF but I don't need to upload a file to imagine the problems.

If you are planning to upload and sell incremental versions of your book as you write, my recommendation is to work with LeanPub and use their *tool chain*. This is what LeanPub was designed for and the publication process is simpler than Amazon's and will get your book on sale sooner.

At the time of writing LeanPub will accept both PDF and Word files. They have a style template to use for Word and I would recommend using it if you write in Word. However, I also suggest that working in this way doesn't leverage the full power of the LeanPub system. Using a simpler notation, Markdown, creates options and removes overheads.

Word processors and style

When you think about writing on a computer you probably reach for Microsoft Word, or perhaps Apple Pages. While other word processors are available, Word dominates the field.

Modern word processor applications offer far more functionality than you need. While adopting many features of desktop publishing tools they have become over-complicated. All those extra features create distractions and diversions, which waste time.

My preference is for simple text editors. While a modern word processor provides better grammar tools, which might be useful, these tools are also distracting. When you are in the flow, when you have an idea you want to express, you want to write – you don't want to be distracted by red or green lines warning you that it is '...with whom I live' and not '...who I live with'.

The second more problematic issue of using Word and other similar applications is that they offer a plethora of formatting options. These are also distracting: is your text best in Times New Roman or Baskerville Regular? 10-point or 12-point?

Formatting options are most obviously a distraction, but they also make layout more difficult. If you do need special formatting then work with styles and style sheets, so when a style is changed all instances of it will change consistently. When writing *Changing Software Development* I was less than religious over style sheets. As a result I had to go back and work over all the formatting styles: it was a nightmare.

Formatting and fonts allow non-standard characters to slip into the text, sometimes invisibly. When you move to ‰another system⌷ or print on ⌷demand you can find unexpected characters showing up in your text.

If you have someone doing a professional layout, perhaps if are working with a publisher, then the more fancy the formatting, the more time you will spend briefing them on what you want and the more time they will spend doing the layout. Even then there is every chance that the layout you have become attached to is not going to be possible. Publishers may have their own house style that determines elements of formatting.

My rule is to keep formatting simple. That is one reason I prefer simple text and Markdown formatting.

Word and friends

If you are working with a publisher they may well specify that your manuscript is delivered in Word file format. While you could write in another application and, at the last moment, convert the files to Word, I'd advise against this. Modern applications are much better at working with different formats to their predecessors, but you can still get problems with formatting.

However you are bringing your manuscript to market, be it via a publisher, LeanPub, Amazon or just website download, at some point you need to pass files to other people. Unfortunately software vendors are moving away from files: Apple Pages and Google Docs offer some kind of document repository that is not clearly file-based. Even Word 365 is moving in this direction. This might make for superior usability – which I doubt – but introduces an extra step, the 'export file'. Sticking to simple text files sidesteps this problem.

If you are working in Word or similar, you probably want to give each chapter a separate file. Historically Word was not stable with big documents – above say 100 pages – or documents with lots of images: it could crash and corrupt the document. So it makes sense to work in smaller chunks and assemble them near the end. This also implies that you need a shared set of styles across your document set.

When you assemble them into a Word master document, you do then, unfortunately, have a big document. When I was writing *Changing Software Development* and *Business Patterns* between 2005 and 2011, my machine struggled with the master document. Hopefully this is a thing of the past: more RAM, faster hard drives, more powerful CPUs and better software should have fixed this, but I'm not planning on trying it anytime soon.

Plain text, Markdown and Markua

Working in plain text (ASCII) may sound very 1980s but has a number of advantages. First, about the only thing on screen is your text: no formatting and no other distractions. Both the distraction (and temptation) of fonts, font size, line spacing and so on is just not there: you have only very basic formatting options.

Second, while there are a few formatting options, they are very limited, so limited that you don't need to worry about style sheets. Files and apps are small, so you don't lose time waiting for a word processor to start or load a large document.

Although you will be working with plain text files – .txt or .md – and very simple editors, if you are working with LeanPub you will also be using a text formatting or 'mark-up' convention. I always use Markdown, which LeanPub has supported from the start. Today LeanPub prefers a similar system called Markua. Other systems also exist, such as ASCIIDoc.

To my programmer's mind the simple text of Markdown is easy, but I do appreciate that to those without my mindset the opposite can be true. To many people a WYSIWYG – *what you see is what you get* – editor like Word is simpler than the raw text world where you have few options to change text size and a change isn't reflected on screen.

You might think of this as the old Microsoft versus Apple debate. In Microsoft applications the user could usually control many options, run the software on many different machines and customize it in many ways. Apple offered a fraction of those options: Apple creates simplicity by not allowing variations or customizations.

Other text editors

Your computer may already have other text editors. Windows machines still ship with Notepad, Macs with TextEdit and the even more basic vim, Linux machines will have some version of vi (maybe vim again), perhaps Emacs and probably others. That does not mean you will want to use any of them. Unless you already know Emacs or vi(m), in which case you may well love them, you probably don't want to spend the time required to master them either.

I do most of my writing in iAWriter[1] from Information Architects, available on Mac, iPad/iPhone, Windows and Android. This is a no-clutter editor with a spelling checker and very basic grammar check options (which I switch off anyway).

As well as the clutter-free design, the big advantage of iAWriter is that is understands Markdown, so I do get some visual indication of how my text will look. Added to this, iAWriter provides good enough support for exporting and importing Word documents, so that when the need arises I can work with the Microsoft world.

Before iAWriter I used TextMate[2] from MacroMates, which is Mac-only. TextMate is much more of a programmer's tool and has add-ins for various programming languages and Markdown. One of my reasons for using it was a passive voice checker, which alerted me to my use of passive voice and nudged me towards a more active voice. Unfortunately that plug-in is no longer available, so I rarely use TextMate now.

Scrivener[3] from Literature and Latte is a writing app for Mac, Windows and iOS which on the face of it looks brilliant: I know several writers who swear by it. Certainly the folding-editor style outliner is very attractive, and Scrivener provides support for Markdown and Word, so should be great. However, although I've tried Scrivener, I've never taken to it. Still, it has been so highly recommended by so many people that I recommend you try it for yourself.

---

[1]https://ia.net/
[2]https://macromates.com/
[3]https://www.literatureandlatte.com

More

I could carry on documenting possible tools and the pros and cons of each one: EverNote, Pages, OpenOffice, the list is endless. I single out those above not because they are the best, but because they are the ones I use, have used or feel I should probably be using.

Personally I love the simple fonts and limited formatting that comes with Markdown and iAWriter; I know that is not to everyone's taste, but it works for me.

46. Formatting tools: Pandoc and LaTeX

You might get by writing a book with Word and publishing on Amazon, or perhaps with your favourite text editor on Markdown and LeanPub. That's just fine, but there are other tools that can come in very useful and might fit your way of working.

Pandoc

Pandoc[1] is one of the most useful pieces of open source software I have ever used. Even after years of using it I am still amazed by it. That said, Pandoc works at the command-line level, so if you are strictly a windows-icon-mouse person it is not for you. There are extra tools[2] to make Pandoc more GUI-friendly however.

It feels something of an understatement to call Pandoc a document converter, but that is what it is. Unlike Word, which can read a variety of file formats, convert them and then export them in different formats, Pandoc will read a vast range of formats and export them in an equally vast range of formats.

Word to Markdown and Markdown to Word, or Markdown to HTML and HTML to Word – I have sometimes taken Markdown files and turned them into web pages on my site to offer book samples. Pandoc saved me a lot of work when a publisher took up *The Art of Agile Product Ownership* and I needed to convert all my Markdown files into Word.

Pandoc can create ePub files, which could be useful if you wish to do something different to LeanPub. It can also – although I don't know why I would want to do this – turn an ePub book into Markdown.

My most regular use of Pandoc is to create PDF documents. If I only want to see a single chapter in print it's far easier to use Pandoc to create a PDF and print the result. Without Pandoc I would need to check all my files into git, log into LeanPub and make a preview book.

---

[1] https://pandoc.org/
[2] http://pandoc.org/extras.html

Being able to use the same source text for HTML, Word documents, web pages and PDF allows text to be repacked, repurposed and reused in different ways.

The other useful feature of Pandoc is that it can include bibliographic databases and processes citation in text files. More of this later when I discuss handling references.

LaTeX

I've been avoiding LaTeX[3] – the markup language, not the clothing material – for about 30 years. One look at its strange syntax of \backslashes, {parameters} and {$funny} conventions was enough to put me off. In fact it is just another programming language, and I should have taken the bull by the horns a long time ago. Unfortunately it never seems to be the right time to learn LaTeX properly.

If you have never come across LaTeX it's not surprising: most people – even authors – can happily live in ignorance of it. LaTeX grew out of Donald Knuth's TeX typesetting system, and while the two are distinct entities in my mind they are pretty synonymous. Together TeX and LaTeX represented one of, if not *the*, first document production systems that were widely available.

Like Markdown, LaTeX uses conventions – markups – embedded in plain text documents, so it is anything but what-you-see-is-what-you-get. It is widely used for academic papers, both because it supports mathematical conventions and because many journals demand LaTeX-formatted documents.

There are three reasons to use LaTeX. First, you want to publish in an academic journal and the journal demands LaTeX submissions. I usually regard this as an added reason not to publish in an academic journal.

The second reason is if you want complete control of your layout – perhaps because you are using a lot of mathematical formula – without paying for an expensive package like InDesign. In this case LaTeX is the system to use because it is open source and many LaTeX tools are free[4]. However, its complexity means you might want a support tool like Overleaf[5], which is a paid-for application.

I find myself using LaTeX, not because I want complete control, but because I want more control than Markdown gives me. Almost everything I write starts life in a plain-text

---

[3]https://www.LaTeX-project.org/
[4]https://www.LaTeX-project.org/get/_
[5]https://www.overleaf.com/

Markdown document. When I want extra formatting I slip in a small bit of LaTeX, and through the magic of Pandoc get the formatting I want.

I haven't tested this in LeanPub, but I believe that small bits of LaTeX would work there too, although I'm not sure about a whole document. Underneath I believe LeanPub runs on LaTeX: the system converts the Markdown-formatted text you supply to LaTeX and generates books from there.

If you want to know more about LaTeX you can find plenty of information online – just remember that when you search you need to add terms like 'Knuth', 'typesetting' or 'document production', or you will be confronted by many pages of clothing.

47. Citations, references and bibliography

Including citations and references is essential if you are writing for an academic publication. For the rest of us references are optional, but there are several reasons why you might want to include them. First, including references adds to your credibility: it demonstrates to readers that you know your subject and you are not just spouting your own opinions. Second, it tells readers where to look if they want to know more. Finally, it is only fair to credit someone if you use their idea or quote.

The easy way to create references in Markdown is to add a footnote every time you reference something[1] or a publication and put the bibliographic details in the footnote. Markdown and LeanPub provide notation for this and Word's footnote feature works too.

This approach to references has some drawbacks. As a writer you can end up littering your text with references, they are easy to forget, and can become distracting when you have a lot. If you find that something is wrong you then need to change it in many places.

Readers might find lots of footnotes distracting too, and as they are distributed throughout the book there is no one place to see all the books and people you have referred to. This is why most books that use them have a bibliography and/or reference section at the end.

It might not occur to you, but using footnotes is only one of many referencing formats. For a start you might choose to use endnotes rather than footnotes – endnotes appear at the end of the book (or chapter), while footnotes appear in the footer at the bottom of the page.

Other formats use the author's name and year of publication, for example (Kelly, 2012) and then list all such references in one place: Kelly, 2012, *Business Patterns*, John Wiley and Sons. That may sound straightforward, but there are a myriad of variations on this: sometimes the first author's name is given, sometimes all the authors are listed, sometimes the reference is set in (regular) braces while at other times in[square braces].

Then there is the question of how the full reference appears in the bibliography: year followed by authors, or authors followed by year? The publisher's name is usually included, but not always, and sometimes the publishers' location is given too – confusing when a publisher

---

[1]This is a footnote.

operates in London, New York and Sydney. Oddly, ISBN is almost never given in these citations, which makes one wonder what the point of it is.

With so many conventions you might not be surprised to learn that they have their own names, usually taken from the publisher or place, such as Harvard, IEEE, Vancouver and Chicago. There are literally hundreds of named referencing conventions, some only differing in tiny details. So it should come as no surprise that publishers may insist you use one particular style. This means that if you start reusing text in different publications – say you publish in a journal and then use the piece as a chapter of a book – you will need to reformat your citations.

Software to the rescue

With so many complications people realised a long time ago that software could help, and there are several packages to help manage and insert citations. Unfortunately LeanPub has no support beyond footnotes and endnotes, so some workarounds are needed.

Software packages help in two ways. First they maintain a database of all your references. Each time you reference a book or article you enter it into the database. Over time you find that most of what you want is already there. Second, the packages make it easy, within your document, to cite something from your database and then generate the bibliography automatically.

While there are many citation packages available I'm going to talk about the three of which I have experience. If citations and references are important to you then it's worth spending time investigating such systems and working out your preferred solution.

Endnote

For several years I used a package called Endnote[2]. It can still be bought outright for about £100 and was the market leader when I acquired it. If you are working in Word then Endnote is probably a no-brainer, as it integrates into Word so that you can just 'cite while you write'. Whenever you insert a reference Endnote automatically adds it to the references at the end of your document.

There are downsides. Endnote costs, paid upgrades are frequent, sometimes I found it would crash Word and I came to feel that it wasn't keeping pace with my needs, for example integration with text editors and Markdown.

---

[2]https://endnote.com/

(Some years ago I found Endnote developers in my class when I was giving an introduction to agile development. From the little conversation we shared over Endnote I got the impression that I was the first user they had met and that it was a Cinderella inside the mega-corporation that then owned it.)

Zotero

Zotero[3] is open source application and therefore a free alternative to Endnote. In fact, Zotero seems to go further than Endnote in the range of word processors it supports, such as LibreOffice and Google Docs. It is one of those software packages that one looks at and thinks *how can this be both better and free?*

The answer to that question is that it started life at George Mason University as a project for academics. It is now developed and supported by the Corporation for Digital Scholarship.

Today I have Zotero installed rather than Endnote, but my writing style has changed, so I use fewer citations and references and don't need to use it very much. While my citation database has decayed, Zotero can access Endnote XML databases, so when need to I can access my old references database.

As with Endnote, Zotero doesn't support plain text and Markdown that I write in for LeanPub directly. This creates problems.

Pandoc

Pandoc can do much of the work Endnote and Zotero does but it does not manage a database. Rather you need to maintain your references database in another system – such as Endnote or Zotero – and then have Pandoc use that database. Using Pandoc implies a two-stage process: write, then create the final document, so 'cite while you write' features are meaningless.

When my writing is not going to LeanPub and into a book this works fine. I usually write my document – say a journal article or report for a client – in Markdown, then process it into PDF using Pandoc. So having Pandoc add references at the same time is easy.

When the files are destined for LeanPub, however, there are problems, because LeanPub is the second step. This means I need some workaround; such workarounds usually involve batch scripts.

---

[3]https://www.zotero.org

My solution

The last book I wrote with formal references was *Xanpan*. For this book production became a three-step process, a process that will be recognizable to most programmers but will be new to many others.

First I wrote the text and embedded references in the text using standard Markdown: [@NameYear]. I imported my Endnote references database to Zotero and used that to manage the references.

Next I 'pre-processed' my files: I ran Pandoc against every file, but instead of producing a PDF I produced a second Markdown document. I had Pandoc convert Markdown to Markdown, but in doing so it completed the references. Unfortunately this also created a few problems between the Markdown that LeanPub accepted (and I had written) and the Markdown that Pandoc outputted. Consequently I ended up writing a shell script to run the process and iron out any problems.

Only then, at the third step, did I have LeanPub process the Markdown files with bibliography into a book.

One extra problem that comes up with Pandoc and plain text is that once the references are added you can't go back to the original document. If you add another reference you need to repeat the processes. This means that you need to maintain two versions of your document: a raw version for you to edit and a processed version where the citations have been fleshed out and the bibliography added for LeanPub to process.

If you don't do this, then changing the new version *with* references will not put those changes into the original: if I add more references I need to process the document again. In the process the bibliography would lose its order. More complicated still would be removing a reference, which would have to be entirely manual.

To work around this I set up a shadow directory where I kept my original documents. I added the references with Pandoc and stored the new, massaged, documents in a directory that LeanPub 'saw'. This worked in DropBox; doing the same thing using git would create an extra commit and push step.

Endnote and Zotero don't work with Markdown editors, but because they work inside Word they can update the bibliography in real time and thus eliminate the need for extra processing steps.

While this all worked for *Xanpan*, it was extra work and could be very frustrating. It was probably one reason why I dropped extensive references in my next books, *Project Myopia* and *Continuous Digital.* That cost me a little bit of credibility and would have made it more difficult to adapt material to the academic world had I wanted to, but it removed a lot of hassle.

Although I have dropped formal citations in recent books I try to keep readers informed of my sources. I now tend to add footnotes and a 'further reading' section at the end. As well as making my writing easier, I think it benefits most of my readers. While academics and the studious may rightly pull me up for being less than rigorous in my writing, I tend to believe that most readers will find my work more readable.

One problem with citations is that they break up the flow of text. With citations writers tend towards a different style of writing, one where every second sentence begins 'According to Kelly (2008)... who was disputed by Jones (2010)...'. While such a style is exact and supports fact checkers, it isn't very readable.

48. A quick guide to Markdown

Markdown might look complicated, but it is no more complicated than changing styles in Word. In fact, because you can't change Markdown styles, it is simpler. It's just that it requires a little imagination.

Everything is text in Markdown; there are just a few conventions you actually need to know. For a start, headings.

Heading 1, the start of a new chapter say, is simply one hash, '#'. The title at the top of this page is '# A quick guide to Markdown'. As you will have noticed, the bit in quotes you just read isn't a heading. That is because Markdown headings only take effect when they are at the start of a line.

Heading 2

The line above this one is '## Heading 2' in the source file, but since the ## isn't hard left at the start of the line it doesn't count and won't be processed as Markdown.

As you might have guessed by now, the more '#' you have, the lower the level of heading. Heading 2 is two hashes or pound signs, '##'; heading 3 is '###' and so on.

Bold, italics and indent

You can make text **bold by** using two asterisk, so this reads as **bold by** in the source file.

Italic text is similar but using only one asterisk, '*'. Unlike headings, you can make text **bold** or *italic* anywhere in a line.

> If you want to indent text you have to start the line with a greater than sign, '>'.

(I can use characters like * and [here without creating the formatting because I have 'escaped' them by placing a backslash \ in front of the character. This negates any special effects.)

Bullets and numbers

- Bullets come at the start of a line, like headings.
- For a bullet you start the line with a minus sign, plus sign or a single asterisk. You will probably need to leave a blank line between bullet points or you will find the text runs together.

1. Finally, if you want to number paragraphs, then start the line with a number, '1', followed by a dot, '1.'
2. When you start the next line with the same number convention Markdown will work out that you actually mean the next number. This sometimes becomes a problem when you want to do something different with the numbers.

Enough

That is all the Markdown you need to get started. In fact there isn't much more – tables being the main thing I've not mentioned here. Some of the text editors mentioned previously, iA Writer for example, can preview Markdown without needing to use Pandoc. While Microsoft Word doesn't recognize Markdown there are plug-ins that allow it to export in Markdown format, so you could avoid the need to learn Markdown.

There is not a lot to learn in Markdown, so I encourage you to try. For me the lack of options creates a simplicity that allows me to concentrate on writing.

Finally, I should point out that LeanPub would rather you write in Markua format. I haven't bitten that bullet yet, so I'll leave it as an exercise.

Please review me

I hope you've enjoyed Books to be Written[1]. I'd be really grateful if you could leave me a nice Amazon review - as I explained these are really important.

The link above will take you to the book page on Amazon - you might need to change it to your local Amazon if this doesn't happen automatically. After that, the more stars the better!

Thanks

Allan Kelly

---

[1]https://www.amazon.com/gp/customer-reviews/B0BSNX433Y

Postscript

As if to show what a dynamic business book publishing has become, things changed even as I wrote this book. Some of them were things I just hadn't kept up to date with, such as Amazon retiring Mobi format and introducing KPF. Others have literally changed in the six months I have spent on the book. Take pricing: if I hadn't written the notes on book prices in Chapter 31 I would not have believed what I see now.

(Don't worry, this book didn't take six months to write. There was an initial six-week burst in April and May, a little work over the summer before another four-week burst in autumn. Now in December, it is a lot more piecemeal while I work with the copy-editor, graphic artist and round up reviewers.)

No hardback?

While I was writing *Books to be Written* Amazon introduced hardback printing. Knowing that hardbacks sell for a higher price, I reasoned that despite the higher printing costs I could still make more on a hardback book than a paperback. (Amazon's printing charge[2] for a 100-page black and white hardback is $6.80 (£5.10, €5.80), while a 100-page paperback costs $2.15 (£1.70, €1.90)).

Traditionally publishers bring out the hardback version first, so those who want early access pay a premium price. As I've published early versions on LeanPub, anyone really keen has probably read the draft. I was imagining a release sequence of Kindle, hardback, paperback and audio, each release being an occasion to make marketing noise and remind people to buy.

While *Books to be Written* was in copy-edit I set about planning the print versions. Obviously there needs to be a different cover for a hardback edition because the dimensions will vary, but beyond that the books would be the same.

Except that Amazon does not offer the same book size options for hardbacks as it does for paperbacks. So, while I had planned to make *Books to be Written* the same size as *Succeeding with OKRs in Agile*, this wasn't an option for the hardback. Now I faced a choice: publish the book in different sizes and so make more work for myself, or change the size of both books?

---

[2]https://kdp.amazon.com/en_US/help/topic/G201723080

ine books taller. When I looked at my bookshelves I couldn't find any books
.uch taller. The taller size wouldn't fit on my shelves. So, a) those books would look
out of place, and b) I would have to resize my bookshelves. So I needed to go smaller.

But going smaller, closer to A5 size, has its own problems. Apart from the fact that
aesthetically I prefer the form factor of *Succeeding with OKRs in Agile* (7.5" x 9.25", 10cm x
23.5cm) to my smaller A5 books, it would also increase the page count. Increasing the page
count means printing costs rise and my return falls.

I could offset some of the page size by reducing the font size, but I don't want to do that
for aesthetic reasons. Besides, to get the page count back to where it started I would need to
reduce the font size several points.

The hardback therefore required compromises that the paperback does not, so I started to
think the editions would be more different: different sizes, different fonts.

That would complicate the production process. I need to produce two print-ready versions
from LeanPub, which it isn't set up to do. So I need to fiddle with settings. Then I need to
check that the images made sense in both. (I missed one image in *Succeeding with OKRs in
Agile* and it really needs to be fixed.)

But for what benefit? The hardback would cost about £5 more per copy to print. This means
it that needs to sell for more than £5 above the paperback. If it sells for £10 more than I'll
make an extra £5 per copy. One of my books has only sold 60 physical copies on Amazon, so
even if all those sold for £10 more in hardback I would only have made £300 more. Of course,
if *Books to be Written* turns out to be a best–seller and sells ten times more in hardback then
it would have been £3,000 more. That would be worthwhile, but my guess is the actual sales
number will fall somewhere in between.

Another option would be to only do a hardback version. Aesthetically that wouldn't make
me happy. It would also mean the price gap between the Kindle version and print version
was bigger, and I'd probably boost the e-book sales while reducing the printed edition sales.
I could estimate that but it would be a lot of guesswork.

In the end I decided to abandon the hardback version.

Dynamic pricing

In Chapter 32 I attempted to draw lessons from the prices of other books. Looking at those
prices now shows how complex or possibly random book pricing is.

Fiona Hill's e-book was £20 on Amazon UK, then a few months later it was available for 99p, and right now, days before Christmas 2022, it is £15. In the US the same Kindle e-book was unavailable for a while and is now back to $17 and the hardback $22. I won't even attempt to explain the changes in price and availability that Jeff Sutherland's Scrum book has gone through. They scramble my brain.

One explanation for this seems to be that Amazon has created dynamic pricing algorithms that override a publishers preferences. Although how much influence big publishers have I don't know.

Recently Amazon has been offering the print version of *Succeeding with OKRs in Agile* at £9.95, reduced from the £16.95 at which I listed it. Worried that I was losing money, I contacted KDP support, who told me Amazon had decided to reduce the price but that I would be paid the full price.

It is worth noting that this occurred before Amazon accepted *Succeeding with OKRs in Agile* into the new Kindle Deals programme (currently in beta). Given Amazon's reputation as a data-savvy company one must assume they know what they are doing.

What I don't know is how much of the pricing I see is different to what you see. About 20 years ago Amazon got bad publicity for adjusting prices based on individuals' previous buying record. Basically, new customers were offered a lower price than regular customers. Presumably their logic was that regular customers don't compare prices in the way that new customers might. Amazon ceased the practice after it was exposed and condemned in the media.

Is it still possible that Amazon is modifying the prices I see based on past behaviour? I tried to counter this by not logging into Amazon and by flushing cookies, but it didn't make any difference. Or perhaps Amazon is offering different prices based on some other parameter such as geolocation or time of day.

Fonts

I haven't said much about fonts, I generally accept defaults and keep things simple. I really don't want to get into font selection or logic. But, occasionally fonts create problems.

For example, take the Rupee symbol, ⊠, I use in chapter 31. While the symbol shows correctly in the ePub edition it doesn't show correctly in the PDF. I've seen similar issues with other symbols so generally try to avoid symbols and non-standard characters.

While I understand some of the issues I don't understand them completely or well enough to attempt an explanation. Basically, it all comes down to a fonts. Not all fonts have all symbols.

While LeanPub offers about 50 font options there are far more to choose from on my Mac or in Word.

Right now I don't know which font to use. Further, changing the font at this late stage will also change layout and page sizes. I don't expect the PDF version to be a big seller so it looks like PDF version will have this problem. But then again, the print version is based on the PDF version and that will sell.

If symbols are important for your work then you either need to delve into this issue or find someone to help.

Always learning

Finally, finally, as you might guess from the postscripts above... even as I finish this book and move it through production and into publishing I'm learning new things, I'm learning to do better.

I'm learning by doing. I'm learning too because, now I've finished my book I am reading others. I am reading what others say about writing, self-publishing and marketing. I am wondering how they make the thousands and thousands they claim when they are doing broadly the same as me.

I see that if I invested more time in researching some of these topics - categories for example - I would understand more and perhaps earn more. I also think I've better things to do than become immersed in categories.

Already I want to go back and change this book. The book has to finish sometime but I will never be finished. This book draws a line in the sand somewhere about September 2022, let's see what happens now.

Also by Allan Kelly

Changing Software Development: Learning to be Agile, John Wiley & Sons, 2008

EuroPLoP 2009 proceedings: 14th annual European Conference on Pattern Languages of Programming, Allan Kelly and Michael Weiss, Hillside Europe (Lulu), 2010

Business Patterns for Software Developers, John Wiley & Sons, 2012

Xanpan: Team Centric Agile Software Development, Software Strategy (LeanPub), 2012–2021

An Agile Reader 2012 (3rd edition), Software Strategy (LeanPub), 2012–2021

A Little Book about Requirements and User Stories, Software Strategy (LeanPub), 2015–2017

Project Myopia: Why Projects Damage Software #NoProjects, Software Strategy (LeanPub), 2015–2018

Continuous Digital: An agile alternative to projects for digital business, Software Strategy (LeanPub), 2016–2018

The Art of Agile Product Ownership, Apress, 2019

Succeeding with OKRs in Agile, Software Strategy (LeanPub), 2021

Thank you

Thank you to Steve Smith, David Daly and the many other people who picked my brains about how I write and self-publish books. Thank you Steve too for saying "You need to write a book about this", and finally thank you Tshilidzi Siphuma for being the straw that broke this camel's back after telling Steve and others that "I have more important things to do than write a book about writing books".

Thanks too to the editors who have tolerated my crazy grammar, punctuation and ideas, and occasionally pushed me in a better direction: John Merrells, Alan Griffiths and Johanna Rothman.

Published by Software Strategy Ltd, London, UK.

contact@softwarestrategy.co.uk

Publication: 31 January 2023

978-1-912832-20-0: ePub format electronic edition

978-1-912832-21-7: PDF format electronic edition

978-1-912832-22-4: hardback edition

978-1-912832-23-1: soft back edition

978-1-912832-24-8: audio edition

Printed in Great Britain
by Amazon